Joseph Allen

**The Worcester Association and its Antecedents**

Joseph Allen

**The Worcester Association and its Antecedents**

ISBN/EAN: 9783744730334

Printed in Europe, USA, Canada, Australia, Japan

Cover: Foto ©ninafisch / pixelio.de

More available books at **www.hansebooks.com**

# THE WORCESTER ASSOCIATION

### AND ITS

# ANTECEDENTS:

### A HISTORY OF

# FOUR MINISTERIAL ASSOCIATIONS:

THE MARLBOROUGH, THE WORCESTER (OLD), THE LANCASTER, AND THE WORCESTER (NEW) ASSOCIATIONS.

*With Biographical Notices of the Members,*

ACCOMPANIED BY PORTRAITS.

By JOSEPH ALLEN,

SENIOR PASTOR OF THE FIRST CONGREGATIONAL SOCIETY IN NORTHBOROUGH.

BOSTON:
NICHOLS AND NOYES.
1868.

Entered according to Act of Congress, in the year 1867, by

JOSEPH ALLEN,

In the Clerk's Office of the District Court of the District of Massachusetts

# NOTICE.

IT is several years since, that, at the request of the Worcester Association, I undertook to write its history, and accordingly prepared a sketch, which was read before that body at one of its regular meetings. It was then proposed, that I should treat the subject more fully, with a view to its publication. With many interruptions and much delay, I have at length completed the work, — a labor of love, — which is respectfully and affectionately dedicated to the brethren at whose instance it was undertaken, — the past and present members of the Worcester Association, — by their brother, the senior member.

JOSEPH ALLEN.

Northborough, Mass., Dec. 5, 1867.

# PREFACE.

AT the time of my settlement in Northborough, half a century ago, there were in the neighborhood three ministerial associations, with members of each of which I had formed an acquaintance. These were the Marlborough Association (the old Marlborough Association revived), and the Worcester and the Lancaster Associations; the two latter soon afterwards uniting to form one, — the Worcester Association, as it now exists.

From an examination of the records of the Marlborough Association, I was led to believe, that the old Worcester Association was nearly related to it, being the identical body formed by the division of that Association in 1762.

It appears, that that body, which was organized in 1725, had gradually extended its bounds, till it embraced, besides a considerable number of towns in

# TABLE OF CONTENTS.

|  | PAGE |
|---|---|
| John Swift | 74 |
| Joseph Davis | 75 |
| John Seccomb | 75 |
| John Mellen | 78 |
| Thaddeus Macarty | 82 |
| Joseph Wheeler | 84 |
| Timothy Harrington | 85 |
| Josiah Bridge | 86 |
| Peter Whitney (portrait) | 90 |
| Joseph Willard | 93 |
| Jacob Bigelow | 95 |
| Jonathan Newell | 96 |
| Joel Foster | 101 |
| Moses Adams | 102 |
| Phineas Wright | 104 |
| Samuel Sumner | 105 |
| David Kellogg | 106 |
| Ezra Ripley | 108 |
| Asa Packard | 114 |
| Jeroboam Parker | 118 |
| Sylvester F. Bucklin | 119 |

Worcester (Old) Association . . . . . . . 123–129

Biographical Notices: —

| Aaron Bancroft (portrait) | 129 |
|---|---|
| Joseph Sumner (portrait) | 147 |
| Joseph Avery | 152 |
| Ward Cotton | 154 |
| William Nash | 156 |
| John Miles | 160 |

TABLE OF CONTENTS.  xi

|  | PAGE |
|---|---|
| LANCASTER ASSOCIATION | 167–173 |

BIOGRAPHICAL NOTICES: —

| | |
|---|---|
| NATHANIEL THAYER (portrait) | 173 |
| ISAAC ALLEN | 183 |
| DAVID DAMON | 193 |
| LEMUEL CAPEN | 203 |
| SAMUEL CLARKE | 214 |

| | |
|---|---|
| WORCESTER ASSOCIATION (NEW) | 229–290 |

BIOGRAPHICAL NOTICES OF DECEASED MEMBERS: —

| | |
|---|---|
| IRA H. T. BLANCHARD (portrait) | 290 |
| SETH ALDEN | 302 |
| HIRAM WITHINGTON | 311 |
| RUFUS A. JOHNSON | 323 |
| PETER OSGOOD | 329 |
| WILLIAM A. WHITWELL | 335 |
| JARED M. HEARD (portrait) | 341 |
| WARREN BURTON | 355 |

| | |
|---|---|
| APPENDIX: CONTAINING NOTICES OF THE LIVING MEMBERS | 316–426 |

# MARLBOROUGH ASSOCIATION.

# MARLBOROUGH ASSOCIATION.

THE MARLBOROUGH ASSOCIATION was formed in 1725, just fifty years before the breaking-out of the war of the Revolution; and it lived and flourished through the long period of eighty-nine years, having been dissolved by a vote of the members, Oct. 14, 1814. It consisted at first of but seven members, who were pastors of churches in towns lying on the western borders of Middlesex County, of which towns Marlborough was the centre. These were Sudbury, including Wayland, on the east; Framingham, on the south-east; Westborough, including what is now Northborough, on the west, with Shrewsbury, including the two Boylstons, still further in the same direction; and Lancaster, including Harvard, Bolton, Sterling, Berlin, and Clinton, on the north-west; and Stow on the north; while Marlborough, the geographical centre, included Hudson and Southborough. All these towns were at this time in Middlesex County; Worcester County not having been incorporated till six years afterwards, viz., April 2, 1731.

The seven townships named, it will be perceived embraced quite an extensive territory, at present subdivided into more than twice the number of incorporated towns. With the exception of Sudbury, Lancaster, and Marlborough, which were among the earliest settlements of the Massachusetts Colony, the towns embraced within the limits of the Marlborough Association had existed in their corporate capacity but a few years. Framingham just a quarter of a century; Westborough, eight years. Shrewsbury, although supplied with a stated ministry from 1723, did not obtain an act of incorporation till four years later, 1727, or two years after the Marlborough Association was formed. Stow was incorporated May 16, 1689.

A much larger territory was afterwards contained within the limits of the Association. On the north, it embraced the towns of Acton and Boxborough; Concord, on the north-east; on the south, Hopkinton and Grafton; and, on the west, Worcester, Holden, and Rutland, — making, in all, twenty-three incorporated towns. Leominster, after the act of incorporation in 1740, which separated it from Lancaster, was not connected with the Marlborough Association. In the absence of any evidence to the contrary, which has come to my knowledge, I presume that the Marlborough Association was the first, in the

MARLBOROUGH ASSOCIATION. 5

ter of time, that was formed in all this region. The Mendon Association, one of the oldest out of the immediate vicinity of Boston, was not formed till more than a quarter of a century afterwards; viz., in 1751. The oldest association in the State and in all New England, unless there was one in the Old Colony, was, I suppose, that formed in Charlestown in 1690, whose meetings were held in the college in Cambridge about once in six weeks.* This was only thirty-five years earlier than the origin of the Marlborough Association. Of the associations in the Old Colony, and on the Connecticut River, I have no knowledge.

It appears from the records of the Marlborough Association, that on the 5th June, 1725, a number of the ministers of the neighboring towns, seven in all, met by appointment at the house of Rev. Robert Breck, the minister of Marlborough; and then and there associated themselves together under a constitution to which they affixed their names, which are as follows: —

Robert Breck . . . . . . . . . . Marlborough.
John Swift . . . . . . . . . . . Framingham.
Israel Loring . . . . . . . . . . Sudbury.
John Gardner . . . . . . . . . . Stow.
John Prentice . . . . . . . . . . Lancaster.
Job Cushing . . . . . . . . . . Shrewsbury.
Ebenezer Parkman . . . . . . . . Westborough.

---

* History of Mendon Association, p. 28.

To these seven were subsequently annexed, in the order in which they are given, the following names:—

| | |
|---|---|
| Solomon Prentice | Grafton. |
| William Cook | East Sudbury, now Wayland. |
| Samuel Barrett | Hopkinton. |
| Thomas Frink | Rutland. |
| Nathan Stone | Southborough. |
| John Martyn | Westborough, now Northborough. |
| Aaron Smith | Marlborough. |
| Ebenezer Morse | Shrewsbury, now Boylston. |
| Thomas Goss | Bolton. |
| Joseph Buckminster | Rutland. |
| John Swift | Acton. |
| Joseph Davis | Holden. |
| John Seccomb | Harvard. |
| John Mellen | Sterling. |
| Thaddeus Macarty | Worcester. |
| Joseph Wheeler | Harvard. |
| Timothy Harrington | Lancaster. |
| Josiah Bridge | East Sudbury, now Wayland. |
| Peter Whitney | Northborough. |
| Joseph Willard | Boxborough. |
| Jacob Bigelow | Sudbury. |
| Jonathan Newell | Stow. |
| Joel Foster | East Sudbury, now Wayland. |
| Moses Adams | Acton. |
| Phineas Wright | Bolton. |
| Samuel Sumner | Southborough. |
| David Kellogg | Framingham. |
| Ezra Ripley | Concord. |

Asa Packard . . . . . . . . . . . Marlborough.
Jeroboam Parker . . . . . . . . . Southborough.
Sylvester Bucklin . . . . . . . . . Marlborough.

These, with the seven original members, make in all thirty-eight, — names intimately connected with the history of the several towns and churches which they represented, and no less with the intellectual and moral culture, and the social and physical condition, of the successive generations who were educated under their ministry, and were guided by their teachings and their example. Most of them are names without reproach, — names borne by men who were honored in their day, and who still live in the hearts of their descendants, and of those who have shared in the fruits of their toil. All have departed: not one survives. To the generation now on the stage of action, how few of those names recall the images of the living men who once bore them! Half a century ago, and down to a somewhat later date, a few venerable forms — the relics of a former generation — might have been seen in the college yard, in Cambridge, on Commencement Day, standing in groups, holding friendly conference with one another, or walking to and fro with a dignified gait, seeking out their classmates and college acquaintance, and forming a very pleasing picture of the olden times.

I remember them well: their erect forms and dignified bearing; their quaint costume; their silver or gold headed canes; their polished silver or steel buckles for the instep and the knee; their sno in white bushwigs, surmounted by the three-cornered broad-brimmed, low-crowned hat; their long-waisted coats and waistcoats; and their shortened nether garments, unsupported by the contrivances of modern art, — all these are fresh in my remembrance, as though they were things of yesterday. Some of the ministers whose names are contained in the above list belonged to a later age; and either never adopted, or at the time referred to had laid aside, the antique style of dress which prevailed all over New England in the middle of the eighteenth, and down so late as the beginning of the nineteenth century.

Of some eight or ten of those whose names are on the catalogue, the writer of these sketches retains a very vivid recollection. With five of the number he has been on terms of intimacy, and has exchanged ministerial labors with them. From authentic history and tradition, we learn that, in respect to a fair proportion of the whole number, their "praise was in all the churches." Many of them, it is true, had their foibles and faults, sufficient at least to show that they were men of like passions with other men; but, with very few exceptions, it is believed they were upright, sincere, devout men, serving God and their generation according to the light that was given them. "Our fathers, — where are they? and the prophets, — do they live for ever?"

"Yes, they are gone; and we are going all:
Like flowers we wither, and like leaves we fall."

But "the righteous shall be had in everlasting remembrance."

"And they that be wise shall shine as the brightness of the firmament; and they that turn many to righteousness, as the stars for ever and ever."

The Marlborough Association was formed, as we have seen, in 1725. Its object, as stated in the records, was "to advance the interest of Christ, the service of our respective charges, and our own mutual edification in our great work." The members were to meet four times a year, Marlborough being selected, on account of its central position, as the regular place of meeting; while, at the request of any member, a meeting might occasionally be held in other towns.

Among the rules which they adopted, one was "to consider any case, that might be laid before them by any member or other person, that should be deemed proper to come under their cognizance." At each meeting, moreover, if circumstances permitted, a *concio ad clerum* was to be delivered by the members in rotation; or, as a substitute for the *concio*, some question, proposed at a previous meeting, was to be discussed by such members as had been designated for that purpose.

But however excellent the plan which they adopted, and however earnest the spirit with which they entered on their labors, their experience was not much unlike that of other similar bodies in more recent times. They had their alternations of zeal and languor, of activity and remissness, of prosperity and declension. Accordingly, some new stimulus and extraordinary efforts were occasionally required in order to keep up an interest in their meetings, and " to prevent the love of God from dying out of their souls." Thus, under date of April 9, 1728, scarcely three years after the Association was formed, the following record was made: "There was a general concern expressed touching our remissness in time past, and that we have met with so many obstructions to the prosecuting the great designs of our Association." In order to revive their interest and to strengthen their good resolutions, it was agreed " that the articles of their Constitution should be read and subscribed anew by all the members; which accordingly was done," followed, no doubt, by similar relapses and other revivals of interest, as in the case of all associations composed of weak and tempted mortals.

It may serve to throw some light on the character of the age, and the state of the New-England churches in the early part of the last century, to state a few cases which were brought before this body for adjudication.

The first on the records is one presented by Rev. Mr. Loring, April 9, 1728, " respecting some *inorthodox* opinions, broached by one Clap, of his church of West Sudbury; the said Clap imagining and believing that we are not beholden to our Lord Jesus Christ for any satisfaction made to God by his blood, except for the sins against God's first precepts to Adam, and the moral law; but, as for *our* sins under the gospel, they are freely forgiven of God without any satisfaction." This "very troublesome affair," as they term it, was again brought up at a subsequent meeting on complaint of said Clap, who, as it seems, demurred at the action of the Association, they having declared their opinion, that the church in Sudbury "had done wisely in suspending said Clap from the sacrament, such doctrines tending immediately to subvert Christian religion." The complainant expressed his readiness to leave the matter of dispute to arbitrators, — "any persons," he says, "ministers or others, a smaller or greater number, as they pleased, or a council (in form), if they (the church) so liked, to examine and consider the case," &c.

With this reasonable request, the Association advised Mr. Loring and his church to comply. How the matter ended, the record does not say.

The next is a case presented by Rev. Mr. Swift, of Framingham, and related to a charge of perjury brought by Colonel Buckminster against three members of the church. This case was wisely disposed of, by advising that "Colonel Buckminster be desired to prosecute them in the common law, rather than involve the church in debates about titles to lands, as that affair will unavoidably run them into."

At the same meeting, a "Mr. Axtell, of Marlborough, came in with his complaint of being so long debarred from communion with the church there." On which complaint, the Association desired he would acknowledge what irregularity or unadvised management he had known himself chargeable with, relating to one T. O. [the initials only are given]. Accordingly, "the moderator drew up a confession, and gave him; which he, being desired well to consider of and to sign, took with him for those ends." The result will be found on a following page.

The importance attached by these good men to infant baptism, and the care taken to exclude from the privilege all who were not considered proper subjects of the ordinance, may be inferred from the following cases, which were brought before the Association: —

One case presented by Rev. Mr. Parkman related to a child whose misfortune it was to be born too soon after the marriage of its parents. It was asked, first, "whether such a child might be baptized?" and, in the second place, "whether if the church should, by a great majority, express their willingness to have it baptized, yet we may proceed if three or four members offered objection, with plausible reasons to support the same?" The advice given was, that the child "be baptized."

Another case, presented by Mr. Cushing, of Shrewsbury (June 23, 1741), for advice, was, "whether he ought to baptize a child whose parent (the father) is reported to be an Arminian, perhaps an Arian?" Mr. Cushing is advised not to do it, "without making diligent inquiry into both his conduct and faith;" and they further remark, "The already common report is supposed to be sufficient ground for such inquiry."

Another case was submitted, June 11, 1745, by Rev. Joseph Buckminster, of Rutland, father of the Rev. Dr. Buckminster, of Portsmouth, asking advice "respecting his gratifying a Presbyterian of the Church of Scotland," a stiff old Covenanter no doubt, "with administering the ordinance in the form and manner of that church." It was agreed, that, "though great condescension and catholic charity and unity were much to be recommended and practised, yet, upon hearing the circumstances of the case, they were of the opinion, that Mr. Buckminster, for the present, strictly adhere to our own customs," stiff old Congregationalists as they were, "discharging faithfully his duty of public preaching on that sacrament, setting forth the duties of parents in offering their children, and privately and personally instructing and charging those parents who do, from time to time, present their desires," &c.

The next case is somewhat more complicated; and the decision, though apparently harsh, shows that the baptism of infants was not then regarded as an unmeaning ceremony.

Rev. Joseph Davis, of Holden (Aug. 17, 1745), "proposed a case relating to a base-born child, whose mother was now dead, without any confession or sense of her sin; nay," as the relator testifies, "without so much as mention of it to him at any time of her sickness, though she died of consumption, and lay some time, and he was sundry times with her: but she gave her child to a sister ("of none of the best behavior," it is added in a parenthesis), who, that it might be baptized, gives it to her mother; and now the grandmother offers it accordingly." The question to be decided was, "Has this child a right, on the account of the grandmother? and may it be baptized?" — "It was answered in the negative, and that the child be not baptized, unless the grandmother (as another person will) in special and solemn manner declare and promise, that she will engage for its education (as another might), and if the grandmother be trusty and faithful."

Under date of May 13, 1729, we find the following record, which appears to relate to some case of peculiar hardship or suffering, which appealed to the sympathy and compassion of the brethren: "Rev. Oliver Peabody (pastor of the Indian Church in Natick) gave us the present circumstances of Mr. Cotton, at Providence;" and, on the following July, "the Association requested Rev. Mr. Baxter, of Medfield, who had been the receiver of the Providence subscriptions, who was present, to look into that account, and call for what was yet behind." Then it is added, " Upon his doing so, every one present paid the full of his subscription ; " reminding us of the practice of the early disciples.

At a meeting of the brethren at Lancaster, April 6, 1731, it was agreed "to turn the Association meetings into fasts, for the reviving religion and imploring the Divine blessing upon the rising generation." This was done ; and the course lasted till the June of the following year, the ministers preaching in rotation.

Under date of Oct. 16, 1733, Framingham, we find the following record : " The Rev. Mr. Swift had invited the Southern Association (which were to have met this day at his son's-in-law, Mr. Stone's of Holliston), by which means we had the benefit of their advice and assistance in the difficulty before us, relating to Mr. Benjamin Kent, ordained at Marlborough ; great complaint being made, about the world, of his principles. Mr. Kent was present, and very freely submitted himself to our inquiries and examinations. Mr. Loring interrogated upon the Articles drawn up in New-England Confession of Faith, chiefly relating to the controversy with the Remonstrants : and he gave such a declaration of his belief, and with such professions of honesty and sincerity in all, that the Association manifested their satisfaction therein, upon condition they should find, that his preaching and conversation had been, and should for the future be, agreeable to such declaration; in short, as long as they should see what he had exhibited were his *real* sentiments." It would seem, from this somewhat equivocal testimonial, that it was with some doubts and misgivings as to the soundness of Mr. Kent's faith, or other ministerial qualifications, that they regarded their young brother from Marlborough. Mr. Kent remained the minister of Marlborough but little more than one year, having been dismissed, by mutual consent, in February, 1735. His dismission was followed by a state of anarchy and division in the church, that prevented the settlement of a minister for the space of four years.

At a meeting of the Association at Hassenemisco (as the name is spelt in the records), the Indian name of Grafton, Oct. 29, 1734, a letter from the Presbytery at Londonderry, N.H., to be communicated to the Association, touching a brotherly and Christian agreement and communion between Congregationalists and Presbyterians, was read and referred to consideration to-morrow morning, Oct. 30. "*Voted*, That an answer be prepared to be sent to the Rev. Presbytery aforesaid, expressing our readiness to comply with their request; but," it is added, " not without complaining of, and resenting, the disorders of late in several Scotch assemblies in those parts, and irregular administrations of the holy communion;" which accordingly was done.

of Lancaster, Aug. 26, 1735. — Several members of
 the Association asked advice respecting the dismission of such members as requested it from their own churches where they dwell, if (or because) they have not ruling elders, to such churches in other towns where they *have*, but yet craving liberty of occasional communion. Many reasons were offered against this practice; and therefore, as the record reads, "it could not be advised to by any means."

It appears, that, about this time, the Convention of Congregationalist Ministers, at their annual meeting in Boston, had passed a vote, " touching the examination of candidates for the ministry, previous to their admission into our pulpits." In accordance with this vote, the Association (Aug. 27, 1735) agreed, that they would not " invite any person to preach, nor countenance any one's preaching, till he has passed through an examination, by this or some other Association, into his qualifications for the ministerial work." The subject had been introduced and discussed at a previous meeting, when " the members present were desired to prepare their minds respecting so weighty an affair, and concerning particularly the best manner of examination, *so as to be secure against deceit and evasion*."

On the inquiry, "What are the qualifications of a candidate for the ministry," they reply: " He must be, — 1. Learned; 2. Orthodox; 3. Of good conversation.

Under the first head are specified, — 1st, Knowledge of the principles of the Christian religion, and some considerable degree of aptness and expertness to teach; 2d, Acquaintance with the tongues, arts and sciences, &c.

Under the second head, we are simply referred to "our Confession of Faith."

Under the third head, he must be, — 1st, Of sober, honest, pious, behavior; and, 2d, Of prudence in conduct. These "heads" were "voted to be our general rule in examination of candidates."

At the same meeting when these rules were adopted, a proposal was made by Rev. Mr. Frink, of Rutland, for forming a *Consociation* in the county of Worcester, which was "considered and left to further consideration still."

As we hear nothing further of this project, we conclude that no further attempt was made to introduce this new form of church government into Worcester County. Mr. Frink was dismissed from his charge in Rutland four years afterwards (1740), was resettled a short time in Plymouth, installed at Barre in 1753, whence he was again dismissed in 1766.

June 14, 1737. — "The conversation turned very much upon the wonderful power and grace of God where he has been pleased to work a revival of religion." Again, Aug. 13, "Conversation turned upon the remarkable dispensations of

Divine Providence in the world within some few last years."

August, 1738. — "A proposal and request came from Rev. Mr. Adams, of Lunenburg, to the effect, that the Association should dismiss Rev. Mr. Prentice, of Lancaster, " in order, it is suggested, to joining with a number of ministers in the north, who were endeavoring to form into one." — " But on consideration," the record proceeds, " that our number was not large in the whole, but that the number who commonly associated was but six or seven, while they who were ready to join and make up their number were nigh as many as we, and great likelihood of much enlargement, which *we* could not have in *ours* in any proportion to them, *it was declined.*"

The old difficulty relating to Mr. Axtell, of Marlborough, came up again June 19, 1739, when Mr. Axtell himself appeared, accompanied by Deacon Keyes and Mr. Daniel Steward. " Upon which there was much debate, and long and affectionate reasoning with Mr. Axtell, but to little purpose." Again, Aug. 29, the case was disposed of by a vote, recommending to the church of Marlborough that it might be best to extend their compassions towards him, and, he having removed his habitation to Grafton, to dismiss him thereto."

But the matter did not rest here. For, the following year (April, 1740), two messengers from the church in Grafton (Captain Joseph Willard and

Deacon Cooper) waited upon the Association at Lancaster (having travelled about twenty miles), asking advice "touching the admission of Mr. Thomas Axtell into their communion, upon the dismission which he had obtained from the church of Marlborough, it being without any recommendation, for want of which they thought it lean and imperfect; and they supposed they could discover, from the form of the draught of the Marlborough vote, a design to exhibit no other than what was the most *slender* and indifferent." The Association advised, in a written communication addressed to the church in Grafton, "that they receive Mr. Axtell." Thus ended, so far as we are informed, this troublesome affair.

The Marlborough Association, as is evident from their records, was, at least during the period now under review, a living, working body. The meetings appear to have been well attended; and the exercises were varied to meet the exigencies of the times.

Besides the fasts, the *concio*, and the questions of theology and casuistry, and cases of church discipline, to which they attended, they voted in June, 1739, "that every member make and bring written collections of what remarkable occurs in his reading, studies, conversation, &c., from one time of Association to another, and communicate the same for our mutual emolument and advantage." Accordingly, this was done for several years, though irregularly, and sometimes after long intervals.

Some of the questions brought before them may seem to us impertinent or puerile, and unworthy the attention of so grave and dignified a body. Such are several of the questions already cited, and many others of a like character are contained in the records. As characteristic of the times, they are not unworthy our notice.

One, proposed by Rev. Mr. Loring, of Sudbury, was " touching the proof of a person's being drunk." Another, by the same, " Whether it is lawful for a man to marry his wife's sister?" a question not yet definitely settled, we believe, in the ecclesiastical courts of England or our own country. Mr. Bridge, of East Sudbury, proposed a case, " Whether a man might marry his wife's sister's daughter?" The answer was, " We know of no special law of God, but yet it was so near as that the man should exercise his best wisdom and prudence;" excellent advice, which, however, is not always heeded in such matters.

Oct. 19, 1743. — The following significant notice appears on the records: " Mr. Goddard, of Leicester, preached yesterday at the Itinerant Preacher's Meeting-house in Framingham, both A. and P. M., to our sorrow." From Whitney's " History of Worcester County," we learn that this Mr. Goddard died a few years afterwards (1754) at Framingham, being seized with a fever while on a journey to that place, in the forty-eighth year of his age and thirteenth of his ministry.

While the principal attention of the Association was directed to the affairs of the churches within their own jurisdiction, they did not forget their brethren without, or overlook the spiritual destitution of places less favored than their own.

April 14, 1741. — "Rev. Mr. Hall, of Sutton, present, and related somewhat of the melancholy state of Smithfield in Providence, being much without the gospel." — "*Voted* by the Association, that Mr. Parkman be desired to go with Mr. Hall and Mr. Webb to Smithfield, to inquire into the state of religion there, and whether any thing can be done to promote the kingdom of Christ among them; and that Mr. Prentice be desired to write to Mr. Webb" (Rev. Nathan Webb, of Uxbridge), "to inform him hereof."

The Association was also occasionally applied to for advice in difficulties between pastors and churches, beyond its own limits; an evidence of the respect which it commanded, and of the deference which was paid to it.

Oct. 28, 1740. — "Rev. Mr. Dorr, of Mendon (who was occasionally with us), asked advice of the Association under his and his church's difficulties." And again, in August of the following year, "Rev. Mr. Dorr and Mr. Rawson, of South Hadley [were] present for advice respecting some difficulties arising among them, in each of their flocks." Rev. Joseph Dorr is said to have been "the projector and first moderator of the Mendon Association" (see History of the Mendon Association, p. 86). Three of the grandsons of Mr. Dorr were respectable merchants and honored citizens of Boston.

In the following extract, reference is made to difficulties in the church at Concord, of the nature of which we are not informed. June 19, 1744. — "Conversation turned very much upon Concord circumstances, and what may be advisable for the neighboring ministers and churches to do, if the members of Concord should desire occasional communion."

"The chief conversation at one of the meetings [Lancaster, Oct. 20, 1741] was upon the works of God among us, the unusual flood of water by the late rains, there having been no such flood in Lancaster for twenty years; also the wondrous influence of the Spirit of God of late, in some parts of the land; also the greater success of the gospel of late in Sudbury, and more numerous additions to the church there," &c. And the following year, April 13, 1742, after a sermon by Rev. Solomon Prentice, of Grafton, the record states that "conference after turned upon some passages of the sermon against such ministers as oppose the present work of God." On another occasion (April 13, 1743), we learn that this Mr. Prentice took exception to some sentiments advanced by Rev. Mr. Barrett, of Hopkinton, in a sermon preached at Westborough on the previous February, at a fast, on John x. 27, 28 ("My sheep hear my voice," &c.). "Upon which, Mr. Barrett was desired to repeat said sermon, which he did; and Mr. Prentice was requested to make his exceptions anew and distinctly, but answered that the sermon did not appear to him as it did at first hearing; yet a reconcilement between these gentlemen was not accomplished."

After this, as appears from the records, Mr. Prentice commonly absented himself from the meetings of the Association; till at length, at a meeting held in Marlborough, Jan. 22, 1745, — at which time "Mr. Morse, of Boylston, and Mr. Mellen, of Sterling, upon their desire, were admitted members of the Association," — that body having drawn up and signed, in order to the publication of it, what is called "A Testimony against Mr. Whitefield and his Conduct," "Mr. Prentice, of Grafton, desired to be dismissed from the Association, and have his name *raized* out of the Association's books; which was consented to."

We learn from Whitney's "History of Worcester County," p. 167, that Mr. Prentice became what was called in that day "a zealous New Light, or, more properly," the historian remarks, "a raving enthusiast." He was dismissed, we are told, from Grafton, July 8, 1747, and became an itinerant preacher." It should have been added to this statement, that Mr. Prentice was installed pastor of the church in Easton on the following November (Nov. 18, 1747). We learn moreover, from Emery's "Ministry of Taunton," that Mr. Prentice (born in Cambridge, May 11, 1705, H.C. 1727) had a short, stormy, and unsatisfactory ministry in Easton. A council was called in 1752, which sat two days; but the result was not satisfactory to either party, at least it failed to bring about a reconciliation. At length, Mr. Prentice, with a majority of the church, joined a presbytery, but with no better result. "The presbytery at a session in Easter, Nov. 12, 1754, judged Mr. Prentice unqualified for 'the office of a bishop,' and gave him a temporary discharge from pastoral labor." Mr. Prentice complains of this treatment as harsh and unkind, in the following terms: "Because I had received a few of my fellow-creatures (and fellow-Christians so far as I knew) into my house, and suffered them to pray and talk about the Scriptures, and could not make any acknowledgment to some of my brethren who were offended thereat, nor to the presbytery, *Voted*, That he, the said S. Prentice, be suspended, &c. Because by said vote I was deprived of the small subsistence I had among my people in Easton, I thought it necessary for the honor of God and good of my family to remove to Grafton; which accordingly was done, April 9, 1755." Mr. Prentice died in Grafton, May 22, 1773, aged sixty-eight.

Aug. 16, 1848, the Association voted, "That, from

the next spring and forwards, the meetings of the Association be turned into fasts, for the prevention of further degeneracy, the reviving religion, and the advancement of the kingdom of the Lord Jesus Christ." The question had been proposed at a former meeting, "What shall best be done in our several flocks for the preventing the awful threatening degeneracy and backsliding in religion in the present day?" and the subject had been committed to four of their number, — Rev. Messrs. Loring, Cushing, Parkman, and Stone (Stone, of Southborough); who, at a meeting in Holden, Aug. 15, 1748, made an elaborate report, embodying, we are told, "the sum and substance of the answers given by the Association at several meetings in the year 1747." This report was adopted Aug. 16, 1748; and it is no more than justice to say of it, that it is drawn up with a good deal of ability, and contains thoughts and suggestions of weighty import, and such as are adapted to all times.

I have already spoken of the care taken in the examination of candidates, to guard the pulpit against abuse. At the examination of Mr. John Martyn, of Bolton (afterwards the worthy minister of Northborough), Mr. Gardner, of Stow (the former residence of Mr. Martyn), made some objections against him, which led to a debate in the Association, and a private conference between Mr. Gardner and the candidate, which resulted in a reconciliation, and a certificate of approbation signed by every member of the Association present. At the next meeting, however, which was at Bolton, June 11, Mr. Martyn, it seems, had advanced some sentiments, in an exercise on Matt. xvi. 27, delivered before the Association, which were received with some doubts and misgivings in respect to their soundness. The record says, under date of June 12, "Conference with *Mr. Martyn*, on his sermon yesterday, which contained some expressions which 'twas thought needed further opening; and, in said exercise, he advanced some notions of the future state and of the last day which were conceived to be very new, and not easily to be come into. After not a little discourse thereon, he said he would take those things into further thought." And afterwards, Oct. 15, 1745, when an application was made to the Association by the people of Northborough (then the second precinct in Westborough) for advice in regard to the settlement of Mr. Martyn, who had preached among them to their great acceptance, the Association, after saying that "they know not why they might not proceed with reference to Mr. Martyn," add the following remark: "But it is to be noted, that the Association (first of all) received satisfaction from Mr. Martyn touching the sermon which he had delivered at *Bolton;* and this was by a retraction of the sentiments contained therein, which was signed by his own hand;" and then

they refer to a document " among the loose papers."
It would be interesting to know what were the
heterodox views Mr. Martyn had advanced, in the
sermon at Bolton, respecting "the future state and
the last day."

At a meeting of the Association at Marlborough,
April 12, 1748, " Mr. Morse, of Boylston, mentioned *his* circumstances and manner of living among
his people, for now above a year, without a salary or
assessment made to pay him any thing, and would
be glad of advice."

At the same meeting, in the evening, a letter
addressed to the Association was handed in, written
by a Mr. William Jennison, a schoolmaster at this
time in Marlborough; to which a reply was made in
writing, signed by Rev. Mr. Cushing, of Shrewsbury, which seems to have been not very palatable
to the said Jennison, as it provoked a rejoinder,
which is spoken of in the records in the following
terms: " N.B. — A contemptuous letter of Mr. William Jennison was treated with the neglect it deserved."

At a meeting in Holden, Aug. 16, 1748, " Mr.
Harrington laid his case, with respect to his relation
to his late church at *Ashuelot*, Keene, N.H. (now
scattered into all parts of the country by reason of
the war), before the Association; he having received
a call from Lancaster First Parish to resettle in the
gospel ministry."

At the same meeting, "another contemptuous letter," as it is called, "signed by William Jennison, treated with deserved neglect."

It appears, that, besides the instance already mentioned, on two subsequent occasions, — namely, about the years 1749 and 1758, — the meetings of the Association were converted into fasts: in the former case, "for preventing further degeneracy," &c.; in the latter, "considering the great increase of the public troubles and dangers." This, it will be observed, was about the time of the repulse of the English, under Abercrombie, at Ticonderoga, which, it is well known, cast a gloom over the English colonies.

The following year (April 17, 1759), another series of fasts was appointed, agreeably to the following vote: "Whether, considering the present aspects of Providence with respect, not only to Great Britain and its allies, but to these American governments, we judge it suitable to recommend to the several congregations to join with us in keeping days for prayer and fasting? Voted unanimously." On the following June, a fast was appointed by the public authorities to be held throughout the province.

The following record appears under date of Aug. 28, 1759: "There was no meeting at Mr. Macarty's (Worcester), by reason of so great a meeting there the week before, at the time of the court, when Mr.

Rogers and the town of Leominster had their case tried." *

Oct. 21, 1760, Mr. Gardner, of Stow, stated in his *concio* from 2 Kings xiii. 20, " that, of late, six ministers, within his knowledge, had died," whom he thus designates : " Venerable Mr. Stoddard (H.C. 1697), of Woodbury ; venerable Allen (H.C. 1703), of Greenland ; Rev. Messrs. Trowbridge (H.C. 1710), of Groton ; Hemingway (H.C. 1730), of Townshend ; Cushing (H.C. 1714), of Shrewsbury ; and Joseph Seccomb (H.C. 1731), of Kingstown," formerly of Harvard.

Under date of June 16, 1762 (Lancaster), we find the following memorandum : " The Scribe having received from Mr. Marsh, one of the tutors of Harvard College, Dr. Leland's 'View of Deistical Writers,' in 3 vols. 8vo, a present from Rev. Dr. Hales, Clerk of the Closet to Her Royal Highness the Princess Dowager of Wales, and the Rev. Dr. Thomas Wilson, Prebendary of Westminster and Rector of Walbrook, London, which benefaction was put into the hands of the Corporation of the above-mentioned college for distribution, and accordingly sent to us this set, the Association was informed of it, and one of the volumes offered ; upon which thanks voted to be returned to Mr. Marsh," &c.

---

\* Rev. John Rogers was the first minister of Leominster. He was dismissed for heresy in 1758 ; and in 1759 commenced a suit for arrearages of salary, and finally obtained a favorable decision in court, which is the case referred to in the text.

"The Association voted, that each member have them, in his order, for the space of two months, to read them, and is obliged then to send the volumes carefully to his next junior."*

Sept. 19, 1775. — "Conversation was upon the general distresses; viz., by the war, and by the terrible sickness (the dysentery). N.B. — In Marlborough four have been buried in a day, — three times this has occurred, — and nineteen have been buried in a week. The ministers were agreed to recommend the keeping fasts in our respective parishes."

Aug. 19, 1777. — "The public calamities are so increased, and the occurrences have been of late so very observable, various, and distressing, that our

---

* The following items, for which I am indebted to Rev. E. E. Hale, of Boston, are taken from the records of the Corporation of Harvard College: After a vote of thanks acknowledging the present of a hundred and one copies of "Leland" from Dr. Hales and Mr. Wilson, the records go on: "And that, whereas the only direction which came with the same present was, 'To the Rev. President and Fellows of the Colleges in New England,' that the said gentlemen be desired to explain themselves, — whether they meant the said present wholly to the colleges in Cambridge (which are indeed three buildings, yet but one body corporate), or any part of it to any other colleges in New England." Subsequently (Oct. 6, 1761), this entry was made in the records of the Corporation: "That, whereas there is a number of Dr. Leland's 'View,' &c., put into the hands of the Corporation, to be disposed of as they shall judge proper; in order, therefore, to render the said valuable work more extensively useful, *voted*, That one set of octavo books be given to the several associations of ministers in the Province, and that the said set be put into the hands of the senior minister of the respective associations, to be by him lent out to the several ministers of the said associations; and, when that senior minister dies or is removed, to be lodged with the next senior minister from time to time."

whole time was taken up with conversations thereon, together with what Mr. Smith has lately met with at Marlborough, several guns having been shot into his study at midnight, as if aimed to take away his life; but he survived unhurt."

The trials of ministers during the war seem to have been peculiarly great. Owing to the depreciation of the currency, their small salaries were reduced to a mere pittance; and, owing to this and other causes, many ministers were brought into collision with their parishes, and lost their livings and their places.

At a meeting of the Association at Stow, in September, 1778, Mr. Stone, of Southborough, read the conclusion of a sermon — probably a manuscript sermon of his own — *on murder*, but in special," as it is explained, "on a peculiar kind of murder; viz., the murdering ministers by withholding support and destroying their characters."

Oct. 19, 1779. — "The Association were requested by Rev. Messrs. Bridge of East Sudbury, and Bigelow, of Sudbury, to enter into some serious consideration of the burden and wrong the ministers, and they themselves in particular, labored under, on account of the depreciation of the medium, and no proportional provision made for their support."

This indifference to religion and neglect of the ministry afford a good illustration of the principle, that seasons of public calamity are not commonly the most propitious to the growth and prosperous condition of the churches.

Aug. 21, 1781. — Mr. Adams, of Acton, gave the Association an account of the strange conduct and temper of a number of people who were come to Harvard, who are called "Shakers," and under the guidance of an "elect lady."

We come down at length to more quiet and prosperous times, — those immediately preceding the war of 1812. It was in the early part of the present century that several of those philanthropic institutions, which have for their object the diffusion and influence of the gospel of Jesus Christ, entered on their beneficent course. Of one of these, the Evangelical Missionary Society, of Mass., the origin is connected with the history of the Marlborough Association. In September of the year 1806, a Committee, consisting of Messrs. Whitney, of Northborough; Adams, of Acton; and Ripley, of Concord, — who had been chosen some time before to meet delegates from other associations at Rutland, — made a report of their doings: upon which the same persons were requested to attend another meeting of delegates for the purpose of adopting a constitution, and organizing a society. This society, composed at first of ministers and laymen in the contiguous counties of Middlesex and Worcester, was afterwards enlarged, so as to receive members and donations from other parts of the State; and, for a succession of years, was liberally patronized, and became an efficient instrument of good to feeble churches throughout the land. Although at present in the hands of Liberal or Unitarian Christians, its affairs, it is believed, have been conducted, and its bounty distributed, in a spirit of catholicity that is worthy of all commendation.

With a succinct account of the division of the Association into two branches, the eastern and western, and of the dissolution of each, we take leave of the venerable Marlborough Association.

It appears that as early as 1750, at the end of the first quarter of a century, proposals were made to divide the body, which had now spread itself over a very extensive territory. A formal division, however, was not effected till several years later, although, from this date, it was customary for the two sections to hold separate meetings for special purposes, while both continued to attend the regular meetings.

At length, Aug. 10, 1762, at a full meeting of the Association at Lancaster, after mature deliberation it was voted to divide the Association, the line of division to run thus: "for the east part, Messrs. Loring, Gardner, Smith, Stone, Martyn, Parkman, Goss, and Wheeler; Mr. Barrett [the only member absent], if he pleases."

For the west, the ministers of the two Shrewsburys, two Lancasters, Worcester, Holden, Rutland; "and [they added] there may be likelihood of several others to join them."

The west division to retain their right in Dr. Leland's "View of Deistical Writers."

I am not aware that any records are extant of this division, after the separation. As its domain lay wholly in Worcester County, it probably took the name of the Worcester Association, and was the identical body that was dissolved in the year 1791, on occasion of a refusal, on the part of a majority of its members, to fraternize with the minister of the Second Church in Worcester, the late Rev. Dr. Bancroft, then a young man and a reputed Arminian. An account of the whole affair, written by Rev. Dr. Bancroft, and found among his private papers, I shall introduce in its appropriate place. Shortly after the dissolution of the old society, a new one was formed, retaining the same name, which lasted till its union with the Lancaster Association in 1820.

The eastern branch, retaining the name of the Marlborough Association, was sustained, with various fortunes, till Oct. 18, 1814, when, as the record states, "sentiments were expressed on the existing state of the Association; and, for important reasons, it was moved and seconded, that this Association dissolve and be dissolved after this day; which, being put to vote, passed in the affirmative." — "The Moderator, Rev. Dr. Ripley, of Concord, then declared the Association to be dissolved."

The immediate cause of its dissolution appears to have been the breaking-out of the great controversy between the Liberal and Orthodox sections of the New-England churches, which took place about this time; and matters seem to have been brought to a crisis by the opposition that was made in the Association to the receiving into their body, as a member, Rev. Timothy Hilliard, who had been recently ordained over the Congregational Church and Society in Sudbury; only five, it is stated, voting for his admission, five of the members not voting. With brief notices of those who became members after the time of its organization in 1725, we take leave of the Marlborough Association, with feelings of deep respect for the good service, which, during its protracted existence of fourscore years and ten, it rendered to the cause of religion and good morals. It lived to a good old age: peace to its memory!

## ROBERT BRECK.

The leading man in the Association during the first five years of its existence, or till his lamented death, was unquestionably Rev. Robert Breck, of Marlborough. This pre-eminence seems to have been accorded to him by his brethren, as due to his talents, his high character, and his eminent attainments.

He was born in Dorchester, Dec. 7, 1682, and was the son of Captain John Breck, and grandson of

Edward Breck, who came from England, and settled in Dorchester in 1636. After the death of his father, he was sent to Harvard College, where he graduated in the class of 1700. Having prepared for the ministry, and received license to preach, he passed some time on Long Island in the practice of his profession; after which he returned to his native State, and on the 24th October, 1704, being then only twenty-two years of age, he was ordained over the church in Marlborough, as the successor of Rev. William Brimsmead, the first minister of that ancient town.

In September, 1707, he was married to Elizabeth Wainwright, of Haverhill, by whom he had six children, four of whom survived their parents, and became heads of families. His widow lived a little more than five years after her husband's death. Of these four children, Robert (H.C. 1730) was for many years the minister of Springfield, died in 1784; Sarah married Dr. Benjamin Gott, a respectable physician in Marlborough; Hannah married Rev. Ebenezer Parkman, of Westborough; and Samuel (H.C. 1742) was surgeon in the army during the French wars, and died in 1764. Rev. Robert Breck, the father, died, after a distressing sickness, Jan. 6, 1731, in the midst of an honorable and useful life; having just completed the forty-ninth year of his life, and the twenty-sixth of his ministry.

The first notice of his illness is found in the

records of the Marlborough Association, dated Framingham, Sept. 1, 1730; from which it appears, that he had been prevented from attending by "a grievous sore in his mouth." On the 15th of the following month, the Association met again in Marlborough, at the house of Benjamin Wood, Esq., one of Mr. Breck's parishioners; and the day was kept as a fast, on account of the alarming sickness of this beloved brother. On this occasion, the Rev. John Prentice, of Lancaster, preached in the morning, and Rev. John Swift, of Framingham, in the afternoon; the day having been set apart by the town with special reference to the sickness of their minister.

Three sermons were preached, on successive sabbaths, in his pulpit, after his death; which were published together in a small, thick pamplet, a few copies of which have been preserved. These were by the ministers respectively of Framingham, Sudbury, and Lancaster.

Mr. Breck published during his life four discourses; viz., the Election Sermon in 1728; a sermon preached in Shrewsbury in 1720, being the first ever preached in that town.* Two other discourses, addressed to the young on occasion of a large accession to his church of about fifty persons, most of them in early life, were printed in 1728.

---

* Only two copies of this discourse are known to be in existence; one in the possession of Rev. William B. Sprague, D.D. of Albany, and the other of Rev. George Allen, of Worcester.

As an evidence of the high estimation in which he was held, we present the following testimonials: —

The writer of an obituary in the "Weekly Journal" for January, 1731 (No. CC.), which is appended to the funeral discourse by Rev. Mr. Prentice, says that "he was a man of strong natural powers, clear head, and solid judgment; and, by the blessing of God on his unwearied diligence and study, he attained great skill in the learned languages [uncommon in the Hebrew, using to read out of the Hebrew Bible to his family], as also in philosophy, the mathematics, history, as well as in divinity, in which he was sound and orthodox; a good casuist, a strong disputant, a methodical and close preacher. He has left," it is added, "a sorrowful widow and four children."

A writer in the "Weekly News-letter," No. 1408, for Jan. 21, 1731, employs the following eulogistic terms: —

"As a clergyman, he was an able minister of the New Testament, and he obtained mercy to be faithful; the Holy Ghost, who made him an overseer, having richly furnished him with grace and gifts for that sacred office. The *Classis*, or Association of Ministers he belonged to, hung much of their glory on him; had an high esteem of his judgment upon all emergencies that came before them; and he likewise took care upon all occasions, with great courage and prudence, to support the honor and rights of the presbytery, when he thought them invaded or any ways diminished. . . . At the same time, he was of a candid, catholic spirit, far from being rigid or censorious; but he dare not receive for doctrine the commandments of men. . . . As to his learning, I suppose it will be no offence to say, there were few of his standing that were even his equals. He was such a master of the learned languages, that he could, and did frequently, to the capacity of his family, read a chapter of the Hebrew Bible into English; and the Greek was still easier to him. . . . His religion was vital and undisguised. Pride, hypocrisy, and affectation were his aversion; and covetousness was what he was a perfect stranger to. His temper was grave and thoughtful, and yet cheerful at times, especially with his friends and acquaintance, and his conversation entertaining and agreeable.

"In his conduct, he was prudent and careful of his character, both as a minister and a Christian; rather sparing of speech, and more inclined to hear and learn from others.

"His house was open to strangers, and his heart to his friends; and he took great delight in entertaining such as he might in any ways improve by, and treated them with good manners. He was a great lover of government and good order, and would express himself with warmth against that levelling spirit which too much prevails.

"The languishment and pains he went through before his death were very great; but God enabled him to bear the affliction with patience and submission." *

### REV. JOHN SWIFT, FRAMINGHAM.

Mr. Swift was the senior minister of the Marlborough Association at the time of its formation, although the name of Robert Breck stands first on the list of members.

He was a native of Milton, where he was born March 14, 1679, and was the son of Thomas and Elizabeth (Vose) Swift, and grandson of Thomas, one of the first settlers of Dorchester, who came over in 1630. He graduated at Harvard College, in the class of 1697, and was ordained as the first minister of Framingham, Oct. 8, 1701. Soon after his settlement, he was married to Sarah, daughter of Timothy Tileston, of Dorchester, by whom he had one son and five daughters. The son, John Swift, jun., was a graduate of Harvard College, in the class of 1733, and became the minister of Acton. His daughter Sarah married Ebenezer Roby, of Sudbury; Elizabeth was the wife of Rev. James Stone, of Holliston; Anne married Rev. Philip Payson, of Walpole, and was the mother of Rev. Dr. Seth

---

\* It is a noticeable coincidence, that a lineal descendant of Mr. Breck, of the third generation, Deacon Isaac Davis, of Northborough, father of Ex-Governor John Davis, of Worcester, was afflicted with what seems to have been a similar disease, which occasioned his death, in 1826.

Payson, of Rindge, N.H., father of Rev. Edward Payson, D.D., of Portland, Maine; another daughter, Mary, was unmarried; Martha, the youngest, married Major John Farrar, of Framingham.

"His ministry in this town," says the historian of Framingham, Rev. William Barry, one of his successors in the ministry, now living in Chicago, Ill., "as far as is known to us, was conducted with faithfulness and prudence; and not a notice occurs, in all the transactions of the town and church, in any degree qualifying the respect and estimation in which he was held. . . . Of his ability as a preacher we have no means of judging. His printed sermons are marked with a pure and classical taste. He was free from all affectation of style, as well as extravagance of zeal, or rashness of opinion. The subjects of his ordinary discourses, as one may infer from his own diary, were often suggested by passing events. Some of these discourses bear marks of extemporaneous composition. Thus, he notes on one occasion his preaching from the words, 'The voice of the Lord is upon the waters: the God of glory thundereth;' adding, 'it being a day of thunder.' . . . A day of extreme severity suggested the text, 'Who can stand before his cold?' And a few weeks later, doubtless while the snow drifted through the crevices of the ancient and dilapidated meeting-house, the motto of his sermon was, 'a covert from the storm.' The halt of a detachment of soldiers in the village induced him to discourse from the words, 'a devout soldier.'"

Mr. Swift preached the Election Sermon in 1732; also a discourse on occasion of the death of Rev. Robert Breck, of Marlborough, in 1731; both of which were printed. He is spoken of as "a wise counsellor and a good man, of a well-cultivated mind, and held in great esteem in the churches."

We learn from a note to Mr. Barry's account of Mr. Swift, that his salary was £70, equal to $233.33; to which in the latter part of his ministry, on account of the protracted sickness of his wife, an additional grant of £10 was added. He died, April 24, 1745, in the forty-fifth year of his ministry, and the sixty-seventh of his age.

A monument was erected over his remains, with the following inscription in Latin: —

HIC JACET
Qui obiit A.D. 1745, Aprilis 24⁰
Ætatisque anno 67ᵐᵒ
VIR ILLE REVERENDUS D. JOHANNES SWIFT,
Dotibus et nativis et acquisitis ornatus;
Docendi Artifex, Exemplar vivendi,
Felix, dum vixit,
Mores exhibens secundum Divinas Regulas
Episcopo necessarios
Commiscens Prudentiam Serpentis, Columbæque
Innocentiam:
Commercium cum eo habentibus
In vita percharus,
Atque gratam sui, etsi mœstam, Memoriam
Post mortem, Iis relinquens:
Qui per varios casus, variaque Rerum Discrimina

> Atque usque ad mortem,
> Raram discretionem, Modestiam, Patientiam,
> Voluntatique Supremi Numinis Submissionem
> Spectandam præbens:
> Jam tandem in Domino requievit
> Adoptionem
> Scilicet, Corporis obruti Redemptionem
> Expectabundus.

### REV. ISRAEL LORING.

Mr. Loring was born in Hull, April 15, 1682, and was the son of John and Rachel (Wheatley) Loring, his father's second wife.

He entered Harvard College at the age of fifteen, and graduated in the class of 1701. Increase Mather, who was then at the head of that institution, bears this honorable testimony to his character while a student in college. It is taken from the introduction to a sermon of Mr. Loring's on Early Piety, published in 1718: —

"As for the author of this discourse, I have known him from his youth. When he was in the college, into which society I admitted him, and there graduated him, I observed that he was there studious, blameless, and serious, in his young years; the fitter to exhort young men to remember their Creator in the days of their youth. Since he has been called to public service, he has found great and deserved respect and acceptance with the Lord's people."

He was ordained as minister of Sudbury, Nov. 20,

1706; and May 25, 1709, he was married, at Hull, to Mary, daughter of Nathan Hayman, of Charlestown, by whom he had seven children, two of whom were graduates of Harvard College. One of these, John, settled as a physician in Boston. Of the other children we have no knowledge.

During the first sixteen years of his ministry, his charge embraced the whole town, including East Sudbury, now Wayland, which was set off in 1722 as a distinct corporation. Having the choice of the two parishes thus created, he concluded to take the west, where he remained through his long ministry till his death, which took place on the 9th of March, 1772, at the age of ninety years. His ministry lasted sixty-six years. It is said that he preached twice on the last sabbath but one preceding his death, and that, on the following day, he offered a prayer at a town-meeting, where he was taken ill, and thence conveyed to his house, where he shortly departed this life. His wife, who was about two months younger than her husband, had preceded him a little more than two years, having died Dec. 24, 1769, in her eighty-eighth year. It is related of her, that, for forty-five of the last years of her life, she ate but one meal in twenty-four hours, and that was ordinarily a little bread and cheese shortly before she retired at night; and yet her health was such that she was able to conduct her domestic affairs till about ten days before her death. The remarkable fact is also mentioned, that, on the sabbath that she was a corpse, a child of her great-grand-daughter was baptized by the aged minister, and called by her name. At the time of his death, Mr. Loring had been a member of the Marlborough Association nearly half a century.

Mr. Loring preached the Election Sermon in 1737, in the presence of Governor Belcher, in which he makes a manly and high-minded appeal to the "Honorable Great and General Assembly," in behalf of the families of those unfortunate persons who had suffered from the witchcraft delusion, near the close of the preceding century. "The question is," he writes "(if it be not beyond all question), whether a restitution is not due from the public to them, and we are not bound in justice to make it?"

In 1742, he preached the Convention Sermon in Boston, in which he strongly reprobates the practice, introduced by Whitefield and others, of ignorant persons "setting themselves up for teachers and exhorters of the people." — " Knowledge in the liberal arts and original tongues," he remarks, "is an handmaid to divinity, and a great help to attain it. But this our exhorters are destitute of. Christ's ministers get their knowledge in a course of hard study, with the blessing of Christ upon their endeavors; but the teachers that I am speaking of spring up, as it were, in the night, and have very little time for the gaining of divine knowledge in an ordinary way. . . .

"May we not conclude, then," he asks, "that the exhorters of the present day are utterly unqualified for the work which they have so temerariously undertaken, and consequently that Jesus Christ never called them to it, and that he will never assist them in it, nor reward them for it?"

In 1745, after Mr. Whitefield's second visit to this country, most of the members of the Marlborough Association, to which he belonged, signed a remonstrance, entitled a "Testimony against the Rev. Mr. George Whitefield and his Conduct," Mr. Loring being one of the number; in which they say, in reference to the course pursued by that remarkable man, —

"We cannot, therefore, but lament it, that he meets with so much countenance and encouragement among us, and especially that any of our fathers and brethren in the ministry should give such countenance to one so erroneous in his doctrines, and so disorderly in his conduct, by inviting and admitting him into their pulpits, and more especially by allowing him to administer the ordinance of the Lord's Supper in their churches."

Reference is here probably made to Rev. John Seccomb, of Harvard, and Rev. Solomon Prentice, of Grafton, whose conduct in this regard, in opposition to the views of their parishioners, caused great divisions, and led to their dismission.

Mr. Loring was a stanch Calvinist, and a strenuous opponent of Arminianism, the liberal theology of that day; but he was as strenuous a defender of the ecclesiastical order and the rights of an ordained clergy, and would give no countenance to itinerant preachers and interlopers, whatever the doctrines they preached.

As an evidence of his steadfast adherence to the Genevan faith, we quote from a communication from Rev. Edmund H. Sears, formerly of Wayland, now of Weston: —

"Mr. Loring had his choice to stay in the east side of the river, or go to the west side. He chose the latter, which made a vacancy in the east parish, over which Rev. William Cook was ordained in 1723. Mr. Cook seems to have been a man of more than common attainments. It was during his ministry that two great parties began to appear more distinctly in the Congregational churches, known as the Arminian and the Calvinistic. Father Loring was rigidly and implacably Calvinistic: Mr. Cook took Arminian grounds, and preached a more genial theology. It does not appear, however, that any other than friendly, fraternal relations subsisted between Mr. Cook and Mr. Loring. Mr. Cook's ministry was peaceful and happy; and he died, extensively beloved and lamented, in 1760.

"At the time of Mr. Cook's settlement, he was a young man of vigor and promise. Mr. Loring was in middle life, but in feeble health; and people thought his parish was soon to become vacant. While they congratulated the east parish on the settlement of their young minister, they were fixing their features into postures ready to condole with the west parish for the loss of theirs. And yet Mr. Loring, notwithstanding the predictions of friends and doctors, survived Mr. Cook, preached his funeral sermon, helped ordain his successor, and was active in his calling for years afterwards."

"At Mr. Cook's funeral, according to tradition, Father Loring took his text from Ps. li. 18, — 'Do good, in thy good pleasure, unto Zion,' &c.; and his first remark was, that 'God did good unto Zion by removing ungodly ministers.' This was a covert thrust at Mr. Cook's Arminianism; and the people were shocked and indignant, as the corpse of their beloved pastor lay before them upon his bier. However, the remark seemed disconnected with what followed; for Father Loring went on, and spoke well of Mr. Cook and his ministry. Not many days after, Father Loring was in Boston, and met Dr. Chauncey in the street, who accosted him in his blunt way, and demanded, 'What did you mean by abusing brother Cook so, the other day, at his funeral?' Father Loring did not make much reply, but was rather disposed to defend the offensive remark, made at the opening of his sermon; whereupon Dr. Chauncey rejoined, 'Well, sir, I hope I shall have to preach *your* funeral sermon ; and I will abuse *you* as much as you did our brother Cook.' " *

Mr. Loring published a Sermon on the Nature and Necessity of the New Birth, in 1728 ; on the Death of Rev. Robert Breck, in 1731 ; on the Torments of Hell, 1732 ; an Election Sermon, 1737 ; a Convention Sermon, 1742 ; on Justification, in 1749 ; and at the Ordination of Rev. Gideon Richardson, at Wells, 1754.

The first-named of these discourses was delivered at the Thursday Lecture in Boston ; and, in an introductory notice by Rev. Thomas Prince, the author is spoken of in the following commendatory terms : —

"He was so plain and easy in his expression and method, so familiar and moving in his delivery, so affected himself with the momentous truths he would inculcate on us, that we must have hearts of adamant to resist the impressions, or continue indifferent whether we pass through so great a change as he clearly explained and earnestly urged as of the last necessity. Nor could the assembly separate without expressing their great satisfaction, and wishes that such an important discourse might be in this capacity to make further impression on those that heard it, and to extend its influence also to others."

---

* Mr. Sears received this, and other anecdotes relating to Mr. Loring, from the late Rev. David Damon, D.D., who was a native of East Sudbury.

This was at the time when the Thursday Lecture was attended by multitudes from Boston and the neighboring towns, and was regarded as the great event of the week.

"Mr. Loring," we are told,* "left a manuscript journal of thirty volumes, of two hundred and twenty-four pages each, closely written; containing, not only a record of all the more important events connected with his ministry, but a great amount of important biographical and historical material. But most of these volumes have been irrecoverably lost.

All that is known of the personal appearance of the venerable patriot is on the authority of a lady who died in 1851, at the age of ninety-three. She knew him in her childhood; and her testimony was, that "he was of a tall, slender form; apostolic in his manner; possessing warm domestic affections; and often calling her one of his dear little orphans."

It is said, that " he divided his library between his own children, and those of his son, Dr. John Loring, of Boston."

## REV. JOHN GARDNER, STOW.

Rev. John Gardner, son of John and Elizabeth Gardner, " descended from a reputable family," was born in the corner of Charlestown contiguous to

---

* See Annals of the American Pulpit, by Rev. Dr. Sprague, of Albany, vol. i. pp. 257-260.

Woburn, called "Charlestown End" and "Gardner Row," after the name of most of the inhabitants. His ancestors, and their descendants there resident, from the first attended public worship at Woburn, where Mr. Gardner's name is recorded. He was born July 22, 1696, O.S.; was graduated at Harvard College, in 1715; and was ordained at Stow as successor of Rev. John Eveleth (H.C. 1689), Nov. 26, 1718. He continued in the ministry till his death, 10th January, 1775, at the age of fourscore years. A few months before his death, viz. 11th October, 1774, Rev. Jonathan Newell was ordained as his colleague, whose ministry lasted fifty-six years, or till the time of his decease, Oct. 4, 1830.

Mr. Gardner was married, 1719, to Mary, eldest daughter of Rev. Joseph Baxter, of Medfield (H.C. 1693), when she was but nineteen years old. By her he had eight children, of whom three of the sons were educated at Harvard College.

1. Samuel (H.C. 1746), born 6th March, 1724, who married Mary, youngest daughter of Rev. William Cooper of Boston, and died at Milton, 18th January, 1778.

2. Hon. Henry Gardner, born Nov. 14, 1731 (H.C. 1750), died at Dorchester, Oct. 7, 1782. He was the first Treasurer of the Commonwealth, and was the father of Dr. Henry Gardner (H.C. 1798), and grandfather of Hon. Henry Joseph Gardner, ex-Governor of Massachusetts.

3. Rev. Francis Gardner, born Feb. 17, 1735, O.S. (H.C. 1756); ordained at Leominster, Dec. 22, 1762; and who died suddenly at Watertown, June, 1814. He was grandfather of Francis Gardner (H.C. 1831), now at the head of the public Latin School, Boston.

All the children of Rev. John Gardner survived their parents, and filled their places with honor.

"Mr. Gardner," says one of his contemporaries, Rev. Mr. Parkman, of Westborough (see Church Records of Stow), "was a gentleman of good intellectual abilities, had collected valuable treasures of learning and observation on mankind. He was sound in the principles of religion, and steady in the practice of the duties and virtues thereof. He was prudent, peaceable, hospitable, and very faithful in the discharge of his pastoral office. He was stanch for the privileges of the people, but a strenuous assertor of the rights of the gospel ministry. He lamented the divisions in many churches, and had deeply at heart the deplorable state of public political affairs."—"He is still remembered," says Dr. Thayer, in his sermon at the funeral of his son, Rev. Francis Gardner of Leominster, "for the soundness of his understanding, for fidelity in his sacred offices, and for exemplary piety."—"He was," says the librarian of Harvard College, Rev. John L. Sibley (one of the successors of Rev. Mr. Gardner in the ministry, to whom I am indebted for several valuable communications), — "he was strenuously opposed to the Whitefieldian movement. In his deportment, he probably exceeded the ministerial sternness and imperiousness of his time. A very aged man told me, more than thirty years ago, that he always stood in awe of him and his great wig. He recollected distinctly, that once, when Mr. Gardner had called at the house of his father, who lived at some distance from the road, his father told him to go down to the road, and open the gate to let the minister pass through. Full of trepidation, he ran in advance; and as soon as Mr. Gardner, with his great wig, had got through the gate, he fled back to the house with the greatest speed with which his legs could carry him."

## REV. JOHN PRENTICE, LANCASTER.

Rev. John Prentice, of Lancaster, was a native of Newton, where he was born in 1680. He was a graduate of Harvard College of the class of 1700, being a classmate of Rev. Robert Breck. He was ordained March 29, 1708, and died Jan. 6, 1746, at the age of sixty-six.

In the "History of Lancaster," by the late Joseph Willard, Esq., of Boston, we find the following testimony to his learning and character, in an extract from the sermon preached at the installation of his successor, Rev. Timothy Harrington, Nov. 16, 1748, by Rev. John Hancock, of Lexington, grandfather of John Hancock of revolutionary memory :—

"God gave him the tongue of the learned: so he knew how to speak a word unto him that was weary. The God of the spirits of all flesh fitted him for his work, and taught him how to behave himself in the house of God. They that knew him esteemed him for his piety, his probity, his peaceableness, and gentleness, and for his commendable steadiness in these uncertain times" (referring, no doubt, to the great revivals under the preaching of Whitefield, Tennant, and others). "He was a practical, scriptural, profitable preacher. As to his secular affairs," he pleasantly remarks, "with the help of that Prudence God gave him" (meaning his wife of that name, as well as the virtue so called), "he managed them with discretion."

Three of the daughters of Mr. Prentice were married to clergymen of the vicinity: viz., Mary, to Rev. Job Cushing, of Shrewsbury; Relief, to Rev. John Rogers, of Leominster; and Rebecca, to Rev. John Mellen, of Sterling, who thus became the mother of John Mellen, Esq., of Cambridge, and of Hon. Prentice Mellen, of Maine, named for his maternal grandfather.

Mr. Prentice preached the Election Sermon in 1735, which was printed; also a sermon at the opening of the first court in the new county of Worcester, Aug. 10, 1731. His sermon at the ordination of

Rev. Ebenezer Parkman, of Westborough, was also printed.

### REV. JOB CUSHING, OF SHREWSBURY.

Mr. Cushing was born in Hingham, in 1694, graduated at Harvard College in 1714, and was ordained as the first minister of Shrewsbury, Dec. 4, 1723.

After a useful and peaceful ministry of nearly thirty-seven years, he died, much lamented, Aug. 6, 1760, in the sixty-seventh year of his age.

The following memorandum is found in the records of the Association: —

"Our dear brother Cushing being removed by death, most of the religious exercises bewailed it, or pointed to it. He died suddenly on the 6th inst." (Aug. 6, 1760).

Mr. Cushing married Mary Prentice, a daughter of the minister of Lancaster.

Some of his descendants still live in Shrewsbury and Northborough.

### REV. EBENEZER PARKMAN, OF WESTBOROUGH.

Mr. Parkman was the youngest of the seven original members of the Marlborough Association, having been but one year in the ministry at the time of its formation. He was born in Boston, Sept. 5, 1703, and was the son of William Parkman, whose grandfather, Elias, lived in Dorchester as early as 1633, but who afterwards removed to Windsor, Conn. (Savage).

Mr. Parkman was graduated at Harvard College in 1721; ordained in Westborough, Oct. 28, 1724, at the early age of twenty-one. He died Dec. 9, 1782, in the eightieth year of his age, and the fifty-ninth of his ministry, having been a member of the Association a little more than fifty-seven years. He was the last survivor of the original seven who formed the Association.

Rev. Mr. Parkman was the father of the well-known Boston merchant, Samuel Parkman, Esq., and grandfather of the late Rev. Dr. Francis Parkman, the respected and lamented minister of the New North Church, Boston. Rev. Elisha Rockwood, one of the successors of Mr. Parkman in the ministry, and who married one of his grand-daughters, speaks of him in the following terms:—

"His preaching was evangelical, his deportment dignified; and, in his daily intercourse with his people, he was distinguished for dropping those words which are as apples of gold in pictures of silver."

From an examination of a number of manuscript sermons of Mr. Parkman, which have come into my possession, I should judge that he was, for the age in which he lived, a respectable scholar, a good writer, and a man of a catholic spirit, as were most of the ministers of the Marlborough Association. He was much respected by his own people and in the neighboring churches; and he left for his children and friends a name without reproach.

One of his sons, Breck Parkman, named for his maternal grandfather, Rev. Robert Breck, of Marlborough, was for many years a respectable merchant in Westborough, who is remembered by many now living.

### REV. SOLOMON PRENTICE, GRAFTON.

Mr. Prentice was born in Cambridge, May 11, 1705, and was the son of Solomon Prentice, of that place. He was graduated at Harvard College, 1727, and was a classmate of Governors Hutchinson and Trumbull. His ordination over the church in Grafton, of which he was the first minister, took place Dec. 29, 1731; Rev. Mr. Appleton, of Cambridge, preaching the ordination sermon.

In 1740, the celebrated Whitefield came over to this country, whose preaching excited a great deal of enthusiasm, and was the occasion of much controversy among the clergy, and of many unhappy divisions in the churches of New England. Mr. Prentice was a great admirer of Whitefield, and became one of what were called "the New Lights." His course was not approved by his society; and a controversy arose which led to his dismission, July 10, 1747.

He was afterwards settled in Easton, Bristol County, where he remained about seven years. He then joined the Presbyterians, but was suspended by the presbytery in 1754; after which he returned to Grafton, where he lived till his death, May 22, 1773, at the age of sixty-eight.

### REV. WILLIAM COOK, EAST SUDBURY.

Rev. William Cook, the first minister of East Sudbury (now Wayland), was a native of Hadley, on the Connecticut River, and was born about 1696 or 1697. He received his collegiate education at Harvard College, Cambridge, where he graduated in 1716. Before his settlement in the ministry, he filled the place of librarian of the college for one year, — 1720–1721.

His ordination took place March 20, 1723; and, after a ministry of thirty-six years, he died Nov. 12, 1760, in the sixty-fourth year of his age.

He preached the sermon at the ordination of Rev. Elisha Marsh, at Westminster, Oct. 20, 1742, and at the ordination of Rev. Samuel Baldwin, of Hanover, in Plymouth County, in 1751. These two discourses, with an anniversary sermon delivered in Plymouth in 1755, were published.

We learn from Sprague's "Annals," that he was on the council that ordained the Rev. Robert Breck, son of the respected minister of Marlborough, at

Springfield, July 26, 1736, whose ordination was opposed by most of the Hampshire Association.

## REV. SAMUEL BARRETT, HOPKINTON.

Mr. Barrett was born in Boston, about 1700; was graduated at Harvard College, 1721; and was ordained in Hopkinton in 1724, Sept. 2. He died Dec. 11, 1772, in the seventy-second year of his age and the forty-ninth of his ministry. The Historical Society of Massachusetts speaks of him as "a pious, good Christian; a man of great candor and good nature." — "They ought to have added," says Rev. Mr. Howe in his Century Sermon, "a man of great stability and perseverance." Mr. Howe also speaks of his ministry as "lengthy, honorable, and successful."

About a year before his death, — viz., Jan. 15, 1772, — Rev. Elijah Fitch was settled as his colleague. Mr. Barrett was the first minister of Hopkinton, a town named in honor of Edward Hopkins, Esq., an English gentleman of wealth and benevolence, who was one of the early benefactors of Harvard College, and whose munificent bequest of eight hundred pounds sterling, made in 1657, was, in 1710, invested in the purchase of a large tract of land, including the town of Hopkinton, and parts of the adjoining towns of Upton and Holliston; the land to be leased to tenants for the term of ninety-nine years, at the annual rent of a penny sterling the acre. Mr. Barrett's salary was fixed at thirty-five pounds, in addition to the cutting and carting his firewood. This was for the first three years; after which, his salary was raised to seventy pounds, which, with the firewood, was his annual salary during his ministry.

From the account given of him in Rev. Mr. Howe's celebrated Century Sermon, we infer that he was a man of sound judgment and practical good sense; one who stood steadfast and immovable in what Mr. Howe terms "troublous times," referring to the disorders and divisions occasioned by the labors of Whitefield, Tennant, and other itinerant preachers of that day.

An only son of Mr. Barrett died in 1800, leaving a son, who, with many eccentricities, had a remarkable memory, and had some acquaintance with Latin and Greek. He used to travel from place to place; and I well remember, at the time I was fitting for college, hearing him repeat, *memoriter*, long passages from Virgil and the Greek Testament; and how we wondered that —

"One small head could carry all he knew."

Some fifty years since, he published a small treatise on English Grammar, a copy of which, with the author's autograph, is now in my possession, and is a work of considerable merit.

### REV. THOMAS FRINK, RUTLAND.

Mr. Frink was the first minister of Rutland, where he was ordained Nov. 1, 1727. His ministry in that place lasted a little more than thirteen years, till Sept. 8, 1740, when, for what reasons I do not learn, he was dismissed. He was installed at Plymouth, Nov. 3, 1743, and afterwards at Barre, October, 1753, from which charge he was dismissed a third time, July 17, 1766. In 1758, he preached the Election Sermon. Of the time and place of his death I find no record.

He was born in Sudbury, and graduated at Harvard College in 1722; married, Feb. 13, 1729, to Isabelle, daughter of Samuel Wright, Esq., of Rutland.*

### REV. NATHAN STONE, SOUTHBOROUGH.

Mr. Stone was a native of Harwich, now Brewster, where he was born Feb. 18, 1708, being the son of Rev. Nathaniel Stone (H.C. 1690) minister of that place. His mother was a daughter of Governor Hinckley. The grandfather of Rev. Nathaniel Stone (Simon Stone) came over in the "Increase," in 1634, with his wife Joan and several children. Rev. James Stone, of Holliston (H.C. 1724), was

---
* A. Q. Reg., x. 128.

the son of Ebenezer Stone, uncle of Rev. Nathan Stone, of Southborough.

Rev. Nathan Stone was graduated at Harvard College, 1726; ordained at Southborough, Oct. 21, 1730.

By his wife Judith, he had nine children, three sons and six daughters; and by a second wife, Mary, two sons. His first wife died, Feb. 9, 1748–9, aged thirty-six. "He was," says Whitney, in his "History of Worcester County," "a judicious, prudent, and faithful minister of Christ, and was continued serving God in the gospel of his Son, to the great satisfaction of his people, until May 31, 1781, when he departed this life, in the seventy-fourth year of his life and the fifty-first of his ministry." \*

## REV. JOHN MARTYN, NORTHBOROUGH.

Rev. John Martyn, the first minister of Northborough, was the son of Captain Edward Martyn, a shipmaster in Boston, where he was born in 1706, and where he spent his early life under the care of an excellent mother, who had been left a widow in easy circumstances, some time previous to Mr. Martyn's entering college. He graduated at Harvard College in 1724. For several years after he left college, he devoted his attention to secular pursuits, and was for some time a citizen of Harvard. He

---

\* Mass. Spy, June 21, 1781.  Geneal. Reg., x. 230; x. 128.

was married to Miss Mary Marrett, of Cambridge, by whom he had four sons, — John, Michael, Richard, and Nathaniel: the two former marrying, and living in Northborough; the other two removing, one to Windsor, Conn., the other to one of the Southern States. Mary, the only daughter, married a Minot, of Concord, Mass. A daughter of John (Abigail) married Thaddeus Fay, jun., of Northborough, and died April 23, 1740, at the age of seventy-nine. A daughter of Michael (Seraphina) married Oliver Eager, whose daughter Zilpah married Colonel William Whitney, son of Rev. Peter Whitney.

Mr. Martyn, at about the age of forty, turned his attention to theological pursuits, prepared for the ministry, and was ordained as the first minister of the North Precinct in Westborough, now Northborough, May 21, 1746, O.S., answering to June 1.

After a ministry of twenty years, during which he faithfully and acceptably discharged the duties of the pastoral office, April 30, 1767, after a short illness, Mr. Martyn departed this life, in the sixty-first year of his age and the twenty-first of his ministry. His widow died Sept. 8, 1775, aged seventy.*

The following epitaph is inscribed on his gravestone: —

"Under this sepulchral stone lies interred, in Christian hope of a blessed resurrection, what was mortal of the Rev. John Martyn, A.M., the late worthy pastor of this flock, son of the

---

* A. Q. Reg., x. 127; and Massachusetts Historical Collections, x. 85.

late Captain Edward Martyn, of Boston. Educated at Harvard College, Cambridge. Was ordained in this place, May 21, 1746. Approved himself an assiduous, orthodox, eminent preacher of the great redemption by Jesus Christ. After a few days' illness, to the inexpressible grief of his family, flock, and friends, expired April 30, 1767, aged sixty-one.

"Si vitam fide Christi egimus sanctam, si quid præclare gessimus hoc sit nostri monumentum." *

### REV. AARON SMITH, MARLBOROUGH.

Mr. Smith was born in Ipswich, Oct. 25, 1713, was graduated at Harvard College, 1735, and was ordained over the church in Marlborough as the successor of Rev. Benjamin Kent, June 11, 1740, on a salary of eighty pounds a year, equal to $266⅔. The same year, he married Martha Allen, daughter of Joseph and Mary Allen, of Gloucester. His father-in-law, we are told, was the oldest of seventeen children of Joseph Allen, sen., by his first wife, Rachel. Mr. Smith's wife, Martha, died the year after their marriage; having given birth, Aug. 22, 1741, to twins, one of whom died in infancy. The other, Martha, became the wife of Rev. Josiah Bridge, of East Sudbury (Wayland). After the death of his wife, he remained a widower during the remainder of his life.

---

* Only two descendants of Rev. John Martyn, and not one of Rev. Peter Whitney, are now living in Northborough.

After a comparatively peaceful and prosperous ministry of twenty years or more, some dissatisfaction manifested itself among his people, which was increased by the suspicion that his sympathies were rather with the royalists than with the friends of freedom. In 1777 two guns were discharged into his sleeping apartment after he had retired to rest, the contents of which were lodged in a beam near the bed on which he was lying. Whether this was done with murderous intentions, or only as a warning to leave the place, cannot now be known. The perpetrators of the deed were never discovered, although the town offered a reward of one hundred pounds for their apprehension. Owing partly to ill health, and partly, no doubt, to his growing unpopularity, in January, 1778, he asked a dismission, which was granted, April 29, the same year, " on account," as is stated in the result of a council, " of his infirmity and weakness, which greatly affected his lungs, and voice in particular."

After his dismission, he removed to East Sudbury, where, in the family of Rev. Josiah Bridge, his son-in-law, he passed the remainder of his days. His death took place March 25, 1781, at the age of sixty-seven.

Mr. Smith had the reputation of being a faithful minister and a good man; nor is there any sufficient reason for calling in question his patriotism. He lived in troublous times, for which, as well as for protracted ill health, due allowance should be made, in forming an estimate of his character. "Judge not, that ye be not judged." *

### REV EBENEZER MORSE, BOYLSTON.

Mr. Morse was born in Medfield, March 2, 1718, and was the son of Hon. Joshua and Mary (Partridge) Morse. He was a graduate of Harvard College, of the class of 1737, and was ordained as the first minister of the North Parish in Shrewsbury (now Boylston), Oct. 26, 1743.

He retained his place, deriving part of his support from his practice as a physician, till the commencement of the Revolutionary War, when, as stated by Rev. Mr. Whitney in the "History of Worcester County," "he was dismissed, more especially on account of his political sentiments respecting the controversy between Great Britain and America." His dismission took place Nov. 10, 1775. After his dismission, he remained in Boylston, continuing his practice as a physician till the infirmities of age came upon him. He died Jan. 3, 1802, at the advanced age of eighty-four. One of his sons, Dr. Eliakim Morse, of Watertown, died Jan. 9, 1858, wanting only one year and one month of completing a century of years.

---

\* See Mass. Hist. Coll , vol. iv. 47; xxii. 312; x. 309.

Rev. Mr. Morse, of Boylston, is spoken of as a man of strong passions, resolute, fixed in his purpose, unyielding.

"He possessed," says Rev. Abner Morse, "a strong, clear, and vigorous mind, a bold and independent spirit, keen and ready wit, and a kind, benevolent, and Christian heart."

The following lines were written by Rev. Thaddeus M. Harris, D.D., of Dorchester, on hearing of the death of his friend and benefactor. Dr. Harris had been placed in the family of Dr. Morse at the early age of ten, his parents having been made homeless by the conflagration of Charlestown at the battle of Bunker Hill. He remained in the family for many years, where he was fitted for college.

> " Hast thou read rightly, Mary ? Is he dead, —
> My early friend, protector, more than father ?
> Oh, had I but been present at the scene,
> With filial tenderness to smooth his couch,
> And kneel beside him for his dying blessing !
> But he has blessed me : I remember yet,
> When in kind charity he took me home,
> And in the evening prayer, with lifted hands,
> And voice and look inspired with heavenly grace,
> Devoutly he commended me to Him
> In whom the fatherless find help and mercy.
> He blessed me, too, in his benignant care
> To soothe my grief, to satisfy my wants,
> And to improve and store my youthful mind
> With the best fruits of knowledge and of virtue.
> Nay, more : a parting blessing I have shared.
> When last I saw him, the devout old man
> Wished me Heaven's favor, health and happiness,

A long and useful life, and peaceful death,
And then to meet him in the realms of bliss.
  That I may worthy prove to meet him there,
Let me not fail those counsels to observe.
He gave, to guide my youth, those maxims sage,
Which formed my early principles, and fixed
The purpose and the tenor of my life.
And let me copy fair, as my safe model,
His exemplary conduct, where appeared
The candor and benevolence refined
Of Christian charity, the graceful joy
And winning loveliness of piety,
And the firm faith and elevated hope
Which smiled and triumphed in the hour of death."
                          "DORCASTRIENSIS."

## REV. THOMAS GOSS, BOLTON.

Bolton, formerly a part of Lancaster, was incorporated in 1738; and Mr. Goss was the first minister of the town. Of the place of his birth we have no knowledge. From his age at the time of his death, he must have been born about the year 1717. He graduated at Cambridge with the class of 1737, and was a classmate of the Rev. Andrew Elliot and Rev. Peter Thacher, also of his near neighbor, Rev. Timothy Harrington, of Lancaster. The exact date of his ordination is not known. Rev. Mr. Edes places it somewhere between September, 1741, and March, 1742, probably Nov. 5. His ministry lasted about thirty years, his dismission taking place Aug. 13, 1771. Difficulties between the minister and the parish began to show themselves in May of the preceding year, when various complaints were brought by the church against their pastor. " A council was called, which exculpated him from the charges. A great controversy ensued, when the church, finding they could obtain no relief from the advice of sister churches, proceeded to dissolve the pastoral relation between them and their minister. The neighboring churches, considering this a high-handed piece of assumption of power on the part of the laity, proceeded in council to pass censures upon the Bolton church in their corporate capacity, to deprive them of covenant privileges, and to exclude them from all communion and fellowship with other churches. The people, being thus put upon the defensive, made a common cause of their troubles through all the towns in the vicinity." *

We shall have occasion to speak more fully of this controversy in our notice of Rev. Mr. Mellen, of Sterling, whose dismission, a few years later, was occasioned in principal part by his connection with this great controversy between the clergy and the laity.

"From this time," — the time of his dismission, — writes Rev. Mr. Edes, "Mr. Goss maintained a constant running fight with his old parish. A portion, withdrawing and becoming his adherents, held Sunday services with him in the house lately occupied

---

* Goodwin's History of Sterling, in Worcester Magazine.

by General Holman; while the larger portion held the meeting-house, and settled another minister, Rev. John Walley, formerly settled in Ipswich.

After the death of Mr. Goss in 1780, and the dismission of Mr. Walley, which took place some time before Aug. 22, 1783, the two parties came together, and united in the settlement of Rev. Phineas Wright, who was ordained Oct. 26, 1785, and was the immediate predecessor of Rev. Isaac Allen.

Mr. Goss has been described to me, by those who remembered him, as a tall, spare man, of stern aspect, and not of gentle or winning manners. He appears to have been a man of an indomitable will and somewhat forbidding presence. With many of his brethren, he entertained high notions of clerical authority, — *a high-church Puritan*, as he might be styled. In the war of our Independence, he took sides with the royalists, and was a thorough-going Tory, as was his son Thomas, who fled to Annapolis, N.S., where he ended his days.

A monument erected in the old burying-ground at Bolton contains the following inscription: —

MEMORIÆ SACRUM

Rev<sup>di</sup> Thomæ Goss, A.M.

qui supra xxxix annos, sacro Ecclesiæ apud Boltonienses Pastoris functus officio, é vita cessit Jan<sup>rii</sup> Die 17<sup>mo</sup> MDCCLXXX.

Ætatis 63.

Vir Pietate, Hospitalitate, Amicitia, aliisq: virtutibus, et publicis et privatis ornatus:

> Corpore quidem infractus, Animi tamen robustus, miraq: Fortitudine præditus.
> primus inter Clericos
> Temporibus hisce infaustis,
> Statum Ecclesiarum labefactantes fortiter oppugnando
> et pro se ecclesiastica, sic ut a Majoribus tradita
> Heroice obluctando
> graviter perpessus est.
>
> ---
>
> Hoc monumentum Amici posuere.

## REV. JOSEPH BUCKMINSTER, RUTLAND.

Mr. Buckminster, "the able, faithful, and worthy minister of Rutland," as Whitney designates him, was a native of Framingham, where he was born March 1, 1719–20; being the son of Colonel Joseph Buckminster, jun., and grandson of Colonel Joseph Buckminster, sen., one of the early settlers and leading citizens of Framingham. His mother was Sarah Lawson, of Hopkinton. He graduated at Harvard College in 1739, and was ordained in Rutland, as the successor of Rev. Thomas Frink, Sept. 15, 1752.

He was married in Weston, June 30, 1743, to Lucy Williams, daughter of Rev. William Williams, who was a son of Rev. William Williams, of Hatfield. Her mother was daughter of Rev. Dr. Solomon Stoddard, of Northampton, and first cousin to the celebrated Jonathan Edwards. Dr. Stoddard is spoken of in a quotation given in Mrs. Eliza Buckminster Lee's Memoirs of her father and brother, as "that great divine, who was considered by many as the light of the New-England churches, as John Calvin was of the Reformation." President Styles, however, thinks he has been overrated, and that his son-in-law, Williams, of Hatfield, was "the greater man."

"Mr. Buckminster continued," says the historian of Worcester County, "the able, faithful, and worthy minister of Rutland, until Nov. 3, 1792, when he died, in the seventy-third year of his age and the fifty-first of his ministry." In Allen's Biographies, he is styled "a Sublapsarian Calvinist." — "It is a comfort to think," writes Mrs. Lee, "that the thing itself is not so harsh as its name; for it seems an effort to soften the stern features of Calvinism, and to mingle a little human clay in the iron and granite of its image."

Mr. Buckminster had, by his wife Lucy, nine children; one of whom, Joseph, born Oct. 4, 1751, was educated at Yale College, where he graduated in 1770. This was the eminent Dr. Buckminster, of Portsmouth, father of Joseph Stevens Buckminster, the talented and eloquent minister of Brattle-street Church, Boston, both of whom died within twenty-four hours of each other, June 10, 1812. Memoirs of the father and son, by Mrs. Eliza Buckminster Lee, forms a volume that should be in every library. Mr. Buckminster, of Rutland, published two Discourses on Family Religion; a Sermon at the Ordination of Rev. E. Sparhawk; a Sermon on the Covenant with Abraham; and several other pieces.

### REV. JOHN SWIFT, ACTON.

I have been able to obtain but few facts in relation to the life and ministry of Mr. Swift. He was born in Framingham, Jan. 14, 1714, and was the only son of Rev. John and Mrs. Sarah (Tileston) Swift. He was educated at Harvard College, being a graduate of the class of 1733. Of his father, one of the original members of the Marlborough Association, we have already given an account. Two of his sisters married clergymen: one, Elizabeth, became the wife of Rev. James Stone, of Holliston; another, Anne, married Rev. Philip Payson, the first minister of Walpole, in this State, whose grandson, Rev. Dr. Payson, of Portland, was distinguished in his day.

Mr. Swift was ordained as minister of Acton, where he continued to labor in the work of the ministry till his death, which took place Nov. 7, 1775, in the sixty-first year of his age and the thirty-seventh of his ministry. He died of the small-pox, as did also, the same year, his son John, who was a practising physician in Acton.

## REV. JOSEPH DAVIS, HOLDEN.

Mr. Davis, the first minister of Holden, was born in Lexington or Concord, in the year 1720, and was the son of Simon Davis, sen., whose son Simon was the father of Deacon Isaac Davis, of Northborough, and grandfather of Hon. John Davis, of Worcester, Ex-Governor of this Commonwealth. Mr. Davis was a graduate of Harvard College, of the class of 1740, and ordained as the minister of Holden, Dec. 22, 1742. After a faithful ministry of thirty years, his connection with his parish was dissolved, Oct. 18, 1772. He lived twenty-seven years after his dismission, and "was employed," says Whitney, "in preaching the gospel in various places; and on Wednesday, the second day of January, 1793, he preached a special lecture to the people of Holden, as on that day half a century from the imbodying the church and his ordination expired." The sermon was printed. He died March 4, 1799.

## REV. JOHN SECCOMB, HARVARD.

John Seccomb, son of Peter and Hannah (Willis) Seccomb, was born in Medford, April, 1708, and was educated at Harvard College, having graduated in 1728. The late Rev. Dr. Thaddeus Mason Harris states on the authority of Thaddeus Mason, Esq., of

Cambridge, a classmate of Mr. Seccomb, that he resided in Cambridge after he graduated; and informs us, that, among other poetical effusions, he was the author, in 1730, of the famous ditty, entitled "Father Abbey's Will," which has often been reprinted both in England and in this country.*

Mr. Seccomb was ordained as the minister of Harvard, Oct. 10, 1733, the year following the incorporation of that town, the day on which the first church was organized. He was married, March 10, 1737, to Mercy, daughter of Rev. William Williams, of Weston, whose father, Rev. William Williams, of Hatfield, married a daughter of the celebrated Solomon Stoddard, minister of Northampton, who, accordingly was the grandfather of Mrs. Seccomb.

By his own request, as he states in the church records of Harvard, he was dismissed by an ecclesiastical council, Sept. 7, 1757. Of the causes of his dismission, the record is wholly silent. After his dismission, he removed to Nova Scotia, and was installed over a Dissenting church in Chester, where he passed the remainder of his days, and where he died in 1792, making his wife executrix of his will.

It was during his ministry at Harvard that "the great awakening," as it was called, under the preaching of Whitefield, Tennant, and others, took place; and Mr. Seccomb is reputed to have been one of

---

* See Mass. Mag. for 1794, vol. vi p. 696; and Cambridge Chronicle for Nov. 18, 1854.

the few ministers of this region who approved of the measures of those enthusiastic itinerants. Whether this had any thing to do with his subsequent dismission, we are unable to say: but it is said, that he filled up life with duty and usefulness; that he was calvinistic in his sentiments, pungent in his preaching; that his ministrations were blessed to the people in Harvard; and that "a revival continued three years, and resulted in bringing about one hundred into the Redeemer's kingdom." *

We learn, moreover, that, after his settlement in Chester, he retained " in a remarkable degree his mental powers, popularity, and usefulness; and continued to preach to his people, to good acceptance, when he required the aid of others in walking to visit the sanctuary of God."

While at Harvard, he built the large three-story mansion near the common, which afterwards came into the possession of Henry Bromfield, Esq., and subsequently of his son-in-law, Rev. Dr. Pearson.

The venerable mansion, embosomed in a grove of ancient elms, a few years since, while in possession of Dr. Pearson's son, Henry B. Pearson, Esq., was destroyed by fire.

Besides "Father Abbey's Will" and several other poetical effusions, written before he entered the ministry, he was the author of two discourses, printed

---

* American Quarterly Review, x. 58.

during his ministry in Chester: one, an ordination sermon; the other, occasioned by the death of the Hon. Abigail Belcher, wife of Lieutenant-Governor Belcher, then Chief-Justice of Nova Scotia, delivered at Halifax, Oct. 20, 1771.

### REV. JOHN MELLEN, STERLING.

Born in Hopkinton, March 14, 1722, O.S.; educated at Cambridge; a graduate of Harvard College, of the class of 1741,— Mr. Mellen became the first minister of Sterling, where he was ordained on the 19th of December, 1744. After a ministry of a little more than one-third of a century, he was dismissed by mutual consent, Dec. 14, 1778. After an interval of a little more than five years, during which time he continued to reside in Sterling, he received a call, and was installed as minister of Hanover, Feb. 11, 1784. Here he remained twenty-one years, till the infirmities of age induced him to retire from the ministry. He was dismissed February, 1805; and, on the following September, he removed to Reading, where, in the family of his daughter, the widow of Rev. Caleb Prentice (H.C. 1765), he passed the remainder of his days. He died July 4, 1807, aged eighty-five.

Rebecca, wife of Rev. John Mellen, born Sept. 22, 1727, was the daughter of Rev. John Prentice, of Lancaster, three of whose daughters were married to neighboring ministers: viz., Cushing, of Shrewsbury; Rogers, of Leominster; and Mellen, of Sterling.

The three sons of Rev. Mr. Mellen — John, Henry, and Prentice — received a collegiate education, all being graduates of Harvard College: the eldest, John, in 1770; the other two in 1784.

John, born July 8, 1752, was a tutor in college from 1780 to 1783. On retiring from the ministry, he returned to Cambridge, where he lived, honored and respected, till his death in 1828. His daughter Catherine was married, first, to Professor Levi Frisbie, and, after his death to Professor James Hayward, of Harvard College.

Henry Mellen, born 1757, died at Dover, N.H.

Prentice Mellen, born 1764, was Chief-Justice of the Supreme Court of Maine from the separation of that State from Massachusetts, in 1820, till his death in 1840. He was the father of the late Granville Mellen (H.C. 1818).

The wife of Rev. Mr. Mellen, born Sept. 22, 1727, lived with the husband of her youth fifty-three years, and died at Hanover, Jan. 11, 1802, aged seventy-five.

For about twenty years from the commencement of Mr. Mellen's ministry in Sterling, nothing occurred to seriously interrupt the harmony of pastor and people. But about this time, just before the beginning of the Revolutionary War, a serious controversy arose between several of the ministers in this vicinity and the churches over which they presided. It related in part to the assumption of ecclesiastical power by the clergy, and in part also to the introduction of more liberal views into the pulpit than the people were ready to receive.

"Most of the churches in this vicinity were, at that time, supplied by clergymen distinguished among their brethren for strength of intellect, depth of research, and energy of character. Such were Mr Harrington, of Lancaster; Mr. Adams, of Lunenburg; Mr. Rogers, of Leominster; Mr. Goss, of Bolton; Mr. Fuller, of Princeton; Mr. Morse, of Boylston; and particularly Mr. Mellen, of Sterling, who, in his time, probably stood at the head of the clergy of the county. The two first of these fathers, by uniting the wisdom of the serpent with the innocence of the dove, had so permanently won the affections of their people, that they alone were enabled to maintain their places. The other five were compelled to sacrifice their livings to the spirit of the times." (Goodwin's History of Sterling, p. 217, in the second volume of the Worcester Magazine.)

Rev. John Rogers was the first to suffer for heresy, by being deposed from his office by sentence of an ecclesiastical council of fifteen churches.

Mr. Mellen was understood to hold views substantially the same as his neighbor, Mr. Rogers, but was less open in avowing them; and, in 1765, he published a volume of sermons, highly creditable to his scholarship and ability, in which he takes "a middle course between the two opposite extremes of Calvin and Arminius."

It was not, however, so much on account of the doctrinal views he entertained and preached that he incurred censure and reproach, as on account of his assumption of authority in matters relating to church discipline. On this point, an unhappy controversy arose between Mr. Mellen and his church, which, after the calling of several councils, resulted in his dismission, by a vote of his church, confirmed by the parish, November, 1774.

"Liberally endowed by nature with a strong and energetic mind, which was highly improved by diligent and successful cultivation, he obtained a high rank, both as a preacher and a scholar."

The publications of Mr. Mellen, so far as known to us, are the following: A series of Discourses, addressed to Parents, Children, and Youth, 1756; a volume of Sermons upon the Doctrines of Christianity, 1765; Thanksgiving Sermon on the Reduction of Canada, 1760; Sermon on Account of the Sickness, 1756; Sermon at the General Muster, 1756; Sermon occasioned by the Death of Sebastian Smith, 1765; Sermon at the Singing Lecture in Marlborough, 1773.

Inscription on his monument at South Reading:—

"Sacred to the memory of Rev. John Mellen, born March 14, 1722; graduated at Harvard University, 1741; thirty-four years pastor of the church at Sterling, twenty-one years at Hanover; died July 4, 1807. Mrs. Rebecca Mellen, daughter of Rev. John Prentice, of Lancaster, born Sept. 22, 1727, having lived fifty-three years with the husband of her youth, died at Hanover, Jan. 11, 1802.

"Their children, in whose bosoms their virtues are faithfully recorded, in testimony of filial respect, affection, and gratitude, have erected this monument."

## REV. THADDEUS MACARTY, WORCESTER.

Thaddeus, son of Captain Thaddeus Macarty, of Boston, was born in 1721, and graduated at Harvard College in 1739, at the early age of eighteen. He was ordained as minister of Kingston, in the Old Colony, Nov. 3, 1742, where he remained just three years, being dismissed Nov. 3, 1745. He preached a farewell discourse from the text, "Therefore, watch, and remember, that, by the space of three years, I ceased not to warn every one night and day with tears" (Acts xx. 31). His dismission from the church in Kingston, it is said, was occasioned by his supposed sympathy with Whitefield. He had invited that eloquent enthusiast, so it was reported, to preach in his pulpit at a communion lecture; to prevent which the people of Kingston fastened the doors of the church against him. Regarding this as a personal insult, as well as an encroachment on his rights as a minister, he omitted the lecture, and immediately asked a dismission. June 10, 1747, he was installed over the church in Worcester, where, after a faithful ministry of thirty-seven years, he finished his course, and entered into his rest, July 20, 1784, at the age of sixty-three.

Mr. Macarty was married, Sept. 8, 1743, to Mary, daughter of Francis Gatcomb, a wealthy merchant in Boston, who had emigrated from Wales. They had fifteen children, one of whom was a graduate of Yale College in 1766, was a physician, and died in Keene, N.H., in 1802. Another son settled in Worcester, and is still remembered as a wealthy and respected citizen of that town.

One of the daughters was married to Hon. Benjamin West, of Charlestown, N.H.

Rev. Mr. Macarty is represented as being "tall in stature, in person slender and thin, with a dark and penetrating eye, a distinct and sonorous, though somewhat sharp-toned, voice; his address impressive and solemn." (A writer in the Hist. Col., quoted by Rev. William B. Sprague, D.D., in Annals of the American Pulpit, vol. i. p. 423.)

Several of Mr. Macarty's occasional sermons were published during his lifetime; and one, the farewell sermon at Kingston, in 1804, twenty years after his death. Among the former were the following: —

A Sermon on the Execution of Arthur, a Negro, 1768; a Sermon on the Execution of William Lindsey, 1770; a Sermon on the Execution of Buchanan,

Brooks, Ross, and Mrs. Spooner, for the murder of her husband at Brookfield, in 1778.

### REV. JOSEPH WHEELER, HARVARD.

Mr. Wheeler was born in Concord, March 18, 1736, and graduated at Harvard College in 1757, at the age of twenty-one. Two years afterwards, Dec. 12, 1759, he was ordained as the minister of Harvard, which office he retained about nine years; being dismissed at his request on account of ill-health, July 28, 1768. After his dismission, he continued to live in Harvard, where he sustained various offices of honor and trust, and where he was highly esteemed as a faithful magistrate and a good man.

He afterwards removed to Worcester, having been chosen register of probate for Worcester County, which office he held till his death, Feb. 10, 1793, at the age of fifty-eight.

Shattuck, in his "History of Concord," states that Mr. Wheeler resided at Worcester, where he was representative, justice of the peace, and register of probate, from 1775 to his death in 1793.

His descendants are numerous and highly respectable.

## REV. TIMOTHY HARRINGTON, OF LANCASTER,

was born in Waltham, Feb. 10, 1716; graduated at Cambridge in the class of 1737. He was first settled as the minister of Lower Ashuelot, or Swansey, N.H., whence he was called to take charge of the large parish of Lancaster. His installation took place Nov. 16, 1748. He remained sole pastor of the church and minister of the town, till the settlement of his colleague, Rev. Dr. Thayer, Oct. 9, 1793; which auspicious event he survived a little more than two years. His death took place, after several years of increasing infirmity, which rendered him incapable of active service, Dec. 18, 1795, being fourscore years old.

He married, for his first wife, his cousin, Anna Harrington, born June 2, 1716, who died May 19, 1778. Their daughter, Anna, was married, first, to Dr. Bridge, of Petersham, and afterwards to Dr. Joshua Fisher, of Beverly, "the beloved physician" and eminent citizen, the founder of the professorship of Natural History in Harvard University.

Mr. Harrington's second wife was the widow of Rev. Matthew Bridge, of Framingham, who died May 12, 1805.

"Mr. Harrington continued to live in harmony with his people during a long and useful ministry; no lasting disturbance injured his good influence; no root of bitterness sprang up between him and his people. He is represented as having possessed respectable powers of mind, with great mildness and simplicity of character. Liberal in his feelings, he practised charity in its extended as well as in its narrow sense. True piety, and an habitual exercise of the moral and social virtues, rendered him highly useful in his sacred office, and an interesting and instructive companion in the common walks of life."*

"He is described by one who knew him well,"— I quote from the Centennial Address of the same writer,—"as a model of ministerial excellence; as possessing a good portion of scientific attainments, singular pertinency and fervor in the performance of devotional exercises; a pattern of Christian cheerfulness and affability, of sympathy with the sick and afflicted, and of compassion to the poor. A man thus constituted, well deserves the appellation of the Christian gentleman."

### REV. JOSIAH BRIDGE, EAST SUDBURY (WAYLAND).

Josiah Bridge, a graduate of Harvard College, of the class of 1758, was born in Lexington, Dec. 13, 1739, and was the son of Deacon John and Sarah (Tidd) Bridge. His grandfather, Matthew Bridge,

---

* Willard's Hist. of Lan., vol. i. Wor. Mag., 325.

of Lexington, was son of Matthew, and grandson of Deacon John Bridge, one of the first settlers of Cambridge. Three years after leaving college, Nov. 4, 1761, before he had completed his twenty-second year, he was ordained as minister of the town of East Sudbury, as successor of Rev. William Cook, where he remained till his death, which took place June 19, 1801, in the sixty-second year of his age and the fortieth of his ministry.

Mr. Bridge married Martha, a twin-daughter, and the only surviving child, of Rev. Aaron Smith, of Marlborough, who was born Aug. 22, 1741, and died June 8, 1824, aged eighty-three.

Seven children, four sons and three daughters, were the fruit of this marriage; all of whom — with the exception of Deacon Josiah Bridge, of Lancaster, who died in 1826, at the age of forty-two — lived to a good old age.

1. Martha, born Sept. 8, 1768; married John Prentiss, who early in this century emigrated to Western New York, and lived in Steuben, Steuben County. At the time of her death, a few years since, at the age of upward of ninety years, she left nearly one hundred descendants, almost all living near her.

2. Aaron, born Aug. 11, 1770; unmarried; died in 1850, aged eighty.

3. William, born Oct. 23, 1773; was a merchant first in Boston, and afterwards in London, England. When about forty years old, he retired from business,

and lived with his mother during the remainder of his life. After her death, he married, but died without issue in 1854, aged eighty-one.

4. Anna, born March 15, 1776; married Rev. Luther Wright, of Medway (H.C. 1796); and died Feb. 23, 1861, aged eighty-five.

5. Sarah, born June 3, 1780; married Rev. Alpheus Harding, of New Salem; and died March 23, 1859, aged seventy-nine.

6. Josiah, born Aug. 20, 1782; deacon of the church in Lancaster; afterwards removed to Lowell, where he died in 1827. Two of his sons, Azarelah M. Bridge and William F. Bridge, entered the ministry. The former died in 1866: the latter, a graduate of Harvard College, of the class of 1846, is now settled in the ministry at Peterborough, N.Y. Another son is a teacher at Cincinnati.

7. Charles, born May 30, 1785; unmarried; died 1850, aged sixty-five.

The father of this large family was a highly esteemed and greatly beloved minister. "The praise of Bridge," says Dr. McKean, in his sermon at the ordination of Rev. Mr. Wight, one of his successors, "is still in all our churches."—"His library," writes Rev. Mr. Bridge, of Peterborough, "was in a good state of preservation when I was a child; and I often resorted to it. It numbered four or five hundred volumes, and contained works of history, and many of the writings of the best English divines. It was particularly rich in the writings of the Puritan fathers. There were many volumes in the ancient languages; some in the Hebrew. My grandfather," he adds, "was an Arminian, and must have been somewhat eloquent as a preacher."

I subjoin a list of his publications, so far as known to us. They are,—

A Sermon delivered at Truro, at the Ordination of Rev. Jude Damon, in 1787; the Election Sermon in 1789; the Convention Sermon, 1792; the Dudleian Lecture, Cambridge, 1797; a Charge to his Son-in-law, Rev. Luther Wright, of Medway, in 1798.

The sermon preached at the funeral of Rev. Mr. Bridge, by Rev. Moses Adams, of Acton, speaks of him in the following terms: "Nature had endowed him with a strong mind and sound judgment. Providence had given him opportunities, which he happily improved, for treasuring an ample stock of science, and particularly that theological knowledge which was necessary to shining in his profession. He was furnished with eminent talents for speaking in the pulpit. In addition to his good personal appearance, he had a pleasantness, a solemnity and dignity in his voice, in his style and address, which seldom concentre in any man. . . . Wherever he was called to preach, his appearance gave pleasure, and he was heard with avidity; while you [his parishioners] were considered as an happy people in having such a minister. . . . Among his brethren of the ministry, he was greatly beloved and esteemed. To the Association of which he was a member, his removal is an unspeakable loss. . . . He was enjoyed by all before him while they lived, and by all who were after him while he lived. . . . In a meeting at his house, the present season, he greatly edified and affected the Association, by conversing on his expected dissolution. He seemed to consider it as the last time he should ever receive them at his house, or perhaps meet with them. He conversed as a man of God, as a father who was soon to be taken from our head. He lamented that the members were not all present, as he had hoped to see them once more."

We learn, from a note to the sermon, that he did meet with the Association once more at the Rev. Mr. Whitney's, in Northborough; and that it was on his return through Lancaster, while on a visit to his son, Deacon Josiah Bridge, he was taken ill, and died under the operation of an emetic administered for his relief.

### REV. PETER WHITNEY, NORTHBOROUGH.

Mr. Whitney was the son of Rev. Aaron and Alice (Baker) Whitney, of Petersham, and was born Sept. 6, O.S., 1744. After graduating at Cambridge in 1762, he taught school in Lexington,

where he was admitted as a member of the Congregational Church, Jan. 2, 1763.

He succeeded Rev. John Martyn as minister of Northborough, where he was ordained Nov. 4, 1767, about six months after the death of his predecessor. March 11, 1768, he was married to Julia, daughter of William Lambert, of Reading, born April 9, 1742. By this marriage he had eleven children; viz., —

I. Thomas Lambert, born Dec. 10, 1768; married Mary Lincoln, of Hingham; died June, 1812.

II. Peter (Rev.), born Jan. 19, 1770; H.C. 1791; ordained over the First Congregational Church in Quincy, Feb. 5, 1800; died March 3, 1843. He was married, April 30, 1800, to Jane Lincoln, a sister of his brother Thomas's wife, who died Nov. 11, 1832. Two of his sons, George (H.C. 1824) and Frederic Augustus (H.C. 1833), were clergymen, settled, the former in West Roxbury and Jamaica Plain, and the other in Brighton.

III. Julia, died in infancy.

IV. Julia, born Aug. 25, 1772; married Antipas Brigham, 1799; died Nov. 29, 1800.

V. Margaret, born Feb. 12, 1774; married Deacon Josiah Adams, of Quincy; died Feb. 3, 1849.

VI. Elizabeth, born Sept. 6, 1775; married Ebenezer Adams, brother of Josiah, of Quincy; died Sept. 26, 1856.

VII. William (Colonel), born Dec. 14, 1776;

married Zilpah Eager, of Northborough, where he died July 24, 1834.

VIII. Aaron, born Aug. 11, 1778; removed to one of the Western States, where he died.

IX. Sarah, born Nov. 3, 1781; married Lemuel Brackett, of Quincy. She lived to the age of eighty-four, respected and beloved, and died in the winter of 1864.

X. Abel, born Nov. 3, 1781; married Susanna White, of Brookline. He was a deacon of the First Congregational Church in Cambridge, where he died Feb. 22, 1853. One of his sons, Benjamin White Whitney (H.C. 1838), is a lawyer at Cambridge.

XI. John, born Sept. 29, 1785; married Sophia Vinal, of Scituate. He died at Quincy, where he had been a teacher and merchant, Jan. 2, 1850.

The ministry of Rev. P. Whitney, of Northborough, covers a period of nearly half a century, terminated by his sudden death, Feb. 29, 1816.

The following notice of Mr. Whitney is quoted from the "History of Northborough," by his successor, as a just tribute to his memory: —

"Distinguished for the urbanity of his manners; easy and familiar in his intercourse with his people; hospitable to strangers, and always ready to give a hearty welcome to his numerous friends; punctual to his engagements; observing an exact method in the distribution of his time; having a time for every thing, and doing every thing in its time, without hurry or confusion; conscientious in the discharge of his duties as a Christian minister; catholic in his principles and in his conduct; always taking an interest in whatever concerned the prosperity of the town and the interests of religion, — he was for many years the happy minister of a kind and affectionate people."

*Publications of Rev. Mr. Whitney.*

1. The History of the County of Worcester, 1793.
2. Two Discourses, on the Occasion of a Public Fast, 1774.
3. A Sermon on the Declaration of Independence, 1776.
4. A Half-Century Discourse, 1796.
5. An Ordination Charge at Boylston, 1797.
6. A Sermon at the Ordination of his Son, Quincy, 1800.
7. A Sermon on the Death of Washington, 1800.
8. Address at the Dedication of a Church, Southborough, 1806.
9. A Funeral Sermon at Shrewsbury, on the Wife of Rev. Dr. Sumner, 1810.

### REV. JOSEPH WILLARD, BOXBOROUGH.

Joseph, son of Benjamin and Sarah Willard, was born in Grafton, Dec. 27, 1741; was graduated at Harvard College in 1765. Joseph's grandfather, Major Simon Willard, was the grandson of Major Simon Willard, distinguished in the early annals of New England, whose father, Richard, was from Horsmonden, in Kent, England.

After Joseph began to preach, he was unanimously chosen minister of Bedford, but declined a settlement. He was ordained at Mendon, April 19, 1769, and was dismissed in good standing, Dec. 14, 1782. He was installed at Boxborough, Nov. 2, 1785, where he lived till his death, which took place in September, 1828, having nearly completed the eighty-seventh year of his age. He married Hannah Parker, by whom he had thirteen children, two of whom were educated at Harvard College, having graduated, Joseph in 1793, the other, Benjamin, in 1809. Joseph was minister of the Episcopal Church in Portsmouth, N.H., afterwards of Newark, N.J., and died at Marietta, Ohio, in 1823. Benjamin studied law in Newark, and became a planter in Parkersburg, Va., where he died in 1857. Two of the daughters, Clarissa and Martha, lived many years after the death of their father, a solitary life in the old family mansion in Boxborough, receiving a small annual stipend from the Congregational Charitable Society of Massachusetts.*

Mr. Willard, of Boxborough, had the reputation of a faithful minister and a good man; and I have always heard him spoken of in terms of respect. His sphere was a humble one: but, as head of a large family and pastor of a little flock, he rendered no unimportant service to the public; filling his place with credit to himself, and usefulness to others.

---

* See History of the Willard Family, by Joseph Willard, Esq., of Boston, who mentions the remarkable coincidence, that his father, Joseph Willard, President of Harvard College, and Rev. Joseph Willard, of Boxborough, cousins of several removes, were the fathers each of thirteen children.

### REV. JACOB BIGELOW, SUDBURY.

Mr. Bigelow was born in Waltham in 1742, and was the son of Jacob and Susannah (Mead) Bigelow. He graduated at Harvard College in 1766, and was ordained as minister of Sudbury, Nov. 11, 1772; retaining his connection with the parish till his death, Sept. 12, 1816, at the age of seventy-four. Owing to his infirmities, he was unable, for the few last years of his life, to perform the duties of his office, and accordingly received as a colleague Rev. Timothy Hilliard, who was ordained June 1, 1814, but who was dismissed Sept. 26, 1815.

Mr. Bigelow was married to Widow Elizabeth Wells, daughter of Gershom Flagg, whose first husband was brother-in-law of Governor Samuel Adams. They had three children, — Elizabeth, Henry, and Jacob. Elizabeth married Asahel Wheeler, of Sudbury; Henry, a merchant in Baltimore, married Sophia, daughter of Deacon Joseph Field, of Boston, and sister of Rev. Dr. Field, of Weston. Their only child married J. D. Williams, of Baltimore. The only living child is Dr. Jacob Bigelow, the distinguished physician of Boston, who married Mary Scollay, of Boston. Their son, Dr. Henry J. Bigelow, married Susan Sturgis, whose daughter Catherine married Francis Parkman, of Boston.

"Mr. Bigelow was a faithful and acceptable minister, simple and unostentatious in his life, eminently cheerful and social in his character. Like many other country clergymen, he devoted the first half of the week to laboring on his farm, and the last half to preparing his sermons. He was beloved and greatly respected in his parish, with which he retained his pastoral connection for more than forty years. His widow, an educated, intelligent, and most excellent lady, survived him but a few months. I am sure that to her kind, devoted, and judicious care of my early education and welfare, I owe much of whatever success has attended me in my life." (Manuscript letter of Dr. Jacob Bigelow.)

### REV. JONATHAN NEWELL, STOW.

Mr. Newell was the son of Deacon Josiah Newell, and was born at Needham, Dec. 8, 1749. Having graduated at Harvard College in 1770, he taught school one year in Brookline, and then entered on a course of theology, under the instruction of Rev. Samuel West (H.C. 1761), of Needham, afterwards of Hollis Street, Boston, with whom he remained two years. He was ordained at Stow, Oct. 11, 1774; having received, about the same time, a call from the church in Putney, Vt., and from the church in Stow. "Mr. Newell's ministry was marked," says Mr. Sibley, who was settled as his colleague a short time before his death, " with consummate prudence. In sentiment, he was a moderate Calvinist. Notwithstanding the schism through the community in the latter part of his ministry, he exchanged, as long as he continued to preach, with both divisions of the clergy, with whom he had been in the habit of making exchanges previously. His sermons were sensible, but his delivery was not animated. His mind was strong and discriminating, his judgment good, and he well understood human nature. He was endued with strong passions; but he had the great merit of being their master. He was remarkable for kindness and benevolence. As he went from house to house, the children commonly found his pockets to be the depositories of raisins or other fruits which in those days were scarce. If a man met with misfortune, or was embarrassed with sickness, he gave him an order on the collector to charge to himself the ministerial part of his tax, and frequently more. Thus he sometimes relinquished in a year a quarter part of his salary, which never exceeded $400, and which, in the distress incident to the Revolutionary War, was, for some years, insufficient to pay for the keeping of his horse. His deportment was simple, unobtrusive, and grave, without being austere. He was a large, vigorous man, and had immense physical strength. In conversation, he was animated and very interesting, quite a humorist, and enjoyed a joke so much, that he would often tell one when it had been at his own expense."

He continued his ministry with a united people nearly fifty-five years, till 14th May, 1829, when John Langdon Sibley (H.C. 1825) now Librarian of Harvard University, was ordained as his colleague.

"At this time, he was laboring under the infirmities of age, though he occasionally walked and rode about. He became so deaf that it was very difficult to talk with him; but his conversation was instructive, religious, touching, beautiful, such as always commands admiration when it comes from one who is consciously and quietly passing away to the future world. After the settlement of his colleague, he preached but one sermon. It was carefully prepared, and replete with wisdom and feeling.

Mr. Newell was a good farmer. He kept good stock. He admired and loved his handsome, showy, well-fed horse, and bestowed particular care on him after he was old and almost useless. He worked hard himself, and looked with satisfaction on his well-tilled acres. For reclaiming a bog-meadow, a a time when such improvements were seldom thought of, he received a premium from the Agricultural Society; and by the use of rackets, or snow-shoes, he travelled over the intertwined and matted grass-roots, and cut an immense burden of hay.

Mr. Newell was interested in science, and especially in mechanics; and he left many curious implements, and parts of machinery, contrived by himself. He invented the nail-cutting machine, which, with the addition of some improvements, is still used in England and America. With another gentleman, Mr. Jonathan Ellis, he established nail-works at Needham. But the enterprise resulted in pecuniary loss, and was given up. There was a struggle in his mind, it is said, whether he should not leave his society for an occupation which was likely to be useful and very profitable, at the same time that it was congenial to his tastes; but reflection led him to the determination to remain with his people, and this gave new vigor to his ministry. Still his interest in such subjects continued as long as he lived. Several months before he died, he lost one of his fingers by a circular saw which he was examining. This probably hastened the termination of a life fast waning through the infirmities of years. He died Oct. 4, 1830. Mr. Newell's first wife was Sarah Fiske, of Watertown, or Newton, who is said to have been very beautiful. She died of consumption, within a year after their marriage.

To his second wife, Lucy, daughter of Rev. Daniel Rogers, of Littleton (H.C. 1725), he was married in 1781. She was an extraordinary woman, highly cultivated, refined, universally beloved, disinterested, shining in the most intellectual circles in the metropolis, and performing with dignity and grace every duty pertaining to a farmer's or a minister's wife in the country. She had such a peculiar sense of propriety, and was so devoted to her husband, that, during a happy union of nearly fifty years, she never spent a night away when her husband was at home. She died June 26, 1846, at the age of ninety. She was sister of Mrs. Samuel Parkman, of Boston, and aunt of Rev. Francis Parkman, D.D., the late respected minister of the New North Church, in that city."

Their children were, —

1. Jonathan (H. C. 1805), a physician in Stow.

2. Samuel, a merchant in Boston, and for several years postmaster at Cambridge. He was mortally wounded on the railroad between Andover and Lawrence, Jan. 6, 1853, at the time when the only son of President Pierce was killed.

3. Charles, at one time a merchant in Stow, now a resident in Chattanooga, Tenn. He was one of the forty boys and one girl born in Stow in 1793.

4. George (H.C. 1823), settled as a physician in Petersham; died in Stow, Nov. 4, 1831.

5. Daniel Rogers, born July 5, 1801. When his father, a few years before his death, lost all his property by being a bondsman, this son was enabled, through friends, to retain the homestead, and thus give to his parents a home in the old place.

Mr. Newell published during his life, —

1. A Century Sermon, preached at Stow, May 16, 1783, at the Conclusion of the Revolutionary War.
2. A Charge at the Installation of Rev. William Ritchie, at Needham, Dec. 12, 1825.
3. An Aged Minister's Review of the Events and Duties of Fifty Years, printed in 1825.

### REV. JOEL FOSTER, EAST SUDBURY.

Rev. Mr. Foster was born in Western, now Warren, on the western borders of Worcester County, Mass., and was the son of Nathan and Elizabeth (Loresford) Foster. "His father," writes one of his grand-daughters, "was an independent farmer, a sturdy old Federalist I'll be bound, and an upright and strong-minded man, whom his children honored and reverenced all their lives long. He lived in Western, a very retired village; . . . and there, I think, his large family of sons and daughters were born. . . . Joel was a graduate of Dartmouth, A.D. 1777; and he was twice settled in the ministry, — first, at New Salem [1779], afterwards at East Sudbury, now Wayland [1803]. I remember him as a very genial and pleasant companion. His visits at our parsonage [Brighton, or, as it was then called, Little Cambridge, where his brother John, Rev. John Foster, D.D., was minister] were always welcomed by the children, as well as the elders of the family. He had a good deal of humor, which was rather a family trait; and between him and my father there was always cherished a warm sympathy and fraternal affection."

During three or four of the last years of his life, he was frequently taken from his labors by sickness. His disease indicated to him approaching dissolution. "When the hour drew near" (we quote from an obituary notice in the "Columbian Centinel"), "he looked into the future world with a lively hope; and, in the full possession of his reason, gave his surrounding friends the most comforting evidence that he was prepared for his change, and that for him to die would be gain. As a man and Christian, Mr. Foster was much respected by those who knew him best. As a preacher, he was sensible, serious, and practical; as a son, dutiful; as a husband, kind; as a father, tender; and, as a brother, affectionate."

### REV. MOSES ADAMS, ACTON.

Mr. Adams was born in Framingham, Oct. 4, 1749, and was the son of Moses and Lois (Haven) Adams, and great-great-great-grandson of Henry Adams, one of the early settlers of Medfield. He was married to Abigail, daughter of Hon. Josiah Stone, and lived for several years after his marriage in Framingham, where two of his children, Lois and Ann, were born. His daughter Lois became the wife of Dr. John Park, of Boston, whose school for young ladies was so celebrated in his day. The other daughter, Ann, was married to Rev. Nicholas Bowes Whitney, of South Hingham.

Mr. Adams was graduated at Harvard College in 1771; was ordained as minister of Acton, June 25, 1777, where five other children were born to him.

1. Moses, H.C. 1797.
2. Nabby.
3. Josiah, H.C. 1801, was a lawyer in Framingham.
4. Joseph, H.C. 1803, a lawyer in West Cambridge; married Almira Fiske, daughter of Rev. Thaddeus Fiske, D.D., of that place. His melancholy death took place June 10, 1814.
5. Clarissa.

Rev. Mr. Adams died Oct. 13, 1819, at the age of seventy.

The writer of an obituary notice in the " Columbian Centinel" says of Mr. Adams, that, " as a theologian, he was rational, catholic, and evangelical; and his preaching was sound, practical, and affectionate. In the days of his prosperity, he was at once the social friend, the agreeable gentleman, and the dignified minister of religion. With his people he enjoyed a great share of peace and tranquillity. They esteemed and loved him; and he reciprocated their respect and affection." The writer adds: " It has not perhaps fallen to the lot of any minister to be so severely tried and afflicted as was Mr. Adams; and perhaps, too, no man in our times ever sustained such inexpressible weight of sorrow and grief more like a thorough and practical Christian than he did. Here the greatness of his soul, the strength of his faith, and the power of divine grace, appeared with a lustre that commanded the astonishment and admiration of every enlightened observer."

### REV. PHINEAS WRIGHT, OF BOLTON,

was born in Westford, June 2, 1747; graduated, with the first honors of his class, at Harvard College in 1772. His ordination as minister of Bolton took place Oct. 26, 1785; the sermon on the occasion being preached by Rev. Dr. Cummings, of Billerica.

He was married, May 31, 1787, to Susanna, daughter of Rev. John Gardner, of Stow. They had no children; and, after the death of her husband, Mrs. Wright lived with his successor in the ministry, Rev. Isaac Allen, till her death. Mr. Wright's life and ministry came to an abrupt termination by a paralytic stroke, Dec. 22, 1802, in the fifty-sixth year of his age and the eighteenth of his ministry. He is described as rather tall in stature, a somewhat dark man, stern in manners, "very much of a hell-fire preacher," says one who was brought up by him, "and a great disciplinarian" (manuscript letter of Rev. Mr. Edes).

"Mr. Wright," continues Mr. Edes, "was less fortunate than his predecessor, Mr. Goss, in one respect certainly. He found no friend desirous of airing his Latinity in the composition of an epitaph, or a lying tombstone, or one upright and downright as truth itself. His remains are in the South Burying Ground, with no stone to mark the spot."

In an obituary notice contained in the "Columbian

Centinel" for Jan. 8, 1803, he is represented as one "eminently qualified for the situation which Providence assigned him;" and it is added, that "by the blessing of God, and the wise management, the multiplied labors, the manly, unwearied, spirited, and persevering exertions, of this servant of Christ, the church has become truly respectable for its regularity, peace, and unity, for the numbers of its members, and their religious character. . . .

"In the pulpit, his manner was grave, his style plain and logical. His voice was clear, audible, and of a happy tone for a speaker. He always studied conciseness and simplicity, rather than prolixity and ornament in his pulpit exhibitions. . . . He had little regard to confessions of faith formed by men uninspired, and avowed the adoption of the Sacred Oracles as the only standard of his faith and practice. . . . He was a pleasant and affectionate husband, a sincere and constant friend, a cheerful companion, tender in his feelings towards all his relations, an intrepid advocate for civil and religious liberty, a stable patriot, a most valuable citizen, a devout and exemplary Christian."

## REV. SAMUEL SUMNER, SOUTHBOROUGH.

Mr. Sumner was the son of Rev. Dr. Sumner, of Shrewsbury, and Lucy (Williams) Sumner, and was born Sept. 24, 1765. He graduated at Dartmouth

College in 1786, and was ordained as minister of Southborough, June 1, 1791, where he remained a little more than six years. After his dismission, Dec. 1, 1797, he removed to Bakersfield, Vt., where he was installed, and where he died in 1836, at the age of seventy-one.

Mr. Sumner married a Widow Williams, formerly Taylor, of Southborough.

### REV. DAVID KELLOGG, OF FRAMINGHAM,

was born in Amherst, in 1755, and was the son of Daniel and Esther (Smith) Kellogg. He graduated at Dartmouth College in 1775, and was ordained at Framingham, Jan. 10, 1781. He received the honorary degree of D.D. from his Alma Mater, and continued in the active service of the ministry, till September, 1830, almost half a century, when he voluntarily retired from his pastoral office. During the remainder of his life, he lived in comparative retirement, retaining to the last the respect and confidence of his parish and of the town; and on the 13th of August, 1843, he "slept with his fathers," at the advanced age of eighty-seven.

Mr. Kellogg was married to Sally, daughter of Rev. Matthew Bridge, his predecessor in office. She was born Jan. 9, 1753, and died Feb. 14, 1826, aged seventy-three.

Their children were, —

1. Mary, married Dr. John Ball Kittredge, of Framingham; 2. Sally, married Deacon William Brown, of Boston; 3. Nancy, unmarried; 4. Gardner; 5. Martha; 6. David; 7. Charles.

Rev. Mr. Barry, one of his successors in the pastoral office, pays the following just tribute to his memory: —

"Possessed of respectable talents, united with a character marked by energy, decision, and self-reliance, his manners ripening into mingled dignity and ease, his voice full and commanding, he maintained, through the remarkable vicissitudes of opinion and sentiment which agitated the period of his ministry, — extending through half a century, — a character of unquestioned sincerity, consistency, and uprightness, which commanded respect and confidence. . . .

"Many," he adds, "will recall with pleasure his venerable form, slightly bowed, his tall and robust figure, his fresh yet placid countenance, his dignified and courteous manners, as he moved among us, almost sole survivor of the generation who had welcomed him to the sacred office as their Christian pastor and guide." (Barry's History of Framingham, p. 124.)

His only publications are a Sermon preached at Framingham before the Middlesex Lodge in 1796, and an Address on Presenting the Right Hand of Fellowship, at the Ordination of Rev. Mr. Dickinson, at Holliston.

## REV. EZRA RIPLEY, CONCORD.

Ezra Ripley was born in Woodstock, Conn., May 1, 1751, and was the son of Noah and Lydia (Kent) Ripley. He entered Harvard College in 1772, at the mature age of twenty-one, and graduated in 1776, in a class which numbered among its members Governor Gore, and no less than three distinguished judges of the Superior Court, — viz., Samuel Sewall, George Thatcher, and Royal Tyler; himself holding a respectable rank among his classmates.

He studied theology with Rev. Jason Haven, of Dedham, and was ordained as the minister of Concord, Nov. 7, 1778. During the first forty years of his ministry, the town was united as one parish; and not a single individual, it is said, during this time paid a ministerial tax to any other society. He lived to a great age; having completed, at the time of his death, Sept. 22, 1841, the full period of fourscore and ten years.

Dr. Ripley was married, Nov. 16, 1780, to Mrs. Phœbe (Bliss) Emerson, the widow of Rev. William Emerson, his predecessor in the ministry, and mother of Rev. William Emerson, of Boston. By her he had three children, — a daughter and two sons. His eldest son, Samuel (H.C. 1804), was for many years the minister of the first parish in Waltham.

He died suddenly of disease of the heart, in his carriage, on his way to the old manse in Concord, Nov. 24, 1847, where he was to spend Thanksgiving Day.

Daniel Bliss, the younger son (H.C. 1805), was a lawyer, and died in Alabama in 1825.

His daughter lived and died in Concord.

Mrs. Ripley died Feb. 16, 1825, at the advanced age of eighty-three. Soon after the death of his wife, he was induced by the approaching infirmities of age to ask for a colleague. His parish complied with his request; invited to fill that office Rev. Hersey Bradford Goodwin (H.C. 1826), who was ordained Feb. 17, 1830, and who died, greatly lamented, July 9, 1836.

Rev. Barzillai Frost (H.C. 1830) was chosen to fill his place as colleague, and was ordained in 1838, and, after the death of Dr. Ripley, became sole pastor of the first parish, which office he retained till his death in 1858. Mr. Frost preached a funeral sermon on the death of his venerable colleague, which was printed. Dr. Ripley was fortunate in having for his colleagues men of great moral worth, ripe scholars, and faithful and devoted ministers, under whom the society greatly prospered, "holding the unity of the spirit in the bond of peace."

During his long ministry of sixty-three years, he wrote, as he states in his Half-century Sermon, as many as twenty-five hundred sermons, several of which, delivered at ordinations and on other extraordinary occasions, were published, two in the "Liberal Preacher" for 1827 and 1829. He also wrote a pamphlet of sixty pages, printed in 1827, relating to the battles of Lexington and Concord, the latter of which was fought in the neighborhood of his house.

Dr. Ripley was a man of medium height, very erect, and bearing marks of unwonted vigor even after he had passed the bounds of threescore and ten. He was a gentleman of the old school, stately and dignified in his manners, and retaining the costume of the eighteenth century till near the middle of the nineteenth. To a stranger, there might seem to be something of *hauteur* in his looks and demeanor; but he was accessible to his friends, and genial and affable in his intercourse with them.

He was not a learned theologian, or an eloquent pulpit orator; but he was an animated preacher, had a strong, sonorous voice, and was listened to with interest by his own people, and in the neighboring churches.

A just and honorable testimony is paid to his memory in the biographical notice contained in the annals of the "American Unitarian Pulpit," by Rev. Dr. Sprague, of Albany, from which we take the following extracts.

"Rev. Dr. Hosmer, of Buffalo,* who passed his

---

\* Now President of Antioch College, Yellow Springs, Ohio.

early days under the ministry of Dr. Ripley, states his impressions concerning him in the following terms: —

"It was not true of Dr. Ripley, that the pulpit was his throne. . . . His throne was his character, and he sat upon it a born king. Some might say that he was arbitrary and imperious; but all knew he was a MAN, fearless in his duty, and determined to walk in the ordinances of his God and Saviour, blameless.

"In parochial service, Dr. Ripley was a pattern of fidelity. Every corner of the town, every house, knew his friendly greeting. He knew all about every family and their ancestors, often better than they themselves knew. Before Sunday schools were organized, he met all the children at their schoolhouses for catechizing; and those who did not know their catechism were made to feel that they must know it before the next parochial round. It was a great moment when we stood up for the first time, at the call of our name, before Dr. Ripley. Then he was the main stay of the common schools, and all the benevolent and social organizations of the town. As Dr. Ripley grew old, his nature grew mellow. His will and his thought got into his heart, and he drew the young lovingly about him. He never failed as old men often do: affection kept him young. He preached better after he was seventy-five years old than ever before: indeed, when almost blind, and not long before his departure so full of years, he preached without notes; and they who listened said he never preached so well. I can readily believe it: he was almost home; the light and love of heaven filled his soul; and that last utterance, at the end of his ninety years' pilgrimage, was his saintly benediction to all of us who follow him."

Dr. Jarvis, of Dorchester, who was also a native of Concord, gives us some of the reminiscences of his early days in relation to Dr. Ripley. "All my father's family," he writes, "went to meeting both forenoon and afternoon. There was no law; we were never commanded to go to church; but we all went as a matter of course, as if nothing else was desirable or possible, as we went to our meals or to our beds. We looked on our own minister as the only possible or desirable man to fill that place; and the idea or the wish to have any other no more occurred to us than to have any other man and woman for our parents. I think this was the general feeling of the town, though there were some who thought the doctor was distant, aristocratic, unapproachable. . . .

"He seemed to consider all the children as objects of his care and attention. He recognized them in the street. He followed them after they left the schools; and when they, as many of them did, went abroad, and labored in other towns and States, he still retained his interest in their progress and welfare. He used to speak with manifest pleasure of his extensive parish, which had its representatives in almost every State of the Union, and in a large portion of the towns of Massachusetts. He made no secret of his gratification when they prospered, or of his sorrow when they failed in fortune, or of his mortification when they failed in character. He seemed to feel that their success was due in great measure to the training they had received at home and in the schools of Concord. . . . He always had a small salary; but, as he was a very careful economist and an excellent administrator, he was enabled to gratify his inclination to be very generous. He, in the earlier or middle part of his ministry, took some boarders; he and his daughters taught some private scholars; and thus money was raised to send his two sons to Harvard College. According to the earlier custom, much was given to him by the farmers and others, to eke out his salary. Thus he lived comfortably, and within the means granted to him, or rather earned by him; and I never knew of his being embarrassed in his pecuniary matters. He owned his house, and several acres of very valuable land, which he cultivated with the ordinary skill and success. . . .

"Dr. Ripley had great confidence in the progress of society. He used to talk with much satisfaction on this subject. He thought each generation improved upon their fathers. He said there was much more religion of heart and life, though perhaps less of the language of religion, in his later than in his earlier years. He often said he loved to associate with young men and women, because they were so much better than the contemporaries of his youth. Consequently, he drew many young people about him. He entered into their feelings, and they entered into his plans; and thus they cordially and pleasantly cooperated. Even to his latest years, his house was a favorite place for young people of both sexes to visit. . . .

"The same qualities for which Dr. Ripley had been distinguished during his life continued with him till life's close. Especially his indomitable energy and perseverance, and spirit of self-sacrifice for the benefit of his fellow-creatures, never forsook him. He was eminently honored in his life, and his death was deeply and widely lamented."

### REV. ASA PACKARD, MARLBOROUGH.

Mr. Packard was born in North Bridgewater, May 4, 1758, and was a descendant of the fourth generation of Samuel Packard, who came from Windham, near Hingham, England, in 1638, and settled first in Hingham, and afterwards in Bridgewater. His immediate ancestors were Jacob and Dorothy (Perkins) Packard. At the early age of seventeen, he enlisted as a volunteer fifer in the Revolutionary Army; and in an engagement with the enemy near Harlem Heights, in 1776, received a severe wound from a bullet which lodged against his spine, where it remained, causing partial lameness for life. An ineffectual attempt was made to extract it, which caused him much suffering, and he was confined to the hospital for eight months; after which he returned home, and becoming interested in religion, and wishing to become a minister, he entered on a course of studies preparatory to entering college. He was graduated at Harvard University in 1783; and, after declining a call to settle in Wellfleet, he was ordained at Marlborough, March 23, 1785, at which time the snow was of sufficient depth to cover the fences, and so solid as to bear the weight of heavy teams.

"The people went to the ordination in their sleighs, upon the crust, passing across their lots over the tops of walls and rail-fences without difficulty."

Mr. Packard remained in this place, in sunshine and in storm, — first as minister of the whole town, and afterwards of the Second or West Parish, — more than thirty years, from 1785 to 1819. In 1808, the town was divided into two parishes, owing to a controversy relating to the location of a new meeting-house; the minority forming a new parish and retaining their old minister, who had previously obtained a dismission from his former charge. Mr. Packard was installed over the West Parish on the 23d of March, 1808, just twenty-three years to a day from his ordination. His connection with this society continued till May 12, 1819, when he took a dismission, and soon afterwards removed to Lancaster, where he died very suddenly while sitting in his chair, March 20, 1843, at the age of eighty-five.

Mr. Packard was in easy circumstances, having come into the possession of considerable property, I believe, through his wife. He was married July 2, 1790, to Nancy Quincy, daughter of Josiah Quincy, and aunt of the late President Quincy of Harvard College.

They had six children, two of whom died before their father: one a child of five years; the other, Eliza Quincy Packard, in 1816, at the age of twenty-four. Two have since died: Asa, in 1851, aged fifty-four; and Ann M., born March 17, 1798, married James Gordon Carter, of Lancaster (H.C. 1820), died Dec. 15, 1853. Mr. Carter was distinguished for his interest in the cause of popular education, to which he rendered valuable service by his writings and his speeches in the Legislature. He died in 1849, while a resident in one of the Western States. They left one daughter. Another son of Rev. Mr. Packard was Frederic Adolphus, born Sept. 26, 1794 (H.C. 1814). He studied law, and commenced practice in Springfield; married Elizabeth D., daughter of Judge Hooker; represented Springfield in the Legislature in 1828 and 1829; removed to Philadelphia, and in 1847 was elected

President of Girard College. He received the degree of LL.D. from Princeton College.

Ruth F., the youngest daughter of Rev. Mr. Packard, was born March 22, 1800; married Rev. George Trask, of Fitchburg, formerly pastor of churches in Framingham and Warren. For several years past, he has carried on, almost single-handed and at his own cost, an incessant warfare against the use of tobacco in all its forms; for which he is entitled to the thanks of the public, and to something more than empty thanks.

Mr. Packard was not a close reasoner or a profound theologian. During his ministry he was classed with the Liberal or Unitarian denomination; but, after his dismission, his associations were principally with the Orthodox, in whose pulpits he occasionally preached. He was commonly listened to with interest as a public speaker; and he excelled in conversational talent, having a fund of anecdotes which he often introduced with happy effect, both in the parlor and the pulpit. His sermons were practical, his style simple, his delivery animated, and his manner often impressive. I knew him well, and passed many pleasant hours in his family, both before and after his dismission; and, while not insensible to his eccentricities and faults, I retain a lively sense of his many redeeming qualities, and end with a *requiescat in pace.*

### REV. JEROBOAM PARKER, SOUTHBOROUGH.

Mr. Parker was a native of Southborough, and was the son of Benjamin and Abigail Parker. He was born April 3, 1769, and graduated at Harvard College with the class of 1797. Two years after his graduation, he received a call from his native town to be their minister, and was ordained Oct. 9, 1799, at the mature age of thirty years.

He was married to Ann How, of Hopkinton, by whom he had eight children; viz., —

Mary Ann, married Dana Fay, of Boston; died June 10, 1828.

Emma, died Dec. 17, 1855.

Martha, married Dana Fay, who died Oct. 31, 1860.

Selima, married a Mr. Rawson, of Chicago.

Lucius, removed to the western part of New York.

Nancy, died Dec. 22, 1829.

Caroline, married Charles Meriam, of Worcester.

Charles Lowell, married Abby Penniman.

July 17, 1827, Mr. Parker preached a centennial discourse commemorative of the incorporation of the town, which was published. His connection with the parish, as its minister, was dissolved Feb. 14, 1832; after which he continued to live in the town, cultivating a small farm, and acting the part of a good and useful citizen. He died March 22, 1850, at the age of eighty-one.

## REV. SYLVESTER F. BUCKLIN, MARLBOROUGH.

Mr. Bucklin was born in Rehoboth, now Seekonk, July 2, 1784, and was the son of John and Jemima (Peck) Bucklin, of that place. He was a graduate of Brown University, Providence, R.I., of the class of 1805; studied divinity with Rev. Dr. Perez Forbes, of Raynham, and was ordained over the First (East) Parish in Marlborough, Nov. 2, 1808; in which office he continued, respected and beloved, till at his request, he was honorably dismissed, passing the remainder of his life in retirement, and retaining his physical strength and mental vigor to a good old age. He died, much lamented, May 25, 1860, at the age of seventy-six.

He married, Sept. 9, 1809, Nancy Balcom, daughter of Jacob and Tryphena (Everett) Balcom, of Providence, R.I. Their children were as follows: —

1. Elizabeth, born 1810; married James T. Rhoades, of Providence.

2. Mary Balch, died in infancy.

3. Henry, born 1814; died in 1825.

4 and 5. Sylvester and Ann, twins, born 1815. Ann married Lucius M. Scammel, and died in 1851. Sylvester lives in Marlborough.

6. Mary Ide, born 1820; married E. F. Wood, of Savannah, Ga. She died in 1860.

7. Sarah Hunt, born 1825; married Albert Richards, of Sharon. She died in 1857.

# WORCESTER ASSOCIATION (OLD).

# WORCESTER ASSOCIATION (OLD).

THE Marlborough Association was divided, as we have seen, in 1762, into two branches, the Eastern and Western: the former retaining the name of the old association; and the latter, as is supposed, taking the name of the Worcester Association.

Of the occasion of the dissolution of this body, and of the formation of a new one retaining the same name, we have a graphic account found among the private papers of the late Rev. Dr. Bancroft. The record is as follows: —

"On the 1st of February, 1786, I received ordination. The Unitarian controversy, at that period, had not been agitated. But the society (the Second Congregational Society in Worcester) was viewed as Arminian; and, as an Arminian, I was to be inducted into office.

"So general then was the Calvinism of the county, that it was not deemed prudent to invite but two churches to assist in this religious ceremony; viz., the church in Lancaster and that in Lunenburg, then under the pastoral care of the Rev. Timothy Harrington and Rev. Zabdiel Adams.

"For several years I stood almost alone. Two or three times within this period, I exchanged with Mr. Harrington, and about once a year with Mr. Adams; and, in a few instances, — not more than three or four, — I had the benefit of exchanges with a clergyman in Boston, and one in Salem.

"While struggling with difficulties in my own society, I was pointedly opposed by most of the clergymen around me; and those who were friendly to me as a citizen kept aloof from ministerial intercourse. At this period, Dr. Fiske, of Brookfield, did once exchange with me. With pleasure I state this exception.

"At the expiration of seven years,* I received a note from Mr. Avery, of Holden, containing an invitation to meet the association of ministers at his house on a given day, and dine with them. In reply, I stated that no member of this association had extended to me any act of ministerial communion, and therefore they could not wish for my presence at their clerical deliberations; that, as a private friend, I should with great satisfaction meet him [Mr. Avery] at his own table or at mine; but that he

---

* As we have before us the original record of this transaction, in the handwriting of Dr. Bancroft, dated Jan. 3, 1791, it must have been *five* instead of seven years.

must excuse me for not accepting his invitation to meet with the associated body.*

"Subsequently I received a letter in which it was stated, that it was not the custom of the Worcester Association to invite ministers, ordained within their circle, to join them; but, if I offered myself as a candidate for membership, they would readily admit me. I soon waited on the moderator, and stated to him that I had ever felt a disposition to interchange ministerial offices with clergymen of the neighborhood; and that I desired him, in my name, to propose me in the usual form to his association. He did. Opposition was made by some of the members, and the subject was put over to the next meeting. At this meeting of the association, Mr. — now Dr. — Austin proposed himself for the body, and was immediately admitted. When the question respecting my

---

\* The following is a copy of the letter referred to: —

"Mr. Bancroft acknowledges the reception of Mr. Avery's invitation of the last week, and must rely on his candor to accept his apology for declining it. No individual of the association of this vicinity has, in any instance, extended the least act of fellowship to Mr. B. since his ordination, or in any way proffered an interchange of ministerial communion. He cannot therefore persuade himself that his presence as a clergyman is desired. As a private gentleman, Mr. B. shall with pleasure embrace any opportunity to spend a day with Mr. Avery, as a man whom he respects, as a friend whom he esteems. Mr. B. considers ministers as members of the same body, and called upon by the gospel of Christ to co-operate with each other to promote the common interests. Yet he is too well satisfied, that the church, of which he is pastor, is built upon the foundation of the apostles, ever to lean on human support; and his present object is, not to complain, but to assign the reason why he does not comply with Mr. Avery's request.

"Monday, Jan. 3, 1791."

admission was agitated, he warmly opposed it; and altercation arose. In consequence, the association commissioned one of their members to call on me to communicate the facts in the case, and to suggest the expediency of my withdrawing my application. I informed him that I should not complain at a negative vote, but must insist on a decision. The vote was tried, and a majority appeared against my admittance. On this result, Mr. Sumner, of Shrewsbury, and Mr. Avery, of Holden, arose, and declared that they would not belong to a body which passed so illiberal a vote as that of my rejection; that the association might meet where and when they would, but that they would no longer be considered members of it. In consequence of the withdrawal of the above-named gentlemen, the association was broken up.

"Two or three years subsequently, uneasiness was expressed at this state of things; and a conference was held by the clergymen of the vicinity. Much discussion ensued. It was proposed that a new association should be formed, of which Dr. Austin and myself should be members. The pious doctor declared that he could not, in conscience, and would not join me in a society formed voluntarily by individual ministers; for, by doing it, he should virtually acknowledge me as a regular minister, and allow that I truly preached the gospel of Christ.

"A new association was formed, of which I was

a constituent member, and which Dr. Austin never joined."

Such was the origin of the old "Worcester Association," as it is called, to distinguish it from the body which now bears that name; and which, after lasting a little more than a quarter of a century, at length regained new life and vigor by forming a union with the "Lancaster Association," then rejoicing in the freshness of its youth.

The records of this association (the old Worcester) cannot be found, and it is feared they are lost. We are unable, therefore, to give its history, and must content ourselves with a very few reminiscences relating to its last years of decrepitude and decay.

In 1815, when my acquaintance with it began, it consisted of the following ministers; viz., Dr. Sumner, of Shrewsbury; Dr. Bancroft, of Worcester; Rev. Messrs. Cotton, of Boylston; Miles, of Grafton; Avery, of Holden; and last, though not least, the sickly but talented Nash, of West Boylston.

Most of these men were, at this time, "old and full of years." Their numbers had been reduced, by death and removal, till only these six remained; and two of these, Avery and Nash, by reason of their many infirmities, seldom attended the meetings of the association. Those meetings, as I remember, were of a *social* character; and, although never dull or unprofitable, — especially when graced by the presence of Dr. Bancroft, — they held out but few attractions to young men, fresh from "the School of the Prophets."

Of these good men I would speak in terms of affectionate respect. With one or two exceptions, they were not distinguished for genius or scholarship or eloquence; but they were good ministers of Jesus Christ, serving God and their generation according to his will, with only such imperfections as are common to men.

With all but one of the number I was personally, and with most of them intimately, acquainted. During the first years of my ministry, and even before my settlement, it was my privilege to enjoy their friendship, and to receive the benefit of their fatherly counsels.

Besides my personal recollections, I have been furnished, from reliable sources, with facts and statements relating to their ministry and lives, of which I am at liberty to avail myself in writing these sketches.

My earliest connection with Worcester County was as a resident for several weeks in the family of Dr. Bancroft, in the summer of 1815, while supplying his pulpit in his absence. To this brief sojourn, and to the opportunity it gave me of forming an acquaintance with clergymen and others in this vicinity, I feel that I am indebted in no small

A. Bancroft.

measure for my settlement the following year in the pleasant place I have so long occupied, where I have passed so many prosperous and happy years.

Worcester was at that time an inconsiderable village of some two or three thousand inhabitants. Most of the buildings were on the main street; and, with few exceptions, the houses were of wood, of moderate dimensions, and without much ornament. Some of them are still standing, occupying the same ground as before, but converted to different uses. Some have been demolished, or removed to less conspicuous places, to make way for the large and handsome blocks which now adorn the street; and a new and beautiful city has taken the place of the small country village, containing a population of thirty thousand.

### REV. AARON BANCROFT, D.D., WORCESTER.

Of Dr. Bancroft, his scholarship and practical good sense, his urbanity and open-hearted hospitality, his benignant aspect, his easy and dignified manners, his perfect integrity, moral courage, and catholic spirit, I can speak with great confidence, from personal knowledge and a full heart; for it was my privilege to know him intimately, in private as well as in public life, as he appeared at home as well as abroad.

I shall not, however, rely solely on my own individual judgment of his character and services; but shall appeal to the general testimony borne by his contemporaries to his worth. Nor shall I hesitate to freely use the materials furnished to my hands by the brother who for twelve years was his colleague, and whose discourse preached at his funeral is a just and noble tribute to his memory.

Dr. Bancroft was born in Reading, Essex County, Mass., Nov. 10, 1755, the year made memorable by Braddock's defeat, just twenty years before the breaking out of the War of American Independence. His father, Samuel Bancroft, was a respectable farmer, and is represented as a man of "distinguished abilities, of great benevolence, and compassion," who trained up his children in the ways of virtue and religion. He himself describes his mother as "a pious and affectionate woman, who did every thing for him by her care, precept, and example, that a tender mother, in her situation, could do for a child." She lived to a great age, wanting only three years of a complete century at the time of her death in 1813.

Being possessed of good abilities, and having a thirst for learning, he had his father's consent to pursue a course of preparatory studies in the grammar school of his native village, and under the direction of the minister of the parish, with a view to obtain a collegiate education. He entered Harvard College at the age of nineteen, and was graduated in 1778, at the ripe age of twenty-three. After a short course of preparatory studies, he was licensed to preach in the following year; and, in the spring of 1780, he went on a mission of three years into the neighboring province of Nova Scotia. On his return in 1783, he was invited to supply the pulpit in Worcester, in the place of Rev. Mr. Macarty who was then sick. After the death of Mr. Macarty, which took place the following year, he was invited to preach as a candidate for settlement; and, though he failed to secure a majority of votes, so favorable was the impression he made on many of the influential citizens of the town, that, in order to secure his services, a second parish was formed, over which he was ordained pastor Feb. 1, 1786.

The theological views of the new society and of their minister were what were denominated *Arminian*, — a term as obnoxious at that time as that of Unitarian or Universalist is now; and, though several ministers in Worcester County were suspected of holding essentially the same views, yet few had the moral courage to make them known, or even to hold ministerial intercourse with one by whom such views were openly professed and publicly taught.

Accordingly, for many years after his settlement, Dr. Bancroft stood almost alone in this region as the champion of a more liberal faith than commonly prevailed. His brethren in the ministry, with few exceptions, avoided him, or at least declined receiving him into their pulpits; and, as we have seen, he was refused admission into the ministerial association, of which Worcester was the centre.

At the time of his settlement, the parish was small, and their resources quite limited; and, as his family was rapidly increasing, the salary he received was quite inadequate to their support. He was under the necessity of practising the most rigid economy; a necessity to which he and his worthy consort submitted without a murmur, trusting in the care of Him "who feedeth the ravens when they cry." But, though in straitened circumstances, he had a large heart; and his house was the seat of an elegant hospitality. It was my good fortune to be an inmate in his family for several weeks in the summer of 1815, where I had opportunity to witness, in the order and peace and mutual love that prevailed, evidence of the wisdom and skill with which it had been presided over by its venerated head, then absent on a distant journey.*

He had much to contend with, as we have seen, in the earlier part of his ministry, both from his straitened circumstances and the unpopularity of the re-

---

* It was during this period — about the first of August — that, late in the week, we were startled by the news of the battle of Waterloo, which had taken place some five or six weeks before. Our afternoons were mostly spent in the parlor, where the members of the family, with occasionally some of the neighbors, used to assemble to listen to the reading of Guy Mannering, the second, in order of time, of that series of wonderful tales, whose authorship was then, and for a long time after, unknown, but which everybody read and admired.

ligious opinions he was supposed to hold. But he stood his ground nobly, submitted to hardship and privation without a murmur, lived down opposition, and earned and secured a high reputation as a theologian, a minister, and a man. He soon became widely known by his publications. His "Life of Washington" appeared in 1807, and was afterwards (1826) stereotyped and published in Boston, and has had an extensive circulation. In 1820, he preached the sermon before the Convention of Congregational Ministers, which was published. He published in 1822 an octavo volume of Sermons on the Doctrines of the Gospel; a work of more than common interest and value, for which he received congratulations and thanks in characteristic letters from the Elder Adams, and Jefferson, and others. And his sermon on the termination of fifty years of his ministry, Jan. 31, 1836, was the last of thirty-six distinct publications that proceeded from his industrious pen.

His house was the resort of distinguished strangers who visited Worcester; and, while the courts were in session, he seldom failed to receive calls from the judges and leading members of the bar. On such occasions, subjects of deep interest and moment were sometimes discussed, to the elucidation of which Dr. Bancroft contributed his full share. However distinguished his guests, he was always listened to with deference and respectful attention; for his remarks were replete with wisdom and learning, with moderation and candor and practical good sense. Often the conversation assumed a more cheerful tone; and those who took part in it indulged in pleasantries and sallies of wit, without, however, descending to unbecoming levity, or approaching the borders of impropriety. On Sunday evenings, he was commonly visited by a few of his more intimate friends and parishioners, who took this method of showing their respect for their venerable pastor, with whom some of them had been intimately associated through nearly the whole period of his ministry. Among these visitors, I recall the familiar faces of the two Allens, brothers, Joseph and Samuel Allen; the Paynes; the Lincolns; of Macarty, son of the minister of that name; of Brazer, father of Dr. Brazer, of Salem; and of many others whom I have met there: all of whom, with a single exception (Governor Lincoln, who still survives in a green old age), have long since been removed from earth. The evenings thus spent were truly *Noctes Ambrosianæ*, spiritual feasts, with which our souls were refreshed; and, I trust, our hearts made better.

To show the estimation in which he was held out of his own parish, it will be sufficient to make the following statement, taken from Lincoln's "History of Worcester," and which is found in the Appendix to Dr. Hill's funeral discourse: —

"Dr. Bancroft was member of the Board of Trustees of Leicester Academy for thirty years, and long its President; President of the Worcester County Bible Society; of the American Unitarian Association, from its organization in 1825 to 1836; and of the Society for Promoting Christian Knowledge, Piety, and Charity; Vice-President of the Worcester and Middlesex Missionary Society, afterward merged in the Evangelical Missionary Society; and of the American Antiquarian Society, from 1816 to 1832; Fellow of the American Academy of Arts and Sciences; and member of other societies. His long-continued and persevering exertions in the cause of education contributed greatly to the establishment of the improved school system of the town. In 1810, he received the degree of Doctor of Divinity from Harvard University."

Of the Worcester Association, both the old and the new that went by that name, Dr. Bancroft was one of the most active and influential members. Of the latter body, after its union with the Lancaster Association, he was the light and the ornament. Seldom did he allow himself to be absent from its regular meetings; and an occasional absence of our respected Moderator was felt as a sore disappointment and a serious loss. It was formerly the custom for the moderator, after the discussion of a subject by the junior members, to give a summary of the reasons, *pro* and *con*, together with his own views in relation to it. This service Dr. Bancroft performed with eminent ability, setting the subject in so clear a light, that its true shape and character could be readily seen. There were few subjects relating to his profession, whether doctrinal or practical, on which he had not read and thought, and formed deliberate opinions; and few, therefore, on which he was not prepared to speak intelligently, and in a scholarly manner, on the spur of the occasion. His presence at our meetings was accordingly always regarded as a benediction.

"Dr. Bancroft continued in the active duties of his profession," I quote from Dr. Hill's Funeral Discourse, "occasionally preaching, — always ready to lighten the burthen and strengthen the hand of his associate, to whom he ever extended a more than fatherly kindness, and who can never cease to be grateful for his long and intimate connection with him, — until the last Sabbath of the last January." This was a little more than six months before his death.

In the following spring, April 27, he met with one of the sorest trials incident to the lot of mortals, — the death of his wife. The separation, after a union of more than half a century, — a union that had been peculiarly happy, — could not fail of being attended with exquisite pain. She had borne him thirteen children: ten of whom lived to the age of manhood and womanhood; and six survived their parents. Among these last are Mrs. Eliza B. Davis, relict of the late Ex-Governor John Davis, of Worcester; and Hon. George Bancroft, the historian. Mrs. Bancroft died April 27, 1839, aged seventy-three years and eleven months. She was the daughter of the late Judge John Chandler, of Worcester, and was the last survivor of a family of seventeen children. She was married to Dr. Bancroft, in 1786, the year of his settlement as minister of the Second Church in Worcester.

Setting out together on their journey, they walked hand in hand, bearing each other's burdens, sharing each other's joys, sustaining with mutual sympathy the trials of their lot, — trials of no ordinary severity; till, laden with rich experience of God's goodness, with thankful and trustful hearts, they reached their journey's end. "Lovely and pleasant in their lives, in their death they were not divided;" and sons and daughters, worthy of such a parentage, "rise up and call them blessed."

From the shock produced by the sudden death of his wife, Dr. Bancroft never recovered. He lingered, for a few months, in a feeble and declining state, without the expectation or hope of recovery; waiting, in "the patience of hope," for the time of his release. "During this whole period," we are told, "amidst many seasons of agony, it is not known that a complaint escaped him." I continue the narrative in the words of the discourse delivered by his colleague at his funeral: "A smile continued to play upon his countenance, and he cheerfully acquiesced in his suffering. PER ARDUA AD ASTRA ; *By a thorny path we mount to the stars, — Bearing the cross, we gain the crown:* this sentiment he quoted on one of my last interviews with him, and on this he acted throughout. And this long period of patient resignation will ever be bright and clear in the recollection of his surviving friends. But there were occasions of more solemn interest. There are incidents and conversations living in their memory, treasured among the best legacies which he has left them. Not that he ever acted or spoke for effect: he was the last man who would have made a deathbed display of his feelings. And I hope his pure spirit, if it is made acquainted with the transactions of this hour, will not be offended by this reference to scenes which I cannot but feel are among the most solemn and impressive I have known. I have asked one who witnessed, to describe one of them; and I am permitted to quote the words of the writer. It occurred in the earlier part of his sickness, and at the hour of midnight. 'To give you an idea of the solemn scene,' writes the eldest daughter, 'and the reverence and awe which pervaded the mind, as we listened to the deep tones of his voice, would be impossible. You must remember the solemn hour of the night; think of the chamber as lighted by a solitary, dim lamp; see the hoary head laid on the pillow, almost in the repose of death;

and, with the feelings of children, watch the fleeting breath of an apparently dying parent. After lying in a sleep of some hours, he suddenly roused, and, calling us to his bedside, spoke of the conviction he felt, that the time was rapidly approaching when he must leave us.

"'I do not pretend,' said he, 'to look forward to that solemn moment without emotion. We cannot bid adieu to the scenes and objects we have loved on earth without pain; and the thought that we are to appear before the judgment-seat of God, and account for the deeds done in the body, renders the contemplation of that event awful in the extreme. But I trust in the mercy of God, who has promised never to forsake those who put their trust in him. I have studied the Bible to obtain a knowledge of his character, and what he reveals, through Jesus our Saviour, of the destiny of man. I think I may without vanity say I have endeavored to make the precepts of the gospel the rule of my life and conversation; and my aim has been to perform the duties assigned me by my Heavenly Father, to the best of my ability. I have not the presumption to claim the merit of sinless obedience; but this I do say, My intentions have ever been to conform, as far as in my power, to the bright example set before us by our blessed Saviour. . . . Death is the portal through which all must pass to reach their home in the heavens; and the gospel alone sheds light on its passage. 'Happy are they who shall sleep in Jesus.'"

"At a period still later, also, deep into night, when, as was not unfrequent, he was denied the refreshing balm of sleep, — at one of those moments, when the soul, awed by the pervading stillness, feels itself alone with God, — he asked the daughter who attended him, to read to him a favorite hymn. It contains the reflections appropriate to an old man. He listened as if the spirit of the song entered his soul; and, when she came to the words expressive of his own peculiar condition, he exclaimed, '*Beautiful, elevated, sublime!*' and, with an almost preternatural fervor, repeated them, line by line, as they were read, —

> "'If piety has marked my steps,
> And love my actions formed;
> And purity possessed my heart,
> And truth my lips adorned;
>
> If I've grown old in serving Him,
> My Father and my God, —
> I need not fear the closing scene,
> Nor dread the appointed road.'

"In this frame he lived, and in this frame he died."

He passed to his final rest on the evening of Monday, Aug. 19, 1839, having nearly reached the great age of fourscore and four years.

On the following Thursday, Aug. 22, his funeral was attended at the church where he had been accustomed to officiate. The occasion brought together a great multitude of sympathizing friends, who were desirous of showing their respect and esteem for the aged servant of God, who had just gone to his reward. An able and impressive discourse was delivered by the junior pastor; an appropriate funeral prayer was offered by Rev. Dr. Thayer, of Lancaster, the oldest surviving member of the Worcester Association; and all the services, together with the drapery of mourning which clothed the pulpit and galleries, served to deepen the impression made by his death. Those who were present cannot fail to recognize the truthfulness and beauty of the following description, taken from a note to the funeral discourse: —

"The afternoon was clear and tranquil. As the procession retired from the grave, the sun, which had shone calmly and benignantly upon the scenes, was just sinking in full-orbed light to his rest; and the whole hemisphere was lighted up, and each cloud tinged, and each object illuminated with the rays of parting glory, — a beautiful emblem of the good man's departure, who, leaving behind the influence of a good life and a bright example, still enlightens the path of the wayfarer and pilgrim, and guides him to his home."

Tidings of the death of their venerable associate and moderator reached the Worcester Association of Ministers, — then in session at Leicester, at the house of Rev. Samuel May, — on the day following his death. The event, though not unexpected, produced a deep impression on the brethren present;

and a committee was appointed to reply to the invitation given to the Association to attend the funeral of our deceased brother; also to prepare and forward, in behalf of the Association, a letter of condolence to his bereaved family.

The letter was in the following terms: —

"The Worcester Association of Ministers, having been informed of the death of Rev. Dr. Bancroft, the senior member and presiding officer of the Association, tender to the family of the deceased their respectful and affectionate sympathies on the sorrowful occasion.

"It has been our privilege to be intimately associated with this good man, some of us for many years; to listen to his wise and paternal counsels, to witness his Christian conversation, to partake of his hospitality, and to enjoy his friendship. We feel, therefore, that we can and do in some measure appreciate your loss, and share in your sorrows. We mourn with you, that the light which has shone so long with undiminished lustre at the domestic altar and fireside, in the golden candlestick, and throughout the wide field of his usefulness and his fame, is extinguished. We mourn that we shall no more be welcomed with that benignant smile and friendly grasp with which we have been greeted, whenever and wherever we have met; that we shall no more be instructed and strengthened and encouraged by his sound judgment, his fatherly counsels, and his blameless life.

"But we feel that you and we have more abundant cause for rejoicing than mourning. We rejoice with you, and give thanks to God, at the remembrance of his faithful labors, — his long and peaceful and prosperous ministry, his literary eminence, his domestic virtues, his honorable and well-spent life.

"We shall not forget the happy home, over which, together with his excellent consort, he presided with so much ease and dignity and grace; nor the serene and cheerful spirit with which he met the visitations of adversity, and drank the bitter cup. We honored him in life: his memory will ever be precious; and we rejoice and will rejoice in the blessed hope and assured belief, that it is but the time-worn tabernacle that is dissolved, while the released spirit of our friend has ascended to purer regions, to be for ever united with the wise and good of all ages and lands; where, if we remain faithful unto death, we shall again meet, to renew an intercourse and friendship that shall be as enduring as the imperishable soul.

"Commending you to the grace of God, and the rich consolations of the gospel, we subscribe ourselves yours in the faith and fellowship of Jesus Christ.

"Nathaniel Thayer.   Washington Gilbert.
Isaac Allen.           Cazneau Palfrey.
Joseph Allen.       Samuel May.
Calvin Lincoln.   Rufus P. Stebbins." *

---

* The other members of the Association were not present at the meeting.

*A List of the Publications of Dr. Bancroft, from a note to Dr. Hill's Sermon, taken from William Lincoln's "History of Worcester."*

1. Sermon at the Ordination of Rev. Samuel Shuttlesworth, June 23, at Windsor, Vt.
2. Sermon before the Grand Lodge of Massachusetts, June 11, 1793, at Worcester.
3. Sermon on the Execution of Samuel Frost, July 16, 1793, at Worcester.
4. Sermon at the Installation of Rev. Clark Brown, June 20, 1798, at Brimfield.
5. Eulogy on General Washington, Feb. 22, 1800, at Worcester.
6. Election Sermon, May 27, 1801.
7. Address on the Importance of Education, at Leicester Academy, July 4, 1806.
8. Life of General Washington. Worcester, 1807. 8vo, pp. 552.
9. Sermon at the Ordination of Rev. Nathan Parker, Sept. 14, 1808, at Portsmouth, N.H.
10. Sermon before Society for Promotion of Christian Knowledge, Piety, and Charity, May 29, 1810, Boston.
11. New Year's Sermon, Jan. 6, 1811.
12. Nature and Worth of Christian Liberty, Sermon, June 28, 1816, Worcester; with an Appendix, containing the History of Consociation. 2 editions.
13. Duties of the Fourth Commandment, Sermon, January, 1817, at Worcester.
14. Vindication of the Result of a Mutual Council at Princeton, March, 1817.
15. Discourse on Conversion, April, 1818.
16. The Leaf an Emblem of Human Life, Sermon on the Death of Mrs. Mary Thomas, Nov. 22, 1818.
17. The Doctrine of Immortality, Christmas Sermon, 1818.
18. Sermon at the Installation of Rev. Luther Wilson, June 23, 1819, at Petersham.

19. Sermon before the Convention of Congregational Ministers, June 1, 1820.
20. Sermons on the Doctrines of the Gospel. Worcester, 1822. 8vo.
21. Mediation and Ministry of Jesus Christ, Sermon, Aug. 15, 1819, at Keene, N.H.
22. Moral Purpose of Ancient Sacrifices, &c., same date.
23. Sermon at the Installation of Rev. Andrew Bigelow, July 9, 1823, at Medford.
24. Duties of Parents, Sermon, Aug. 10, 1823, at Worcester.
25. Sermon before the Auxiliary Society for Meliorating the Condition of Jews, April 23, 1824, Worcester.
26. Sermon at the Funeral of Rev. Dr. Joseph Sumner, Dec. 30, 1824.
27. Sermon on the Death of President John Adams, July 19, 1826.
28. Sermon on the Sabbath following the Ordination of Rev. Alonzo Hill, April 8, 1827.
29. Sermon at the Dedication of the New Unitarian Meeting-House, Aug. 20, 1829.
30. Sermons in "Liberal Preacher:" Office of Reason in Concerns of Religion, July, 1827.
31. Female Duties and Trials, August, 1828.
32. Importance of Salvation, August, 1830.
33. End of the Commandments, Sermon in "Christian Monitor."
34. A Glance at the Past and Present State of Ecclesiastical Affairs in Massachusetts, in "Union Advocate," January, 1831.
35. Moral Power of Christianity, in "Western Messenger."
36. Sermon on the Termination of Fifty Years of his Ministry, January 31, 1836.

A monument has been erected to the memory of Dr. and Mrs. Bancroft, with the following inscription: —

### WEST FACE.

Here rest
the mortal remains
of the Rev. AARON BANCROFT, D.D.
Born in Reading Nov. 10, A.D. 1755;
Ordained Pastor of the
Second Parish in Worcester,
Feb. 1, A.D. 1786.
His spirit ascended to God who gave it,
Aug. 19, A.D. 1839.

### SOUTH FACE.

In honor and gratitude
to a devoted pastor,
who gathered a little flock
of Christian worshippers
in days of opposition, straits, and trials;
vindicating for them
the glorious freedom to worship the one God
according to the teachings and example
of the blessed Saviour;
giving them union, strength, and increase,
by his labors and his life,
in a ministry of fifty-three years, —
the Second Parish in Worcester
erect this monument.

### EAST FACE.

A spirit free to concede as to claim
its dearest treasure, — Christian liberty;
fearlessness in thought and duty;
ready and various powers
of learning and observation;
a clear and forcible expression;
an ardent temper,
subdued to the calmness of Christian philosophy;
uniform prudence in counsel and action;
a warm heart and courteous manners;
and devoted fidelity in all relations
of public and private life, —

gave to our revered pastor
a moral power
which extended to a large circle
beyond those whose happiness it was
to know him best and love him most.

NORTH FACE.
Here rest
the mortal remains
of LUCRETIA BANCROFT,
daughter of Judge
and Mary Church Chandler.
Born June 9th, A.D. 1765.
Married to Rev. Dr. Bancroft, Oct. 24, A.D. 1786.
Died April 27, A.D. 1839.
With zealous and untiring sympathy,
she shared and relieved
the pious labors of her husband,
and was not long separated from him
by an earlier summons to her reward.
Her ardent friendship, her active benevolence,
her many virtues,
and her efforts and sacrifices
for the welfare
of the Second Parish in Worcester,
should ever be held
in grateful remembrance.

## REV. JOSEPH SUMNER, D.D., SHREWSBURY.

Joseph Sumner, son of Samuel and Elizabeth (Griffin) Sumner, was born in Pomfret, Conn., Jan. 30, 1740. He was graduated at Yale College in 1759, and was ordained over the Congregational Church in Shrewsbury, Mass., June 23, 1762, as successor of Rev. Job Cushing, the first pastor of that church. He was married in 1763 to Lucy Williams, of Pomfret, who was the eldest daughter of William Williams, formerly of Roxbury. The honorary degree of D.D. was conferred on him, in 1814, by Harvard University; and, about the same time, he received the same mark of respect from Columbia College, S.C.

Dr. Sumner continued in the ministry, as pastor of the same church, till his death, Dec. 9, 1824; a period of nearly sixty-three years. He died at the age of fourscore and five years, wanting a few days. Mrs. Sumner died Feb. 13, 1810. A discourse was preached at her funeral by Rev. Peter Whitney, of Northborough, which was published. The discourse preached at the funeral of Rev. Dr. Sumner, by his friend and neighbor, Rev. Aaron Bancroft, D.D., of Worcester, was also published.

On the 14th of June, 1820, Rev. Samuel B. Ingersoll was ordained as an associate pastor with Dr. Sumner. He preached but one Sunday after his ordination, being very ill at that time. He was soon removed to his friends in Beverly; where he lingered and languished till the 14th of the following November, when he was released from his sufferings by death.

Dr. Sumner received a second colleague, Rev. Edwards Whipple, formerly settled in the ministry in Charlton, Worcester County, who was installed at Shrewsbury, Sept. 20, 1821. He also died, after a brief ministry of less than one year, Sept. 17, 1822.

A third colleague, Rev. George Allen, of Worcester, son of Hon. Joseph Allen, for many years clerk of the court, was ordained Nov. 19, 1823; who survived Dr. Sumner, and became sole pastor of the church after his death. In the discourse preached at the funeral of Dr. Sumner, it is stated, that, during the period of sixty-two years, he was never absent from the stated communion of his church.

His published discourses are a Sermon preached at the Ordination of his Son, Rev. Samuel Sumner, of Southborough, June 1, 1791; a Thanksgiving Sermon, preached 28th of November, 1799; a Sermon at the Ordination of Rev. Wilkes Allen, at Chelmsford, Nov. 16, 1803; a Half-Century Sermon, preached in Shrewsbury, 23d of June, 1812. This sermon passed through two editions, and is valuable for the information it contains respecting the affairs of the church and town.

Dr. Sumner was settled on a salary of £66. 13s. 4d., a little over $222, which was increased in 1809 to $286.67; and, with this salary, he brought up a family of eight children, one of whom received a collegiate education, leaving at his death a handsome property, mostly in real estate. His eight children, three sons and five daughters, survived their father. The eldest son, Samuel, a graduate of Dartmouth College, of the class of 1786, was, for a little more than six years, the pastor of the Congregational Church in Southborough. After his dismission, he removed to Bakersfield, Vt., where he was again settled in the ministry, and died in 1836, at the age of seventy-one years. All the children of Dr. Sumner, with a single exception, were married; and most of them have left descendants.

Dr. Sumner was respected and honored, not only among his own people, but in all the neighboring churches. He was a man of unblemished integrity, of sound judgment, and practical good sense. Tall and erect in stature, dignified and urbane in manners, retaining to the last the costume of the eighteenth century, — flowing wig, three-cornered hat, knee and shoe buckles, and all, — he appeared, as he was, a true gentleman of the old school. Although he took no part in the theological controversies which were carried on between the Unitarian and Orthodox (so called) portions of the Congregational order, his sympathies and associations were, as is well known, with the former; and he lamented and remonstrated against the great schism, which broke up or enfeebled so many of the churches of New England during the last years of his ministry.

The Worcester Association, after its union with the Lancaster Association, met only once at the house of Dr. Sumner, which was on New Year's Day, 1822; on which occasion, a discourse was preached in his pulpit by the writer, which was printed.

He retained the use of his faculties to the last. The religion which he had proclaimed unto others was his support in sickness, and his hope in death; and, when the time of his departure came, he was ready to meet it. In the very appropriate words taken by his friend, Dr. Bancroft, for the text of his funeral discourse, "he gave up the ghost, and died in a good old age, an old man, and full of years, and was gathered to his people."

*Children of Rev. Dr. Sumner.*

1. Sarah, married to William Jennison, of Worcester.
2. Samuel (D.C. 1786); settled, first as minister of Southborough, afterwards of Sandisfield, Vt.
3. Joseph, married Rebecca Jaffrey, of Salem; died 1825.
4. Joanna, married Edward Sumner, of Roxbury.
5. Lucy, married Joseph Wheeler, of Worcester.
6. Elizabeth, unmarried.
7. Dorothy, married George Merriam, of Worcester.
8. Erastus, married Lavinia Boyd, of Marlborough.

"During the period of sixty-two years," as is stated in Dr. Bancroft's funeral sermon, "he was never absent from the stated communion of his church; and, till bodily infirmity rendered him unable to officiate, through his ministry the public exercises of the sabbath in this place were suspended only seven Sundays, on account of his indisposition, or in consequence of journeying."

### REV. JOSEPH AVERY, HOLDEN.

Rev. Joseph Avery was born in Dedham, Mass., Oct. 14, 1751, and was the son of Deacon William Avery and Bethiah (Metcalf) Avery, who were married Dec. 10, 1714: the former of whom died, Aug. 5, 1796, aged eighty; the latter, Dec. 25, 1793, aged seventy-eight. Deacon William Avery was the son of William, whose father, William, was born in England, and who accompanied *his* father William to New England about 1650.

Rev. Joseph Avery was a graduate of Harvard, of the class of 1771, and was ordained in Holden, Dec. 21, 1774; where he continued in the ministry, respected and beloved, till his death, which took place, March 5, 1824, in the seventy-fourth year of his age. Rev. Horatio Bardwell was ordained as his colleague, Oct. 22, 1823. Rev. Mr. Avery was married, Dec. 22, 1777, to Mary Allen, daughter of James Allen, of Boston, and sister of Joseph and Samuel Allen, in their day respected and honored citizens of Worcester: the former, for many years clerk of the court; and the latter, treasurer of the county. Their mother, Mary, was a daughter of Samuel Adams, sen., and sister of Governor Samuel Adams, the well-known patriot of the Revolution.

She was born in 1717, and was married to James Allen about 1741. Mrs. Avery was born, Feb. 8, 1755, and died, April 1, 1842, at the age of eighty-seven.

The children of Rev. Joseph Avery were two sons, Joseph and Samuel, both of whom died before their father, and four daughters; viz., Mary, who married the late Aaron White, of Boylston; Nancy, wife of the late William White, of Westborough; and Catharine, wife of Samuel B. Bent, of Middlebury, Vt. Bethiah was the wife of Jonathan P. Grosvenor, of Paxton.

Mr. Avery was a man of retiring habits and of unostentatious piety; an "Israelite, indeed, in whom was no guile." My acquaintance with him was very slight; but, in the few interviews I had with him, I was impressed with his humility and candor and modest worth, and felt that I was in the presence of a good man.

He is represented, by those who knew him well, as a scholar and a man of more than ordinary scientific attainments, of which, however, he made no display. Of his catholicity, and hatred of bigotry and intolerance, a striking instance has been given in our memoir of Dr. Bancroft. In him, orthodoxy and liberality were happily blended; a combination not uncommon in the early part of this century, and which I devoutly hope may characterize its close.

## REV. WARD COTTON, BOYLSTON.

Ward Cotton was the youngest child of John and Hannah (Sturtevant) Cotton, and was born at Plymouth, Mass., March 24, 1770. His father was settled in the ministry at Halifax, Mass.; and afterwards removed to Plymouth, where he was chosen Register of Deeds for Plymouth County, in which office he remained till his death. He had, by his wife, Hannah Sturtevant, of Halifax, eleven children, four sons and seven daughters, all of whom lived to adult age; and all became heads of families, except one daughter, who remained unmarried. The father of John, and grandfather of Rev. Ward Cotton, was Rev. John Cotton, who was settled in the ministry in Plymouth, and who preached occasionally as a missionary among the Indians. In a note appended to a memoir of his father, — the celebrated John Cotton, minister of the First Church in Boston, — it is stated, that "he was eminent for his knowledge of the Indian language, and superintended the publication of 'Eliot's Bible.'" He afterwards removed to Charleston, S.C., where he was again settled as a minister of the gospel. Rev. John Cotton, of Boston, New England, came over in the ship "Griffin," September, 1663, from Boston, in Lincolnshire, England, where he had been minister from 1612.

Rev. Ward Cotton, of Boylston, was graduated at

Cambridge in 1793; after which he studied for the ministry under Rev. Zedekiah Sanger, of South Bridgewater, and was ordained as minister of Boylston, — successor of Rev. Ebenezer Morse, — June 7, 1797; in which office he continued till June 22, 1825, when, in consequence of divisions in the church and society, he was dismissed at his own request.*

From the time of his dismission till his death, which took place suddenly, Nov. 15, 1843, he continued to live in Boylston, preaching occasionally, as he had opportunity, and discharging with fidelity his duties as a Christian citizen. For several years, he served as the representative of the town in the Legislature of the State; was respected and esteemed for his private and social virtues; and his friends always found a welcome at his hospitable mansion.

Mr. Cotton married, Feb. 19, 1800, Rebekah Jackson, youngest daughter of Thomas and Sarah (Taylor) Jackson, a descendant of one of the early settlers of Plymouth, though not of the company that came over in the "Mayflower." Mrs. Cotton was a woman of much dignity and grace of manners; one who appreciated and enjoyed cultivated and refined society, and was the object of affectionate respect, not only in her family, but in a large circle of friends with whom she was in the habit of interchanging visits.

---

* The immediate successor of Mr. Morse was Rev. Eleazer Fairbank.

Mrs. Cotton died at Boylston, Oct. 11, 1854, aged eighty-two years and eight months.

The children of Mr. and Mrs. Cotton were two sons and four daughters; viz,—

John Thomas, born Feb. 25, 1801; lives in Southborough.

Ward Mather, born March 11, 1804; married Elizabeth M. Lamson, of Boylston; lives in Leominster.

Lydia Jackson, born Jan. 1, 1806; married Josiah Pope, of Sterling; died April 25, 1829, leaving one daughter, married to Dr. Dickerman, of Foxborough.

Sally Mary, born Nov. 8, 1808; married to Rev. Charles Robinson, of Medfield; died June 6, 1849, leaving one son.

Hannah Sophia Phillips, born Oct. 16, 1810; married to Rev. Daniel S. Whitney, who now resides in Southborough.

A daughter, Mary Atwood, died in infancy.

None of Rev. Mr. Cotton's writings were published, except a sermon delivered at the first annual meeting of the Female Benevolent Society, of Boylston.

### REV. WILLIAM NASH, WEST BOYLSTON.

William Nash was born in Williamsburg, Hampshire County, Aug. 5, 1768; pursued his studies, preparatory to entering college, under Rev. Dr. Strong, of Northampton; graduated at Yale College in the class of 1791. He was ordained as minister of West Boylston, Oct. 11, 1797, where he remained, the able and faithful pastor of his flock, for seventeen years. He was dismissed at his own request, on account of long-continued ill health, Nov. 14, 1814; but continued to reside on his farm, in that place, till his death, which took place March 25, 1829, in the sixty-first year of his age. During the interval between his dismission and his death, he preached occasionally in neighboring churches, especially in Worcester; supplying the place of Dr. Bancroft in his absence, where he was sure to meet a cordial welcome. Knowing this fact, the author of these sketches wrote to Ex-Governor Levi Lincoln to give his recollections of the minister of West Boylston; a request with which he kindly replied in the following just and discriminating terms: —

. . . "With the Rev. William Nash I had no such acquaintance as would enable me to sketch his biography. He was a stranger to me previous to his settlement in the neighboring town of West Boylston; and afterwards I had little personal knowledge of him but as a preacher, and through that intercourse which his exchanges with the late Rev. Dr. Bancroft,— on whose ministry I attended,— and some occasional social interviews, gave me. He has now been dead many years. I recollect him as a tall, spare, pale-looking man, with strongly marked features, and a countenance expressive of thoughtfulness and care. In his deportment, he was modest and retiring, shrinking with peculiar sensitiveness from public observation. His habits were those of a student, with little relaxation, even in ill-health, as I have understood, except in such attention as he might pay, without interference with professional duties, to the cares and labors of his little farm. His classic acquisitions were highly respectable; and, in his social converse, he gave constant evidence of his fresh reading and his ready acquaintance with the best literature of the day. With a mind clear and logical, rather than subtle or metaphysical, his conversation was interesting and instructive, and his public discourses eminently sententious and didactic. In the pulpit, he was plain, simple, cogent; and such was the remarkable *terseness* of his style, that there scarce seemed an expletive in his sermon. Although his manner appeared at first somewhat stiff and awkward, yet such was the distinctness of enunciation, and so pointed and striking his emphasis, that his delivery often approached to the character of eloquence, and never failed to fix the attention and earnest regard of his audience. Few preachers in the Association, of which he was a member, were heard with deeper interest.

"In private and social life, Mr. Nash was spoken of as an amiable man, of genial feelings, hospitable and kind. His friends cherished his society, and delighted in visiting his family roof. He was always the faithful counsellor and the reliable friend. With clear perceptions and cool judgment, he advised wisely; and, with a manly spirit and a firm purpose, he acted ever consistently and well. The good of his pastoral charge was foremost in his heart; and, through many difficulties and discouragements, he was true to it to the uttermost. In the town of his residence, he was faithful to all the duties of a citizen; and, by the influence of high moral culture and an active and useful life, he contributed largely to the promotion of its best interests. In the failure of health, after a long struggle with its decline, he resigned the ministry; and, with a few years more of sickness and suffering, *he passed on.*

"WORCESTER, March 17, 1856."

Having been invited to supply the pulpit at West Boylston during the winter of 1815–1816, I often visited in the family of Mr. Nash, and had the best opportunities of forming an acquaintance with its members; and I have always felt that I was much indebted to this scholarly man for suggestions and counsels relating to the composition of sermons and the duties of the ministry. I only regret that I did not heed them more, and derive from them greater benefit. He was of a bilious temperament, sickly and feeble, and did not always maintain a buoyant, cheerful spirit; but his mind was always active, and his conversation instructive and interesting. He was blessed in his domestic relations; his wife being a lady of cultivated mind, accomplished manners, and uncommon merit. Their three children still live to honor their memory, and "to serve the present age."

The maiden name of Mrs. Nash was Elizabeth Doubleday. She was the daughter of Captain John Doubleday, a respectable ship-master of Boston, who married a daughter of Rev. John Gardner (H.C. 1715), the minister of Stow, one of the original members of the Marlborough Association. Mrs. Nash died Sept. 9, 1849.

They had three children, all of whom are still living: —

Charles Nash, born Oct. 9, 1806, Worcester.

Mary Gardner, born Oct. 17, 1808; married Dr. Thompson, of Lancaster.

Elizabeth S., born Feb. 1, 1812.

Their oldest child, William Henry, died in infancy.

It is not known that any of Mr. Nash's writings are in print.

### REV. JOHN MILES, GRAFTON.

The subject of this notice was born in Westminster, Mass., Nov. 3, 1765, and was a graduate of

Brown University, Providence, R.I., of the class of 1794. After leaving college, he studied for the ministry, under the care of Rev. Dr. Sanger, of Bridgewater.

Mr. Miles was ordained pastor of the Congregational Church in Grafton, Oct. 12, 1796, at which time there was but one religious society in the town. Accordingly, as in the case of most country ministers at that period, he was the minister of the town, and settled for life. On account of the great numbers who assembled to witness his induction into office, the ordination services were held on the Common in the open air.

The marriage of a minister, in those early days, was an occasion of almost equal interest as that of his ordination. Mr. Miles was married, May 1, 1798, to Mary Denny, daughter of Colonel Samuel Denny, of Leicester, — an event which, in the language of another, "did something more than connect him with families well known and highly respected in Worcester County, valuable as that was: it gave him one who, in other than the partial judgment of filial affection, was fitted in no common degree for the place she was called to fill."

For the following sketches, relating to his parents and to the customs of the olden times, the writer is indebted to the same gentleman, Rev. Dr. H. A. Miles, of Boston, son of the subject of this notice: —

"Among the pleasant recollections of her children,

are her — Mrs. Miles's — stories of the troop of horsemen that received the new-married pair at the town lines, and escorted them to their home; where gifts of skeins of yarn, yards of homespun, household furniture, and delicacies of food, attested the affection of their people.

"For a period of nearly thirty years, embracing, beyond doubt, the most embarrassing and trying portion of the history of our Massachusetts Congregational churches, my father was pastor of that society, which, under his ministrations, was in a united and prosperous condition. Attention to public schools, the sole care of which for the most part fell into his hands; and visiting his widely scattered flock, to which duty he always assigned a high place in the sphere of a minister's labors, — absorbed a large part of his time; though he gave a due share also to a little farm of sixteen acres, which he tilled in a skilful and exemplary manner. For study, but little opportunity was found. The fashion and demand of that day required less than is called for now. My father's manuscripts, several of which have come into my hands, show that he always chose practical themes; which he treated in a direct and affectionate manner, though always according to the old fashion of three heads, with minute subdivisions, and the never-failing 'improvement.' I happen to have single manuscripts of many clergymen, which I have collected as objects of some interest; among which are written sermons by Dr. Chauncey, Dr. John Clark, Dr. Osgood, Dr. Ripley, Dr. Puffer, and others of an earlier and later origin than these. Few of them, in the care and neatness with which they are written, compare with those of my father, — a hint of that scrupulous attention to his dress, carriage, garden, grounds, house, and barn, which formed a noticeable element of his character.

"Many scenes of his ministerial life are among the delightful recollections of my childhood. I recall, with special pleasure, the walk to church on a pleasant Sunday morning in summer, when six or eight children would arrange themselves in order, the sons on the side of their father, the daughters on the side of their mother; and the platoon would proceed, with all becoming gravity and solemnity, to the house of prayer. That old square church in the middle of the Common, with porches bulging out on three sides, with its large old-fashioned pews and slamming seats, is before me now. I remember many a ride with my father to distant parts of the town, where he went to attend a funeral, or officiate at a conference meeting.

"The 'working-bees,' too, are not forgotten, when all the farmers of the parish assembled to rid one of our pastures of its ancient inheritance of rocks; and when all the housewives of the parish brought offerings to our house of cloth and yarn, no doubt spinning much of the latter on the spot. These last-named occasions were fruitful, in many ways, of much merriment, and wove fabrics more enduring than those then prized and praised. Town-meeting days brought a display of ceremony nowhere else witnessed by the boys. A large committee of citizens waited on the pastor to conduct him to open the meeting with prayer. The formal procession, the opening to the right and left, the bowing to the pastor, as he passed the line, was something that pleased the keen eyes of youth. When witnessing a similar custom in Holland, a few years ago, I could not doubt that there was the origin of this old New-England ceremony; while I could not but regret that this little tie connecting us with the days of old is now almost obliterated.

"My father belonged to the liberal class of ministers of his day, exchanging pulpits with Rev. Dr. Bancroft, of Worcester, Rev. Dr. Thayer, of Lancaster, Rev. Dr. Ripley, of Concord, and others of the same theological affinity; although, as party-lines were not drawn with the strictness of later days, he maintained fraternal intercourse with more orthodox clergymen of his neighborhood.

"On a salary never amounting to three hundred dollars per annum, he lived in the practice of the hospitality which was then more generous. than now; he brought up a large family of children, one of whom he carried through college, and to all of whom he gave a good education.

"When, at length, divisions arose in the town, he asked a dismission; and his connection with the parish was terminated, Oct. 12, 1825. In the spring of the following year, he removed to the neighboring town of Shrewsbury, where he had purchased a farm. Here he lived till the day of his death; which event took place, after a life active and happy to the last, March 20, 1849, in the eighty-fourth year of his age."

His children, by his wife, Mary, besides three, — two sons and a daughter, — who died in infancy, were, —

1. Mary Denny, married Rev. Seth Alden, of Marlborough, and was the mother of John Carver Alden, a merchant in Boston, and William Bradford, who died in infancy. Mrs. Alden died July 31, 1825.

2. John Russell, died in 1819, at the age of eighteen.

3. Henry Adolphus, the well-known minister of Lowell, afterwards Secretary of the American Unitarian Association, who, by his wife, Augusta H. (Moore) Miles, has seven children, — Henry Townsend, Charles Russell, Francis Denny, Helen Augusta, Sarah Holyoke, Mary Denny, and George Blagden.

4. Sarah Henshaw, married to John Cooledge Mason, of Worcester; whose children are seven, — Henry Ware, George Denny, Albert Russell, Emily

Wood, John Frederick, Sarah Elizabeth, and Mary Augusta.

5. Charles Edward, married Catherine Swan Denny, whose children are, — Mary Elizabeth, Catherine Augusta, Charles Denny, Sarah Swan, Ellen Maria, and William.

6. Elizabeth Denny, married George Allen, formerly principal of the Hancock School, Boston. She died two years after her marriage; leaving an infant child, Elizabeth, who died in childhood. He died in 1864.

7. Augusta Sophia, married Isaac R. Noyes, of Shrewsbury.

# LANCASTER ASSOCIATION.

# LANCASTER ASSOCIATION.

THE LANCASTER ASSOCIATION was formed April 14, 1815, and consisted originally of four members, — Nathaniel Thayer, of Lancaster; Isaac Allen, of Bolton; Lemuel Capen, of Sterling; and David Damon, of Lunenburg. To these names were subsequently added Joseph Allen, of Northborough; Samuel Clark, of Princeton; and Peter Osgood, of Sterling. With the exception of the writer, all have ceased from their mortal labors, and gone to their reward. Of the departed, — "brethren beloved for Jesus' sake," with whom I have taken sweet counsel, and labored together in the Lord's vineyard, — I wish to speak, neither in the language of indiscriminate eulogy nor of cold indifference, but with a deep feeling of responsibility, and a desire to do justice to the memory of departed friends.

A meeting for consultation was held at Lancaster, on Friday, April 14, when it was agreed to form an

Association; and the senior member was requested to prepare a draft of a Constitution to be presented at an adjourned meeting. Accordingly, at the appointed time, June 14, the brethren met at the house of Rev. Isaac Allen, in Bolton; a Constitution was adopted; and the Association was organized by making choice of Rev. N. Thayer as moderator, and Rev. Lemuel Capen as scribe.

A letter of Rev. Mr. Capen, addressed to the writer a short time before his death, states that the Association was intended to embrace two other towns at least, Leominster and Harvard, originally included within the territorial limits of Lancaster, as also were Sterling and Bolton:—

"The Rev. Warren Fay, then of Harvard," according to his statement, "was with us by invitation, and was asked to join with us, but declined. He had exchanged with me the year before; and up to that time, I believe, he used to exchange with the other gentlemen present. Rev. Mr. Bascom, of Leominster, was not with us; though he must have been invited, as he was installed there in the spring of 1815."

As many readers may wish to learn what were the principles and rules adopted for their guidance by the founders of this Association, I present a copy of the Constitution, which they adopted at the meeting in Bolton:—

## Constitution of the Lancaster Association.

With a view to professional and Christian improvement, the subscribers agree to associate, and that the Association shall be called the Lancaster Association.

The members severally engage to conform to the following regulations:—

1. The senior member at each meeting shall be Moderator; and, in addition to his being the presiding officer, shall engage in all discussions, and perform his duty agreeably to the method prescribed in a following article.

2. There shall be a Scribe, whose duty it shall be to keep an impartial record of all proceedings; and, before the Association shall separate, give notice of the place at which the succeeding meeting shall be holden, and also give such notification to absent members as may be necessary.

3. On the second Wednesday of each month, beginning with April, at ten o'clock, A.M., there shall be a meeting of the Association. The first shall be at the house of the senior member, then according to seniority. If there be not a sufficient number of members to have a meeting in each of the seven succeeding months, there shall be such alterations of the time as may be thought expedient.

4. Each meeting shall be opened with prayer by the member at whose house the meeting of the Association may be. He shall also prepare a dissertation, or take the lead in a verbal discussion on some subject assigned at the preceding meeting. The other members shall express their ideas on the subject, and on the dissertation which they have heard, beginning with the junior members.

5. At each meeting, there shall be a public lecture at two o'clock, P.M. The members shall preach according to their standing (reckoning from the time of their ordination), unless local situation or other circumstances prevent. If the person expected to preach be absent, the next in succession shall perform.

6. At the last meeting in the season, the subject of the

sermons for the succeeding year shall be agreed upon, and the respective societies notified on the preceding sabbath of the meeting of the Association and of the topic of the sermon.

7. When the Association are in retirement, each member, who has been a hearer, beginning with the junior, shall in a friendly manner remark on the public performances.

8. It shall be the duty of the Moderator to prevent any conversation or discussion, which may interrupt the regular business of the Association.

To this document, the names of the four original members were subscribed; and, with some unimportant modifications, this Constitution remained in force up to the time of its union with the Old Worcester Association; when, by the articles of agreement entered into between the Lancaster and the Worcester Associations, it became the Constitution of the new Association then formed. Since that time, it has undergone various changes and modifications, of some of which I shall have occasion to speak hereafter.

It existed as a separate body till May, 1820, having received accessions of three new members, — Clarke of Princeton, Allen of Northborough, and Osgood of Sterling; losing, in the mean time, one of their number, by the removal of their first scribe, Rev. Lemuel Capen.

I now present brief biographical sketches of the members of the Lancaster Association.

## REV. NATHANIEL THAYER, D.D.

The senior member of the Lancaster Association was Dr. Thayer; a man eminent in his profession, whose useful ministry lasted nearly half a century, and whose praise was and is in all our churches. Dr. Thayer was born in Hampton, N.H., July 11, 1769, the year so memorable for giving birth to distinguished men. He was the son of Rev. Ebenezer Thayer (H.C. 1753), the worthy minister of that place, " who was " we are told, " remarkable in his day for his learning, for the dignity and suavity of his manners, and the placidity of his temper and disposition." His mother was the daughter of Rev. John Cotton, of Newton, who was a great-grandson of the celebrated John Cotton, the minister of the First Church in Boston.

He fitted for college at Exeter Academy, being a member of the first class of pupils offered for admission by that institution to Harvard College, which he entered at the age of sixteen. He passed the ordeal of college life with safety and honor, gaining distinction as a scholar, in a class that numbered among its members such men as Rev. William Emerson and President Kirkland, whom he reckoned among his personal friends. He graduated in 1789, and at once entered on a course of studies preparatory to the Christian ministry, under the direction of

Rev. Dr. Osgood, of Medford, — a man of reputed orthodox faith, but who breathed the very spirit of freedom, and to whose fervid eloquence in the pulpit no one could listen without emotion. That the pulpit profited by the teachings and example of this champion of religious freedom, this able theologian and eloquent divine, the life and ministry of Dr. Thayer fully evince. He, too, was a champion of religious freedom, and a strenuous vindicator of the right of private judgment in matters of religion, and of the independence of Congregational churches.

Soon after approbation, he preached as a candidate at the church on Church Green, Boston, and received a majority of the votes of the proprietors for settlement. He afterwards passed a year at Wilkesbarre, Pa., on the banks of the Susquehanna, in the family of Hon. Timothy Pickering, Secretary of War in Washington's administration, where he commenced his active ministry. Having received a unanimous invitation to settle as colleague pastor over the large and respectable society in Lancaster, of which the Rev. Timothy Harrington had been sole pastor for nearly half a century, he received ordination Oct. 9, 1793.

The following anecdote relating to the two associate pastors is given in the discourse preached at the funeral of Dr. Thayer, by Rev. Dr. Hill: —

"While the youthful candidate was making his

vows at the altar, and was receiving from his brethren and fathers in the ministry the charge to be faithful and true, the aged and infirm pastor was stretched upon a bed of languishing, to which he had for many weeks been confined. His strength was wasting away, and the fountains of life were drying up within him. But his work was not quite done. One act yet remained, and then he was ready to go. Accordingly, when the rite of ordination was over, and his youthful associate, invested with the sacred office, was passing by with the procession of his parishioners and friends, the old man was borne to the gate of his dwelling, his eyes dim with years and his locks streaming in the wind; and, there supported, he placed his trembling hand on the head of the young pastor, and invoked on him the blessing of Heaven. Almost in the words of Simeon, he gave utterance to his emotions: " I now die in peace. I can go, and bear witness to my brother, from whom I received this people, that I leave them united, prospered, and happy." Mr. Harrington lived a little more than two years from this time; his death having taken place Dec. 18, 1795, at the age of eighty, and in the forty-eighth year of his ministry.

Possessed of good natural abilities, with the advantages of a high intellectual and religious culture, of a dignified aspect, a strong and rich and well-modulated voice, together with easy, graceful, winning manners, Dr. Thayer soon gained the reputation of an accomplished pulpit-orator and able divine. He was at the height of his reputation, and in the full maturity of his powers, when my acquaintance with him commenced, and when I was introduced to the family of which he was the honored and beloved head.

To him more than any one else was the Lancaster Association indebted for the excellent rules and regulations adopted for its basis. It was about this time, 1815–1820, that several young men, who had pursued their theological studies at Cambridge or Boston, under the direction of Drs. Kirkland and Ware and Channing, had obtained a settlement as ministers in this part of Worcester County. Damon of Lunenburg, Capen, and subsequently Osgood, of Sterling, Allen of Northborough, and Clarke of Princeton, were of this number. These, with Father Allen, as he was called, of Bolton, formed a circle of which Dr. Thayer was the centre, drawn together by similarity of views, and unity of spirit. During the brief period between its formation and union with the Worcester Association, Dr. Thayer, as the senior member, presided over it with his accustomed ability, dignity, and suavity of manners. He assumed no superiority over his younger brethren; who, however, as was meet, deferred to his superior wisdom and sounder judgment. He welcomed them to their respective fields of labor, aided them by his counsels, sympathized with them in their trials, and rejoiced in their success; and they, in turn, appreciated his services, valued his friendship, and paid him the tribute of their involuntary respect.

After the union of the two Associations, his place, as moderator, was filled by his senior, Rev. Dr. Bancroft, till the death of the latter; but he still occupied a high position in the body, and did much to keep it alive and in working order. The measures that were adopted, from time to time, to give increased interest and value to the meetings of the Association, or for promoting other objects of Christian philanthropy, if they did not originate with him, were sure to find in him an earnest advocate and a firm and efficient friend. He was never rash and precipitate; but he believed in progress, and held fast only that which time and experience had proved to be good. He was a *liberal Christian* in the best sense of the term, — a worthy associate of such men as Bancroft and Freeman and Kirkland and Thatcher, the elder Ware and Buckminster and Channing, with whom he lived on terms of personal intimacy and friendship. His reputation for integrity and practical wisdom caused him to be often invited to take a seat in ecclesiastical councils for the settlement of difficulties arising between churches and their ministers, — in his day of frequent occurrence, now scarcely known in the churches of our faith.

On these occasions, he frequently acted as moderator; and his counsels and suggestions often dictated the result. Through his exchanges with his brethren, he became known in all the region round about; and, wherever he went, his appearance in the pulpit was the signal for a simultaneous smile of welcome throughout the assembly. He may not have been eloquent in the highest sense of that term; but he was rational and earnest and instructive, "able in prayer," and impressive in delivery. So rich and powerful a voice is seldom heard in the pulpit, at the bar, or in the senate. With such gifts and graces, he could not fail to secure for himself a high place in the public estimation. Accordingly, he was honored abroad, as he was the object of esteem and affection at home.

He was peculiarly happy in his domestic relations; and his home was a model of a well-regulated Christian family, where parental, filial, and fraternal affection were blended in due proportions, forming a threefold cord, which could not be easily broken. Mrs. Sarah Thayer, his excellent wife, was the daughter of Hon. Christopher Toppan, also of Hampton; and from youth to age, through all the vicissitudes of life, she proved herself worthy of such a husband. They had their share of domestic trials; among which was the removal by death of two daughters, one in the freshness and beauty of youth, the other in the ripeness of early womanhood, both highly accomplished, adorned with those graces of person and manners which win affection and inspire respect. These trials they bore with chastened grief, bowing with reverential submission to the behests of the all-wise and all-loving Father. At the time of Dr. Thayer's death, three sons and two daughters survived to comfort their widowed mother during the remnant of her days; one of whom, the late John E. Thayer, of Boston, was removed from earth while yet the aged mother lived. The other two sons, Rev. Christopher T. Thayer, — till recently the minister of the First Church in Beverly, now living in Boston, — and Nathaniel Thayer, Esq., of Boston, with their two sisters, still live, dispensing good within their several spheres, according as God has prospered and blessed them.

Dr. Thayer continued the active labors of the ministry among his people, without any sensible abatement of physical or intellectual power, with but few interruptions from sickness, till a few weeks before his death. In June, 1840, he set out with his daughter, Mary Ann, on a journey for recreation and health, through the State of New York, intending to revisit the scenes of his early ministry on the banks of the Susquehanna in Pennsylvania. He had reached Rochester, N.Y., where, after a pleasant evening, he retired to rest apparently in good health. This was the 22d of June. The closing scene shall be given in the words of another (Dr. Hill's Funeral Discourse, p. 23) : —

"The messenger of death had been sent, and was already on his way; and, in the silence of the night and in a strange city, he came, — and the aged pastor, familiar with his form, perceived that his hand was upon him, and felt his cold breath upon his cheek: but his presence and power created no alarm. Without a murmur or a sigh of discontent, he yielded to the decision of an unerring Providence; and, serene and cheerful, awaited the final issue. His mind was never clearer, or his heart warmer. His thoughts were among his family and the people whom he loved. 'Give them my dying love,' said he to the daughter whose privilege it was to stand by his bedside. 'Tell them I cheerfully submit; I die in the faith I have preached; I die in peace and in the hopes of the gospel.' It was all that he could say; and then, in accordance with his oft-repeated prayer, that he might not survive his usefulness or the possession of his powers, — that he might not die a lingering and painful death, — he sunk to his rest, as calmly and gently as an infant into its slumbers. And they who were there, and witnessed that death, although but strangers the day before, and of a faith differing from his own, took note, and said, "A good man has fallen." He died at two o'clock on the morning of the 23d of June; and his funeral took place on the 29th, in the church in which he had so long ministered at the altar, in the presence of a great assembly which the occasion had brought together from that and the neighboring towns.

It is worthy of notice, that, within the twelve months immediately preceding the death of Dr. Thayer, no less than four of his clerical brethren, eminent in their profession, whose names are intimately associated with the progress of religious freedom, with liberal views of theology, and an enlarged and generous philanthropy, passed on to their reward; viz., Rev. Dr. Bancroft, President Kirkland, and Rev. Drs. Tuckerman and Follen, — men of mark, whose memory is blessed.

*Children of Rev. Dr. Thayer.*

Dr. Thayer married, Oct. 22, 1795, Sarah, daughter of Hon. Christopher Toppan, of Hampton, N.H., by whom he had the following children : —

1. Sarah Toppan, born Aug. 21, 1796; died Oct. 20, 1839.
2. Martha, born April 25, 1798; married John Marston, Esq., for many years consul of the United States at Palermo, Sicily.
3. Mary Ann, born April 13, 1800.
4. Nathaniel, died in infancy.
5. John Eliot, born Aug. 23, 1803; married Ann, daughter of Ebenezer Francis, Esq., of Boston; died Sept. 29, 1857.
6. Christopher Toppan, born June 5, 1805; for a quarter of a century the minister of the First Parish in Beverly. Rev. Christopher Thayer (H.C. 1824)

married Augusta, daughter of Oliver Brewster, Esq., of Boston.

7. Nathaniel, born Sept. 11, 1808; married Cornelia, daughter of General Stephen Van Rensselaer, of Albany, N.Y.

8. Abigail, born Oct. 1, 1812; died Dec. 10, 1834.

*List of Publications of Rev. Dr. Thayer.*

Sermon at the Funeral of his Colleague, Rev. Timothy Harrington, 1795.
On the Annual Fast, 1795.
Masonic Discourse, 1797.
Artillery Election Sermon, 1798.
Sermon at the Ordination of Rev. E. Whitcomb, 1799.
Sermon at the Installation of Rev. William Emerson, Boston, 1799.
Sermon at the Ordination of Rev. John Sabin, Fitzwilliam, 1805.
Sermon at the Ordination of Rev. Samuel Willard, Deerfield, 1807.
Sermon at the National Fast, 1812.
Sermon at the Interment of Rev. Francis Gardner, Leominster, 1814.
Sermon on Leaving the Old Church, Lancaster, 1816.
Sermon on Entering the New Church, 1817.
Sermon at the Funeral of Henry Bromfield, Esq., Harvard, 1820.
Election Sermon, 1823.
Sermon at the Installation of Rev. Winthrop Bailey, Greenfield, 1825.
Sermon on Revivals of Religion in the "Liberal Preacher," 1827.
Sermon at the Dedication of the Church, Stow, 1827.
Sermon at the Ordination of Rev. William H. White, Littleton, 1828.

Discourse at Townsend, 1828.
Discourse at the Ordination of Rev. A. D. Jones, Hubbardston, 1828.
Thanksgiving Discourse, Lancaster, 1828.
Discourse at the Ordination of his Son, Christopher T. Thayer, Beverly, 1830.
Address at Berry-street Conference, 1831.

## REV. ISAAC ALLEN, BOLTON.

Next in seniority to Dr. Thayer was Mr. Allen, of Bolton, a name familiar as household words in all the region embraced by the Worcester Association; for he was so identified with the town of which he had so long been the minister, that their names were associated in the public mind, and were commonly pronounced in the same breath. Indeed, he seemed to be not so much the minister, as the soul, the presiding genius, of that respectable corporation. There he spent forty years in the faithful discharge of his duties as a pastor and Christian minister and citizen: there, without stinginess or meanness, for he was " given to hospitality," — there, without shutting his heart or his hands to the calls of suffering humanity, by a thrift as incomprehensible to most of his brethren as it is rare, at least in the profession to which he belonged, he accumulated a fortune, which made him the wealthiest man in the town; and there, in honor and peace, he ended his days in a good old age, bequeathing to his beloved people the whole of his estate, amounting to more than twenty thousand dollars, and, what was more and better, the remembrance of his many virtues.

Mr. Allen was born in Weston, Oct. 31, 1771, and was the son of a respectable mechanic of that place. Owing to a fall on the ice, when a lad of thirteen, he became a cripple for life; and his halting gait, a robust frame, and full and florid face, together with his rapid and abrupt utterance, his friendly and cordial greetings, his pithy and weighty sayings, reminding one of Dr. Franklin's "Poor Richard," his apt and well-told anecdotes, his easy intercourse with children and young persons, not only in his parish, but in the families of his brother ministers, — these, and other peculiarities and qualities of person and character, are called up before us at the mention of his name.

After spending some years in learning a trade, he was encouraged by his minister, Rev. Dr. Kendall, to seek a collegiate education. Accordingly, he applied himself to the study of the classics, under the direction of his pastor, and entered Harvard College at the age of twenty-three, graduating with the class of 1798, — a class that numbered among its members Judge Story, and Rev. Drs. Tuckerman and Channing, of blessed memory. Having pursued a course of preparatory studies with Dr. Kendall, he began to preach, and soon received a nearly unanimous call from the town of Bolton, to fill the place made vacant by the death of their minister, Rev. Phineas Wright (H.C. 1772). He accepted the invitation, and was ordained March 14, 1804. "At the time of his ordination, I have heard him say," writes Rev. Mr. Edes, his successor in the ministry, "there was an immense body of snow on the ground; and the travelling was difficult and dangerous." \*

He had at this time reached the mature age of thirty-three years; and here he passed in great quiet the remainder of his days, laboring, as occasion called and as inclination prompted, with his own hands, in his garden and on his homestead, but not to the neglect of his duties as a parish minister. During the whole of this period of forty years, with the exception of the last year of his life, when he was disabled by disease, and was relieved of his burden by the settlement of a colleague, Rev. Richard S. Edes, he was prevented from preaching, on account of indisposition, but one Sunday.

Though never married, he did not live in seclusion, or without many of the comforts and joys of domestic life. For many years, he had a pleasant home in the family of Madame Wright, the widow of his predecessor, who, being childless, bequeathed

---

\* I well remember the winter of 1804, that it was one of uncommon severity; that the snow accumulated to a very great depth; and that so late as the 23d of March, — a date fixed in my memory, as on that day my aged grandfather died, — while the sun was so warm as to cause the buds to swell, the snow by the roadsides was even with the walls; and that, on that or the following day, I saw in a sheltered nook, where a warm spring issued, a dandelion in full blossom! — J. A.

to him the principal part of her estate. After her decease, he continued to occupy the same spacious mansion, having the good fortune to secure the services of a housekeeper admirably fitted for the place, who was to him even as a daughter, and who, after many years of faithful services, sickened and died in his house. Her death was felt by him as one of the severest trials of his life, from the effects of which he never fully recovered. He felt his solitariness, and the more as the infirmities of age crept upon him. Almost to the last, however, he retained to a remarkable degree his bodily vigor and his mental activity; nor did his affections grow languid, or his interest in his profession or in his people abate one jot. But he had now completed his "threescore years and ten;" and he was anxious to be relieved of a part of the burden, which began to press too heavily on his aged shoulders. Accordingly, about a year before his death, he asked for a colleague, and his request was granted; and, May 24, 1843, Rev. Richard S. Edes was installed as junior pastor, with his full and cordial approval. But the connection thus happily formed was of brief continuance. In the beginning of the following autumn, he was seized with paralysis, which prostrated his strength, confined him to his room, and made him a helpless invalid during the brief remnant of his days. His mind, however, was still unclouded, and his trust in God unfaltering. He was glad to see his friends, whom he cordially greeted, and with whom he freely conversed, although with imperfect utterance. He continued in much the same state for several months. On the first Sunday of the new year, Jan. 7, 1844, he addressed the following pastoral letter to his church, which was read at the commencement of the communion service on that day : —

"CHRISTIAN FRIENDS, — I wish you a happy new year, and all the happiness which results from a faithful discharge of duty. Your old minister and friend, although weak and helpless, feels the same strong interest in your welfare he has ever felt. During the few remaining days God may see fit to spare me on earth, it will give me heartfelt pleasure to hear of your religious progress, and that you are increasing in numbers and strength, and that you remain united, full of Christian faith and charity, and that you are making daily advancement in every thing excellent and praiseworthy. I would say to those young friends who have recently united with the church, that I hope they will experience all the religious advantages and pleasures they anticipate from this step. I would also express the hope, that others, who have been witnesses of their good example, may be induced to follow it.

"My friends, my own condition may serve to remind you of the duty of action, while health and strength remain. May what I have so often said to you from the pulpit be now indelibly impressed upon your minds, — that the sick-bed is no place to fix the attention or fasten the thoughts on any subject; and that, accordingly, if religious thoughts and principles have not been impressed before, they can hardly yield here their appropriate supports and consolations!

"Ever your friend,     Isaac Allen."

"The attack of paralysis," says Mr. Edes, in his funeral discourse, "was a most grievous affliction. He had hardly known before what it was to be confined to a sick-room. He loved the free air of heaven, and to be moving about among his friends and people. Sad, sad, then, was that allotment of Divine Providence which laid upon him the burden of helplessness. Though he had every comfort of which his case admitted, though unwearied kindness and skill ministered to his relief, and though always submissive and resigned, still, the wish would sometimes burst from his lips, 'I desire to depart, and to be with Christ; nevertheless, God's will be done.'"

Mr. Allen lingered along through the winter months, till March 18, 1844; when, just four days after the fortieth anniversary of his ordination, he "passed on," and entered into his rest, being then in the seventy-third year of his age.

"Our father died," says Mr. Edes, " amidst ministrations to his wishes and comforts which could not have been surpassed, in tenderness and fidelity, by an affectionate son or a devoted daughter. He died at a mature age, looking backward with pleasant memories, and forward with cheering anticipations. He died possessed of the sincere affection and respect of the people who knew him intimately, and whom he had long served. He died with a loving, benevolent, and pious heart. He died a Christian, — so far as we could know, and as far as his humility would allow him to confess it, — with a pure conscience, void certainly of any grave offence either towards God or towards men. After a life, in the main, healthy and happy, he died in the hope of a blessed immortality, 'trusting,' to use his own words, 'in the mercy of God, as made known by Jesus Christ.'"

Mr. Allen was not a theologian, a metaphysician, or a scholar; but he had what is better, — a large fund of plain, good sense, a deep knowledge of human nature, and a straightforward, blunt honesty, which inspired confidence, and made him a wise and safe counsellor.

In confirmation of this statement, we give the following extract from a private letter of Mr. Edes: —

"He was never much of a literary man, never very fond of study, or of writing sermons; but he was a person of strong mind, of accurate and often acute perceptions, of remarkable memory, and of correct, if not fervent, religious feelings. His ready wit, and his quickness at repartee, were quite remarkable, — as in the story told of his college life: Walking across the college yard one day, limping as usual, he overheard a fellow-student behind him say to his companion, 'The legs of the lame are not equal,' quoting Prov. xxvi. 7. At which Allen immediately turned round, and gave the rest of the verse, — the best answer that could be made, — 'So is a parable in the mouth of a fool.'"

"His sermons," Mr. Edes continues, "I should judge, from what I have heard of them, were sound, sensible, often pithy, *evangelical*, in the true sense of the word; but better adapted to meet the approbation of minds already matured, and to strengthen habits of feeling already tending in the right direction, than to arouse slumbering consciences or to awaken souls sunk in apathy. His imagination was sometimes quite active, but never soared high; and, as to rousing appeals, he was entirely a stranger to any thing of the sort; though in keenness and severity of rebuke, when any thing awakened his moral displeasure, very few ever went beyond him. As a parish minister, as a public-spirited citizen, sympathizing with all classes of his parishioners, seeking to say the right word, and to do the right thing, at the right time, in the joyful or the sorrowful occasions of life, always ready with pecuniary or other help where his judgment approved or his feelings were interested, — in these points he deserved, as he has gained, a high place among his brethren."

"His views and his virtues," says Rev. Mr. Sears, then a near neighbor and intimate friend of Mr. Allen, "were all practical. He thought it far less important what men believe, than what they do. His whole mind and character were formed by what is usually called common sense; and this gave tone to all his preaching, and a thorough coloring to his theology. Indeed, I presume that those who heard him preach for nearly forty years knew little about his theology; for I think he never elaborated any opinions, except those which touch directly upon moral practice."

In illustration of this remark, Mr. Sears relates the following anecdote, which is so characteristic of the man, that it could not well be omitted: —

"When called upon once by his brethren in the ministry to give his opinion upon the origin of moral evil, how men become sinners, and what is the true doctrine of human depravity, he replied, as usual, by an illustration: 'A field of corn belonging to one of my neighbors was the other day broken into; and, while they were debating the question how the intruders could have got in, the whole crop was nearly destroyed and eaten up. Go home to your people, and work faithfully in driving sin out of the world; and, when that is accomplished, we will ask how it came in.'"

With the closing paragraph of Mr. Sears's funeral discourse, we take leave of our well-remembered, well-beloved brother, "Father Allen, of Bolton," as, in the latter years of his life, he was commonly called: —

"He was the last of his generation among the Liberal clergy of Worcester County, — those men who stood forth for freedom of thought and opinion among the Congregational churches. May we be faithful to the trust they leave us; using that freedom sacredly in learning and interpreting the only creed they would bind upon us, — the revealed Word of God! Let us learn it with fresh zeal, and kindle our souls anew from its everlasting truths. For so *we*, too, are passing away. So we press on, ministers and people, to join the congregation of the dead, or, rather, the innumerable and immortal company that have gone to the tribunal of the Eternal Judge. May we go as servants that have been faithful, and lie down to life's last slumber, at peace with the world, at peace with ourselves, and at peace with our God!"

At the funeral of Rev. Isaac Allen, March 21, the following order of services was observed: —

The corpse was followed from the late dwelling-house of the deceased by the members of the Worcester Association of Ministers and other clergymen, and by the parish committee of arrangements, to the meeting-house. On arriving there, the corpse was borne into the house, and placed in front of the pulpit.

Hymn 464 of Greenwood's Collection was then sung, — "I heard a voice from heaven," &c.

Prayer was then offered by Rev. Alonzo Hill, of Worcester.

Selections of Scripture were read by Rev. Mr. Sears, of Lancaster.

Hymn 559 — "Servant of God, well done" — was then sung.

The funeral sermon was delivered by Rev. Mr. Edes; and Rev. Mr. Allen, of Northborough, offered the funeral prayer.

Hymn 602 — "Unveil thy bosom, faithful tomb" — was then sung; and the congregation was dismissed by Rev. William H. White, of Littleton.

After the funeral services were over, the people repaired to the Town Hall, and listened to the reading of the will by Rev. Mr. Allen, of Northborough, by which the whole of his property, amounting to over twenty thousand dollars, was bequeathed to the society of which he had so long been the pastor.

REV. DAVID DAMON, LUNENBURG.

Mr. Damon, another of the original members of the Lancaster Association, was connected with the new Worcester Association from its formation in 1820 till 1829, when he removed from this county, to enter another field of service. He was born at East Sudbury, now Wayland, Sept. 12, 1787, and was the son of Aaron and Rachel (Griffin) Damon; was fitted for college at Andover; and was graduated at Cambridge, in the class of 1811, at the ripe age of twenty-four. Among his classmates were Everett, Fuller, Frothingham, Gilman, and many others who have gained an honorable distinction in letters and in professional life. It was no slight indication of merit in Mr. Damon, that he held a high rank in a class containing so large a proportion of good scholars, and so many of distinguished eminence. With good natural abilities, and a good degree of self-reliance, he could easily excel in the recitation-room; and, by the early habit of writing, his compositions were always respectable, and sometimes of superior merit.

Being wholly dependent on his own exertions for support, he maintained himself through the four years of college life, partly by keeping school in the winters, and partly by writing for a literary paper at that time published in Boston. Besides, he availed himself, with many others of high standing as scholars, of the privilege of earning his board by waiting on the table in Commons Hall, where nearly all the students, and most of the officers of college, took their meals. He graduated with distinguished honors, on the best terms with the government, and with the kind regards of his classmates.

After graduation, he entered on a course of theological studies under the direction of President Kirkland, Professor Henry Ware, sen., and Professor Sidney Willard; having for his fellow-students, besides six or eight of his classmates, a number who had graduated at an earlier period, among whom were Charles Eliot, George B. English, Lemuel Capen, and Cyrus Peirce. Having completed his preparatory studies, he offered himself as a candidate for settlement; and having received an invitation from the church and town of Lunenburg, in Worcester County, he received ordination Feb. 1, 1815.\*

The society over which he was placed had diminished somewhat in numbers and strength since the days of the venerable Adams (Zabdiel Adams, H.C. 1759, died in 1801), one of his predecessors. "I found the town," Mr. Damon says in his farewell discourse, "when I came here, in a divided state as to religious opinions; and the society worshipping in this house, already reduced in number." It was

---

\* The day and night preceding the ordination (January 31) were said to be the coldest ever experienced in our climate; the average through the day being ten degrees below zero. Notwithstanding the severity of the weather, Dr. Ware, sen., who preached the ordination sermon, rode in an open sleigh from Cambridge to Lunenburg; taking with him one of his daughters as far as Lexington, which place they reached before sunrise, and arriving at Lunenburg in season for the ordination services. Rev. Dr. Field, of Weston, was ordained on the same day, which, although intensely cold, was fair and pleasant.

hardly to be expected, in those days of religious commotion, just as the great controversy broke out, in Boston and the vicinity, between the adherents of the old and the advocates of the new faith, that, however gifted or faithful, he should be able to heal all divisions, and harmonize all the discordant elements, that he found there. He was a man of peace; and no one ever charged him with being a fomenter of strife or a violent partisan. However he may have been regarded at home, he was one of the most acceptable preachers of our faith in the circle of his exchanges. Without the advantages of a commanding presence, he had a clear and strong voice, perfect self-command, and an easy and graceful delivery, that was quite attractive; all which made him, if not an impressive and powerful, yet an interesting and popular, preacher.

In the meetings of the Worcester Association, he was always ready to do his part; and by his genial spirit, no less than by his learning and his wit, he did much to render those meetings pleasant and useful. His brethren held him in honor; and his removal from their neighborhood, after a pleasant acquaintance of more than twelve years, was an occasion of deep regret.

He was dismissed, at his own request, in December, 1827, after a ministry of nearly thirteen years; and the sermon he preached on the occasion, which was published, contains a calm and dispassionate review of his ministry, and an affectionate farewell to the people whom he had so faithfully served.

He did not long remain without a settlement. He was installed over the church and society of Salisbury and Amesbury, in the north-eastern part of the State, June 25 of the following year, 1828, where he remained about five years when, May 14, 1833, he asked and obtained a dismission from his pastoral charge.

The reasons which led him to make this request are set forth in the following letter, addressed to his church and congregation : —

"CHRISTIAN BRETHREN AND FRIENDS, — Having been informed by members of the society, who are undoubtedly well acquainted with its situation, that a portion of the pecuniary aid promised to the society, previous to my settlement with you, is withheld ; and that influence, which it was then expected would be exerted in favor of our society, has been turned against it ; and that, on these accounts, the society is unable to continue my support, — I therefore respectfully ask a dissolution, &c.

"Your pastor and affectionate brother in Christ,

"DAVID DAMON.

"AMESBURY, Dec. 4, 1832."

The council called to sanction the proceedings relative to his dismission, of which Rev. Charles W. Upham, of Salem, was moderator, and Rev. Thomas

B. Fox, of Newburyport, scribe, bear testimony to his fidelity and worth in the following terms : —

"The council cannot bring this result to a close, without expressing their affectionate sympathy and Christian regard for the pastor and people, whose hallowed and harmonious union has thus unexpectedly been dissolved by influences beyond their control, and for the injurious consequences of which, to themselves and others, they cannot, of course, be considered to any extent answerable. When the council reflect upon the motives which induced Mr. Damon to relinquish his legal claim upon the society for support, and to throw himself and family again upon the world without any other reliance than a good conscience and a trust in God, rather than permit a faithful people to bend under a burden greater than they could bear, or remain among them to kindle the fires of controversy, and conduct a sectarian strife, in a small and industrious village, which, but a few years before, he had entered for the purpose of advancing the cause of peace, charity, and love within its bosom, their hearts are filled with sympathy for his disappointment, and with admiration of the Christian wisdom, fortitude, and self-sacrifice which have marked his course; and when they think of his excellent abilities as a preacher of the gospel, of his large and varied experience, and the virtues of his character and life, they are strong in the belief, that Providence will open to him, in some other field, a path of longer-timed usefulness and happiness."

It appears, from the documents which were published at the time, that this was one of those cases, of which there have been many during the last thirty years, in which, for the sake of peace and union or for some less worthy cause, the friends of Liberal Christianity have yielded to the persistent claims of their Orthodox brethren, and disbanded, — ceased to exist as organized bodies.

Mr. Damon did not long remain without a parish and a home. He was installed as pastor of the First Congregational Church and Society in West Cambridge, April 15, 1835, where he remained for eight years. "Honored," to borrow the words inscribed on his monument, —

> Honored for his genius and learning,
> Revered for his piety and virtue,
> Trusted for his simplicity and integrity
> of character, loved for his kind
> and gentle affections, his people mourn
> the loss of a pastor whose daily life
> repeated the lessons of the pulpit.
> In his family, a husband and parent, whose
> love knew no measure; to the
> public, a valued citizen.

On the reverse is the following : —

> . . . . . . . . . . installed
> over the society in
> West Cambridge, April 15, 1835.
> Seized with apoplexy
> at a funeral service,
> he died on the following

Sunday, June 25, 1843,
in the 56th year of his age.
His body is the first interred
in this cemetery, which was consecrated
by him a few days before his death.
This monument is erected by members
of his late congregation, as a humble
tribute of affection and respect to his memory.

A short time before his death, the degree of doctor of divinity was conferred on him by a vote of the Corporation of Harvard University; but it had not at that time been publicly announced. In 1841, he preached the Election Sermon before the State Legislature, which was printed. He also preached "the Dudleian Lecture" at Cambridge; both appointments being regarded as marks of distinguished honor.

His death was sudden and wholly unexpected, as he seemed to possess a good degree of bodily vigor, and his sound constitution gave the promise of long life. He died in the midst of his useful and acceptable labors, at a time when he seemed to have found at last a field suited to his powers, and a people congenial to his tastes, among whom he might hope to pass the evening of his days in peace and comparative independence. But Heaven ordered it otherwise; and it becomes us to bow in submission to the behests of the All-wise, the All-loving Father. Peace to the memory of our brother and classmate!

It is stated by his son, Norwood Damon, in a note to the address delivered by his father at the consecration of the new cemetery in West Cambridge,

June 14, that, "nine days subsequent to its delivery, he attended the funeral of the Hon. Edmund Parker, in Reading, Mass. He entered the pulpit apparently in good health, but, at the close of the services, was attacked with apoplexy. He was conveyed from the pulpit to the late residence of Mr. Parker, where he died on Sunday morning, June 25, in the fifty-sixth year of his age. He was the first to rest in the new cemetery, at the consecration of which he had so recently assisted."

We close this brief notice of our brother Damon, with the following extract from a letter from his classmate, Hon. Edward Everett: —

"In college, I knew him rather intimately, considering the difference in our years; he being one of the oldest, and I the youngest member of the class. We were brother members, with yourself, of several literary clubs, where you remember he distinguished himself by the maturity of his compositions, as might, indeed, have been expected from his years.

"He was in the habit, even in our Freshman year, of writing essays for one or two literary journals, of rather humble pretensions, published at that time in Boston. I think he told me that he began to do this, even before he came to college. Influenced by his example, I made my own first efforts at writing for the press at this time. Being under fourteen years of age, they were of course crude enough. His pieces, though, if I remember, not marked by much vivacity, were sensible and correctly written. He maintained, as you know, a very respectable rank in the class. He had made great efforts to prepare himself for college, and distinguished himself, while there, among the most diligent and laborious of our number. He was perfectly amiable in his disposition, and exemplary in his habits."

Mr. Damon was married, Oct. 16, 1815, to Rebekah, daughter of John and Sarah (Norwood) Derby, of Lynnfield, by whom he had seven children, — four sons and three daughters. Mrs. Damon died in Boston, May 21, 1852, in the fifty-sixth year of her age.

The following list of Mr. Damon's publications is taken from "The Annals of the American Unitarian Pulpit," by Rev. Dr. Sprague: —

A Sermon preached at Worcester, not far from the Year 1820.

Sketch of the Life and Character of the late Rev. Joseph Motley, of Lynnfield, published in the "Christian Disciple," 1822.

A Sermon preached at Concord, at the Semi-annual Meeting of the Evangelical Society in Massachusetts, 1823.

A Sermon preached at Charlton, Mass., at the Annual Meeting of the Auxiliary Bible Society in the County of Worcester, 1826.

A Sermon delivered at Lunenburg, at the Close of his Ministry there, 1827.

An Address on Temperance, delivered at Amesbury, 1829.

A Sermon, entitled "What is Truth?" about 1830.

A Sermon, entitled "The Common Faith of Christians," published in the "Liberal Preacher," 1830.

A Sermon, entitled "Means of Attaining Religion," published for the Union Ministerial Association, 1832.

A Sermon, entitled "Human Life: a Tale," delivered at Amesbury.

A Sermon, entitled "The Exceeding Sinfulness of Sin."

A Sermon on Acts ii. 22.

An Address delivered before the Ministerial Conference, in Berry Street, Boston, 1840.

A Sermon preached after the Death of Philip Augustus Whittemore, 1841.

A Sermon delivered before the Legislature of Massachusetts at the Annual Election, 1841.

An Address at the Consecration of the New Cemetery at West Cambridge, 1843.

He published also, in the newspapers of the day, a notice of the Rev. William Gray Swett, a poem delivered at West Cambridge, and various other minor productions of his pen.

To this list of publications, it may be added that he was one of the founders of "the Harvard Lyceum," a periodical — we believe the first of its kind — to which he contributed many interesting articles, published in 1810 and 1811, supported chiefly by the class which graduated in the latter year.

### REV. LEMUEL CAPEN, STERLING.

The youngest of the four original members of the Lancaster Association was Rev. Lemuel Capen, for a short time the minister of the First Congregational

Church and Society in Sterling. He was present at the organization of the Association; and, so long as he remained in Sterling, he was an active and efficient member. He was a man of a robust constitution, somewhat above the medium size, of a benignant and cheerful aspect, blest with uninterrupted health and uncommon elasticity of spirits. Without any pretensions to genius or uncommon gifts, he was a sound theologian, an earnest and acceptable preacher, a pleasant companion, a faithful friend, an honest, trustworthy man. My acquaintance with him began in college, was continued through a course of preparatory studies in Cambridge, renewed during his ministry in Sterling, and ripened into a friendship which lasted through life.

His connection with the Association he regarded as a high privilege. "I can speak," he says, in a letter to the writer, Jan. 21, 1856, "in the strongest terms of the satisfactions I enjoyed, and the benefits I received, by my intercourse with that Association. And among the very painful circumstances of leaving Sterling was my separation from those good men, to whom I had become greatly attached. Our intercourse was truly cordial, fraternal, Christian."

Mr. Capen was born in Dorchester, Nov. 25, 1789, and was the son of John and Patience (Davis) Capen. "After enjoying such advantages of early education as his native village and the adjoining town of Milton then afforded, he was at length, in order to be fitted for college, placed under the charge of Rev. Peter Whitney, of Quincy, for whom he ever afterwards entertained feelings of unabated esteem, and of whom he wrote an obituary notice for the 'Christian Register,' soon after his death in 1843." He entered Harvard College in 1806, and graduated with the class of 1810, in which he held a respectable rank. Among his classmates were Judge Willard Phillips, Hon. Joseph G. Kendall, James Gore King, Octavius Pickering, Theodore Lyman, and others more or less distinguished for their public services or their private virtues.

Having deliberately made choice of a profession, he entered on a course of theological studies at Cambridge, under the superintendence of President Kirkland, Professors Henry Ware, sen., and Sidney Willard, with whom was associated, the latter part of the time, that accurate scholar and accomplished theologian, Andrews Norton, who subsequently rendered so important a service to the Divinity School and the cause of biblical learning.

"He often spoke of the satisfaction he felt in regard to his intercourse with Dr. Ware, sen., and of the depth of his obligation to him in particular for the advantages of that season of preparation for the ministry."

Having finished his course of study at Cambridge, he offered himself as a candidate for settlement;

and he was ordained in Sterling, March 22, 1815, at the age of twenty-six. He was the immediate successor of Rev. Reuben Holcomb, who, after his dismission, continued to reside in the town, till the time of his death. The society over which Mr. Capen was ordained pastor was quite large, consisting of nearly all the families in the place. He was, in fact, *the minister of the town;* all the ecclesiastical and all the secular interests of the society being in the hands, and at the disposal, of the citizens at large.

The initiatory step towards the settlement of a minister was, it is true, commonly taken by the church-members, whose action, however, had no legal force, till confirmed by a vote of the town, at a regular meeting called for the purpose.

The salary of the minister was assessed, like any other tax, on the inhabitants of the town, not otherwise legally discharged, and collected and paid over by the town treasurer.

The great meeting-house in Sterling, with galleries on three sides, afterwards destroyed by fire, was not too large for the accommodation of those who attended public worship. The whole front gallery was occupied by the choir, which in Sterling, at the time spoken of, was very large, and composed of some of the finest voices it has ever been my privilege to hear.

Such was the society to the pastoral charge of

which our young brother was called. He filled the place well and acceptably; but, with a growing family, he found his salary quite inadequate to his necessities, and, believing it could not be increased without causing division in a hitherto united parish, he resigned his charge, June 21, 1819, having retained it but little more than four years. I have never understood that there was any disaffection among his people, or any wish on their part to have the connection dissolved; but yet they made no effort, I believe, to retain his services, probably through the same fear of division which prevented him from asking for an increase of salary.

"The reasons for this separation are set forth in the documents published with his 'Farewell Sermon' (a second edition of which was printed), bearing testimony to the good feeling subsisting between him and the parish, and their mutual satisfaction with one another as pastor and people. He ever held them in affectionate remembrance, and was always happy when an opportunity was granted him of visiting them from time to time, and preaching to them."

Of the following twenty years of his life, he gives, in a letter to the writer, the following succinct account: "Removed to Dorchester, and from March, 1819, to November, 1822, was employed there in teaching a private school, and supplying vacant pulpits, in the neighborhood, as opportunity offered.

In the autumn of 1822, during the sickness of their temporary minister, Rev. Zephaniah Wood, who was also master of the public school at South Boston, I was asked to supply the pulpit of the Hawes-place Society. At the decease of Mr. Wood, I was appointed master of the school; and continued in that employ about four years, at the same time preaching to the society. On the 29th of January, 1823, I was invited to become pastor of said society, and consented. But, on account of my connection with the school, my installation was deferred till the autumn of 1827, when the call was unanimously renewed; and the installation took place Oct. 31, 1827. My pastoral relation to the society was dissolved June 22, 1839." Up to the time of his installation, as we learn, he received little or no compensation from the society, but had a small salary of five hundred dollars, as master of the public grammar school. With this inadequate compensation, and the profits of a few acres which he skilfully cultivated with his own hands, he supported a large and growing family for several years.

From 1827, his means were enlarged, so that, by rigid economy, he was able to give four of his sons a collegiate education; a proof of the estimation in which he held good learning, as well as of the self-sacrificing parental love which prompted such action.

After his dismission, he continued to reside in South Boston, finding grateful employment in the cultivation of his land and in literary pursuits, preaching occasionally in neighboring pulpits, and in discharging the duties of public and private life to which he was called.

Twice, viz. in 1836 and in 1847, he was chosen a representative to the State Legislature; and in 1845 he was employed for one year as a missionary to the poor in the city of Baltimore, where he labored with diligence, and where his services were appreciated, as the documents appended to his first quarterly report amply prove.

The latter years of his life he spent in honorable retirement in the bosom of his family, finding pleasure and profit in the cultivation of his grounds, taking an interest in the affairs of church and state, and occasionally writing for the public papers. His habits were domestic, and to him no place was so dear as home. He was of an affectionate disposition, and his affections clustered around the domestic hearth and altar.

He loved the ministry. It was his chosen profession; and his interest in it, and in his ministerial brethren, especially those who belonged to the same household of faith with himself, was strong, and continued without abatement to the last. Liberal Christianity had in him a firm friend and an enlightened advocate; and, while his charity was wide and comprehensive, it was discriminating and just. He not only spoke the truth with love, but he refuted error and rebuked wrong without acrimony or ill-will.

So early as 1813, while yet a resident graduate at Cambridge, he prepared a pamphlet of fifty pages, published without his name, relating to a controversy in the Second Church in Dorchester, growing out of the refusal of its pastor, Rev. Dr. Codman, to hold ministerial intercourse with certain members of the Boston Association. The title of the pamphlet was, "A Memorial of the Proprietors of the New South Meeting-house in Dorchester to the Ministers of the Boston Association;" a recent perusal of which fully justifies the commendation bestowed upon it by the leading Orthodox periodical of the day, which speaks of it as a document "written with more than ordinary care and ability." The controversy resulted in the formation of a new society, — the Third Congregational Society in Dorchester (Rev. T. J. Mumford's). Again, after an interval of more than forty years, he prepared an able and elaborate article, "On Dr. Codman, and the Second Church in Dorchester," contained in the "Christian Examiner" for September, 1855, which may be regarded as the deliberate judgment of a wise and honest and fair-minded man, on the merits of a controversy now nearly forgotten, but which at the time excited not a little interest in the ecclesiastical world.

Besides the publications already mentioned, Mr.

Capen was the writer of a good practical sermon on the "Religious Education of Children," contained in the "Liberal Preacher" for June, 1831, and of a "Discourse on the Character of Mr. John Hawes," preached Feb. 1, 1829, the Sunday after the funeral of his excellent friend, whose name is honorably associated with the society to which he ministered. He was also the writer, as we learn, " of several biographical notices of ministers, and of old residents in South Boston," as well as of valuable articles published in "The New-England Farmer."

Of his last days on earth, we give the account furnished us by one of his sons: "He died of consumption undoubtedly, although no one who had known him would have considered him a subject for that disease. He was, on the contrary, considered very robust for a professional man. I never knew him, but in a single instance, to be obliged to suspend preaching on account of illness. . . . Indeed, he was accustomed, late in life, to speak of his uninterrupted good health as a blessing for which he was most devoutfully thankful. Some time in the year 1856 (I think), on taking a sudden cold, that which, for twenty years, had assumed the form of catarrh, seemed to settle upon his lungs, being succeeded by a wearing cough and difficult respiration. From this time, he gradually but perceptibly failed. . . . His mind and memory seemed giving way in the spring of 1858. He abandoned all at once, and with a sentence incomplete, his diary of passing events, which he had regularly kept for more than thirty years. He attended Commencement for the fifty-sixth time, just before his death. I think you saw him on that occasion, and perhaps may have been surprised that he should be there, seemingly so feeble. But it was his wish to go: it had been his constant habit from boyhood; and, though perhaps the day might have passed by without his being aware of it, still we could not withhold from him such a gratification. He kept about house till two days before he died. His strong religious faith, which all through life had sustained him, did not desert him in the end. He had never any gloomy fears or misgivings in relation to the future, but looked upon death rather as the 'open door' to a new and more glorious life. During his last night on earth, his mind wandered much: but he appeared to know, at times, those who stood around his bed; would at times attempt to speak, but could hardly make himself understood. Towards the close, he said with considerable distinctness, 'To-day I shall be where glory' —— Here his strength failed, and the sentence was not completed. But we can hardly doubt as to what was passing in his mind. He seemed, while laboring for breath, and apparently in great bodily distress, to be favored, now and then, with a glimpse of what was 'within the veil,' 'across the narrow stream of death.'"

And so he passed on to join the goodly company of the "sons of God" who have gone to their reward, where, in "the house of many mansions," we who are left behind, if we hold fast our faith without wavering, may hope to meet our brother again.

"He enjoyed eminently," says the writer of an admirable obituary notice, published in the "Register" for Oct. 2, 1858, "the fellowship of his ministerial brothers. No one was more constant than he at the 'ministers' meetings.' No one was more punctual at the 'Thursday Lecture,' even after that time-hallowed institution had ceased to be hallowed by much else, and when the rooms and the bookstore proved more attractive than the church to the gathering clergy of that famous old day." We heartily join in the sentiment of the closing paragraph: "Associate for so many years in a sacred profession, where the able are infirm, and the best cannot always be commended! we dismiss you from us, in the full confidence that you have not gone into any worse society."

Mr. Capen was married, Oct. 11, 1815, to Mary Ann Hunting, daughter of Asa and Abigail (Blaney) Hunting, of Roxbury. They had six sons and three daughters; the two oldest sons being born in Sterling, the others in Dorchester and Boston. Six of these nine, five sons and one daughter, with their mother, are still living. They are,—

1. Francis L. Capen, clergyman, resides in Boston.
2. John, also resides in Boston.
3. Edward, librarian of the Boston Public Library.
4. Charles J., teacher in the public Latin School, Boston. His residence is in Dedham.
5. Barnard, secretary of the Boston School Committee.
6. Jane, married Jesse Harding, druggist, Boston.

The names of the three not living are, —

7. Mary Ann, died in Boston, Nov. 7, 1844.
8. Sarah Hawes, died Oct. 22, 1844.
9. Eliphalet Porter, died Nov. 19, 1835.

Mrs. Capen still survives, and lives in Boston.

## REV. SAMUEL CLARKE.

"A beloved brother, and faithful minister in the Lord," was the text of a commemorative discourse preached to the bereaved flock of this excellent man, a few weeks after his death, by his relative and friend, Rev. Dr. Hill, of Worcester. Fitter words could not have been chosen; and there are few to whom they more justly apply than to him whose name stands at the head of this sketch. During the fifteen years that he remained pastor of the First Church in Princeton, he was an active member, first of the Lancaster, and then of the Worcester Association as now organized. And from the commencement of his ministry in Uxbridge till his death in November, 1859, though, on account of the distance, he declined an active participation in the doings of the Association, he did not lose his interest in the body; and with some of the brethren he maintained habits of intimacy even to the last. Occasionally he attended our meetings; and his presence was always greeted with a cordial welcome. While an active member, he was seldom absent, and never without a good and sufficient reason; and, though not a man of many words, what he said was judicious, pertinent, and sound.

To the writer he was endeared by habits of intimacy through the long period of more than forty years, and by a substantial harmony of religious views. We were nearly of the same age; we pursued our theological studies at the same time, and under influences very much alike. There was an interval of but a few months between the commencement of our respective ministries. We were members of the same Association; and there was a frequent interchange of ministerial and social visits at each other's houses.

In the notice which is subjoined, while I shall studiously abstain from the language of indiscriminate eulogy, I cannot — I do not wish to — forget that the subject of my remarks was a personal friend. I shall not, however, rely solely on my own impressions, in the judgment I form and the character I give of our beloved brother. I shall avail myself of the privilege, kindly allowed me, of giving extracts from the commemorative discourse of Dr. Hill, who is better qualified, probably, than any other person to portray the character of our common friend.

Mr. Clarke was born in New Boston, N.H., April 21, 1791, and was the son of Ninian Clarke, "a man of large sympathies and a noble spirit, trusted by every one, and famed all the country around for his unflinching integrity." He was of Scotch descent; one of his ancestors having belonged to a company of emigrants, who, flying from persecution at home, had formed settlements in the mountainous region on the south-eastern borders of New Hampshire.

"The tradition of his family is," we are told, "that, in childhood, he was set apart for the ministry;* and never thought, himself, of being any thing else." Nor can we doubt that this early act of self-consecration had a great and lasting influence on his life and character. It may have been the *hinge* on which his future destiny turned.

With this leading object in view, he looked to a collegiate education as the best means of qualifying himself for the office of a Christian minister. Taking leave of the home of his childhood, he pursued his preparatory studies under the care of Rev. Mr.

---

\* "Set apart," not by any formal act, only considered as destined to the ministry.

Beede, of Wilton, N.H., and entered Dartmouth College, graduating with the class of 1812.

On leaving college, he repaired to Boston, and entered on a course of theological studies, under Rev. Dr. William E. Channing, whose character he admired, and whose friendship he enjoyed. Under the instructions of this eminent man, and the influences of the Boston pulpit, then in its glory, under the administration of such men as Freeman, Channing, Thatcher, Lowell, and Ware; living, too, in the neighborhood of the University, then under the administration of President Kirkland, and holding intercourse with the noble band of young men at that time preparing for the ministry under the direction of President Kirkland and Professors Ware and Willard and Andrews Norton, — he enjoyed advantages hardly inferior to those furnished by the best theological schools. It was my own good fortune to be one of the number; and the names of Everett, Frothingham, Damon, Gilman, Prentiss, associated with the names of other fellow-students of earlier classes still continuing their theological studies in the shades of their Alma Mater, — as Charles Eliot, Thomas B. English, Lemuel Capen, Cyrus Peirce, and others, — recall some of the happiest scenes and most valuable experiences of my life. The saintly and gifted John E. Abbot, too, for a brief period the almost idolized minister of the North Church, Salem, was a friend and fellow-student of Mr. Clarke; and Henry Ware, jun., also was just entering on a course of studies at Cambridge, preparatory to his short but devoted and most successful ministry.*

Having received approbation, he was invited to supply the pulpit in Princeton, Mass., made vacant by the resignation of Professor Murdock, of Andover. The pulpit had hitherto been occupied, for a series of years, exclusively by a minister of Calvinistic or Orthodox views; and, under such circumstances, it was not to be expected that all would be united in the choice of a minister who came to them under the auspices of a man like Dr. Channing, who was regarded as one of the champions of the Liberal school of theology. A large majority, however, of the society united in giving Mr. Clarke a call, which he accepted; and his ordination took place June 18, 1817, the remonstrance of the church against his settlement being overruled by the ordaining council. The remonstrants seceded, and formed a new church, while those who remained gave their minister a cordial welcome; and with few, if any, exceptions, stood by him as friends and fellow-

---

* In a letter to the writer of the date of Feb. 4, 1856, speaking of an article in the "Christian Examiner" for January, "On the Unitarian Controversy," he says: "I am very glad to have the subject opened so ably, and think the promised discussion, if conducted in the same spirit, will do great good. The article reviews," he adds, " what was of much interest to myself forty and fifty years since; for I very early became a heretic, renouncing Calvinism, although educated strictly as a Presbyterian."

helpers to the last. His preaching was from the first, and uniformly, serious, earnest, affectionate; in the true sense of a much-abused term, *evangelical.*

"I have ever regarded him," says Dr. Hill, "as a man eminently conscientious and devoted; with whom the spiritual world was near, its concerns an ever-present, a momentous reality; and who, in the ministerial office, felt a weight of responsibleness pressing upon his thought, prompting his language, and spreading a look of unwonted gravity upon his countenance. . . . I do not think he was ever betrayed into light and frivolous talk. Although he could relax at the agreeable sally, he was serious beyond most men. Although he could unbosom himself in the freedom of private friendship, he was habitually contemplative and reserved; loving most to commune with his own thoughts, and to be engaged in the especial duties of his calling."

At the beginning of his ministry in Princeton, owing to the secession of a large part of the church-members, the communion table was surrounded by a very small number of guests; but he had the gratification of welcoming, from time to time, large accessions, so that he had little occasion to mourn, with many of his brethren, that so few came to the holy feast. In this connection, I present another extract from Dr. Hill's commemorative discourse: "The evidence which came to him, from time to time, of his usefulness in Princeton, where he had spent fifteen years of the very flower of his life, was among the most grateful. He knew that he had left impressions there, and was glad when he heard of it. In a conversation which I had with him not long before his death, he told me that few things had ever afforded him such pure satisfaction as what he had just learned from his successor of another denomination, the clergyman of that place. He had just come from the dying bed of a respected officer of his church. He had known him well, and could bear testimony to the purity and blamelessness of his life. He had witnessed his exalted Christian character; and now, as he stood by, he had seen his countenance lighted up with ineffable peace, and heard his voice whispering in tones of triumph, 'Tell Mr. Clarke, if you ever see him, that for the first thought of religion, for the source of life's purest satisfaction, for the tranquillity of this hour, under God, I am indebted to him.'"

After a useful ministry of fifteen years, in consequence of impaired health, he asked a dismission from his pastoral care, which was granted, June 18, 1832, just fifteen years, to a day, from the date of his ordination.

After a respite of a few months, he accepted an invitation to preach in Uxbridge, and was installed as pastor of the First Congregational Church and Society in that town, Jan. 9, 1833; which office he held to the day of his death.

On entering this new field, he found himself surrounded and sustained by a band of earnest and devoted men and women, who gave him their sympathy, their confidence, and their affectionate respect. I well remember the company of aged and venerable men, some of whom had passed the bounds of fourscore years, who occupied the front seat of the old meeting-house, and who continued their regular attendance on the services of the temple till compelled by physical inability to withdraw. It was a beautiful spectacle, and one that often rises up before me, as I call to mind our annual exchanges.

Nor must I omit to speak of the peculiar felicity of his domestic relations. He was married, Sept. 13, 1819, to Sarah Wigglesworth, of Newburyport, daughter of Michael and Charlotte Wigglesworth, and grand-daughter of Colonel Edward Wigglesworth, an officer in the war of the Revolution, and intimately associated with Washington. Colonel Wigglesworth was a lineal descendant of Rev. Michael Wigglesworth, author of the quaint old poem, entitled "The Day of Doom." That kind Providence "that shapes our ends," brought together these kindred souls, and led to a union for which he never ceased to be thankful, and which contributed in no small measure to his happiness and his professional success.

Mrs. Clarke proved in every way fitted for the station she filled with so much grace and dignity.

To natural gifts of a high order, she united a rich intellectual culture, with easy and peculiarly winning manners. She had, previous to her marriage, taught a school for young ladies, in which capacity she had gained a high reputation; and all these gifts and graces she brought with her into her new home, and consecrated them all to the service of her husband, her children, and the community in which they lived.

"Gifted with genius," Dr. Hill writes, "refined tastes, and an active intellect, Mrs. Clarke could not fail to win to her home even those whom no parochial ties could have drawn thither. She was a woman to win; for she combined, to a rare extent, large mental endowments with a capacity for the homeliest duties." With but scanty means, she managed her domestic affairs with so much skill and with so little ado, that the occasional visitor would not suspect, what was nevertheless true, that all the work of the family, even the most menial and distasteful, was done by her own hands or those of her daughters.

Seldom has it been our lot to witness scenes of domestic felicity more attractive than that exhibited in the home over which our brother presided, and of which his companion was a chief ornament. It was a foreshadowing of those brighter scenes which are unfolded only to the vision of glorified spirits.

At length, after a union of thirty-seven years, the time of parting came. The event took place Sept. 8, 1856.

In a communication to the writer of these sketches, Mr. Clarke writes: "Her sickness was borne with wonderful cheerfulness; her departure was long anticipated with perfect composure; and, in the closing scene, she illustrated strikingly the peaceful triumph of our blessed faith. Her disease, in its whole progress and termination, was like that of Mary Ware. You may well say, that 'my loss is irreparable.' It is so. The light of my house is extinguished. But I do not complain. The memories of the past are delightful; and the anticipations of the future are comforting, strengthening, and cheering."

"After the death of his wife," we are told, "Mr. Clarke resumed his duties with unwonted vigor. . . . But this could not last. The blow which had fallen left a wound that time could not heal. Always frail, his whole life interrupted by frequent sicknesses, he could bear the strain upon his faculties no longer." On a Sunday of July, 1859, while in the midst of his discourse, he fell exhausted to the floor of the pulpit, and was conveyed to his house in a state of great feebleness. On the following Sunday, I officiated in his place, and, while together, had much conversation on the scenes of former days, and the friends who had *passed on*. I saw him once for a few moments after this, but only to exchange brief salutations. The time of his departure was drawing near, and it came suddenly at last. On Saturday, Nov. 19, he saw the last of earth; and, in obedience to his Master's call, *he went up higher*. He died ripe in years, rich in Christian experience, rich in the treasures that gold cannot purchase, laid up " where moth and rust do not corrupt, and where thieves cannot break through nor steal."

His funeral was attended by a large concourse of people of the various religious societies (in Uxbridge). The business of the village was suspended; the stores were closed; and, although the day was stormy, the whole community seemed to wish to pay their last tribute of respect to the memory of a good man and a truly Christian minister. It was well remarked by one of the company at the grave, "There lies a man who was more beloved than any other man in the town of Uxbridge."

Jan. 10, 1858, the twenty-fifth anniversary of his installation, Mr. Clarke preached an occasional discourse, which was published. In this discourse, speaking of his ministry in Princeton, he says: "There I was consecrated to the responsible duties of the Christian pastor's office. There, with youthful vigor and earnestness, I entered on the blessed work to which I had devoted my life. There I formed the domestic connection which was so long the light and bliss of my home, and whose memory, so blessed, will accompany me to my grave. There my children were born, whom a kind Father has thus far spared to be my comfort and joy in my declining years, and who, I may frankly and gratefully say, have honored their father and mother. There I formed friendships, Christian friendships, which death will not dissolve, but which will, I trust, be perpetuated in that better land, which is the home of all the pure and good. There I have reason to believe that my ministry was not without healing, saving efficacy; for I know that many who have 'passed on,' in their last peaceful hours looked back to my ministrations as the instrumentalities, under God, of leading them to Christ: and there are those now there who always greet me, when we meet, as their spiritual father."

After a review of the twenty-five years he had spent in Uxbridge, he thus trustingly speaks of the unknown future that lay before him: —

"At the time of life to which I have arrived, and especially with my impaired constitution, it is not wise in me to make any calculations in regard to the future. I have been gradually and gently descending these twenty-five years, and am now approaching the foot of the mountain. How soon I may reach the last step is unknown. If God has yet more work for me to do in his vineyard, I will strive cheerfully to do it, as he shall give me health and strength. I will 'not count my life dear unto myself, so that I may finish my course with joy, and the ministry which I have received of the Lord Jesus, to testify the gospel of the grace of God.' . . .

"The time may have arrived, or may be near, when it shall be expedient for *you* that I retire, and give place to a younger and more vigorous laborer in the vineyard. If so, I will not, for a moment, stand in the way of a more efficient, and, it may be, successful minister of Christ. Years, and the events they have witnessed, and the changes they have wrought, have made you inexpressibly dear to my heart; and my attachments here are as strong as life: but such are my convictions of the importance of an efficient ministry, that I would not suffer my own feelings or wishes to lead me to continue my connection with you, as pastor, after my usefulness was essentially diminished, either in consequence of impaired intellect or continued ill-health. But I leave all with God. His will be done!"

He closes his affectionate address with words of solemn import, well befitting the occasion:—

"And now, my friends, I commend you to God, and to the word of his grace, which is able to build you up, and prepare you for the heavenly inheritance. Live in peace and love, and the God of peace will be with you. And when we shall stand, pastor and flock, in the unveiled presence of the Infinite and

Holy One, may I be able, with inexpressible joy, to say of you all, without an exception, 'Here, Lord, am I, and the children thou hast given me'!"

Mr. Clarke had three children, one son and two daughters, all of whom survived their father.

# WORCESTER ASSOCIATION (NEW).

# WORCESTER ASSOCIATION (NEW).

THE WORCESTER ASSOCIATION, as now constituted, dates back to the year 1820, and, accordingly, has nearly completed a half-century. It was formed by a union of the Old Worcester Association, then in its decrepitude, and of the Lancaster Association, then in the freshness and vigor of youth, having been in existence scarcely five years.

The first motion towards a union was made at a meeting of the Lancaster Association at Lancaster, Nov. 17, 1819, when Dr. Thayer was chosen a committee to confer with Rev. Dr. Sumner, Rev. Dr. Bancroft, and Rev. Ward Cotton, on the subject of uniting the two bodies. At a subsequent meeting of the Lancaster Association at Northborough, May 18, a communication from the Worcester Association was read by Rev. Dr. Bancroft, which was in the following terms : —

"At a special meeting of the Worcester Association of Ministers, holden at the house of Rev.

A. Bancroft, on the 29th of April, 1820, the following resolutions were passed. Representations having been made, that the Lancaster Association is disposed to form the above-mentioned societies into one body on the conditions, —

"First, that the united body take the name of the Worcester Association; and, secondly, that this body adopt the Constitution and forms of the Lancaster Association, — *Voted*, That this Association, with high satisfaction, hereby manifest a disposition to comply with the aforenamed conditions of union.

"*Voted*, That the Scribe be a committee to make communication of the proceedings of this meeting to the Lancaster Association, and in our name to invite them to close the proposed union.

"A. BANCROFT, *Scribe.*
"WORCESTER, May 17, 1820.

"The following vote was then unanimously adopted : —

"*Voted*, That the Lancaster Association, in the hope, that, by a union with the Worcester Association, their mutual improvement will be promoted, hereby express their desire to close with the terms to which that body have consented."

Only three members of the Old Worcester Association were present at this meeting: viz., Rev. Joseph Sumner, D.D., of Shrewsbury; Rev. Aaron

Bancroft, D.D., of Worcester; and Rev. Ward Cotton, of Boylston, — the other members never having expressed a desire to join the new Association.

The new Association was composed of the following brethren, ten in number, named in the order of college seniority, Rev. Seth Alden having joined the Association the day the union was consummated: —

| | | |
|---|---|---|
| Rev. Joseph Sumner, D.D. | Shrewsbury | Y.C. 1759. |
| Rev. Aaron Bancroft, D.D. | Worcester | H.C. 1778. |
| Rev. Nathaniel Thayer, D.D. | Lancaster | H.C. 1789. |
| Rev. Ward Cotton | Boylston | H.C. 1793. |
| Rev. Isaac Allen | Bolton | H.C. 1798. |
| Rev. David Damon, D.D. | Lunenburg | H.C. 1811. |
| Rev. Joseph Allen, D.D. | Northborough | H.C. 1811. |
| Rev. Samuel Clarke | Princeton | D.C. 1812. |
| Rev. Peter Osgood | Sterling | H.C. 1814. |
| Rev. Seth Alden * | Marlborough | B.U. 1814. |

The union thus consummated proved advantageous to both parties. It was a union of hearts as well as of hands. All the members were united in the bonds of a common faith and a true fraternal affection. Dr. Thayer gracefully resigned his place of moderator to his senior, Dr. Bancroft, who from that time was seldom absent from our meetings. More delightful re-unions than were the meetings of the Worcester Association at this time, I have never known; and I recall them with feelings of

---

* We subjoin, in the Appendix, a list of all who have since become members of the Worcester Association, in the order of time in which they became members, together with the years of their graduation.

deep gratitude for the valuable helps I received from them in the early part of my ministry, as well as for the opportunities they afforded for becoming intimately acquainted with the excellent men who then occupied the neighboring pulpits, and whose influence is felt to this day.

Whether for good or for evil, the minister half a century ago held a more commanding position, wielded more ecclesiastical and secular power, than now. With the exception of Dr. Bancroft and Rev. Seth Alden, whose respective charges were made up of seceders from the original town societies, each of the members of the Worcester Association, at the time of its organization, was the minister of the *First Congregational Church and Society* in the place of his settlement, which in most cases comprised nearly all of the families within the territorial limits of the town. Six of the ten — viz., Dr. Sumner, Dr. Thayer, Rev. Mr. Cotton, Rev. Mr. Osgood, and the two Allens — were *ministers of the towns* which they respectively represented; the town in each case, as a corporation, being responsible for the fulfilment of the contract into which it had entered in the settlement of its minister. The salary of the minister was assessed like other taxes, according to property, upon the citizens of the town. Accordingly, the minister was expected to visit all the families socially as a neighbor, and officially as a pastor; to know all, young and old, by sight, and to be able to call them by name; to officiate at all weddings and funerals; to have the general charge and oversight, in conjunction with the board of selectmen, of the public schools; occasionally to draft wills and deeds, and other instruments of a like nature; as well as to take the lead in all measures of reform, and in all plans for improving the physical, social, or moral condition of the people. The visitation of the sick was considered almost as indispensable on the part of the minister, as that of the family physician; and any remissness or neglect in this particular was reckoned a grievous fault, not easily overlooked or forgotten.

In the employment of teachers, and in the selection of class-books for the schools; in the formation and management of libraries; the institution of lyceums and social circles, or sewing societies, for the improvement of the youth of both sexes; in planting trees on the common, and by the roadside, for shade and ornament; in laying out and beautifying grounds for rural cemeteries; and in other labors, quite distinct from what are considered the special and appropriate duties of a pastor, — the minister of the town was expected to take the lead: nor would it have been prudent for any one, however hardly pressed, to decline the labor or the honor thus imposed or proffered.

It was at a somewhat earlier period that a change had taken place in *the costume and the manners* of the clergy. Small clothes, knee-buckles, the three-cornered hat, had been laid aside, and with them the stateliness, and somewhat of the dignified bearing, which characterized the profession at an earlier day. Still, however, the young minister, from the time of his ordination, was expected to appear in the pulpit in flowing gown and cassock and muslin bands, commonly the gifts of the ladies of his parish; which, when soiled by use or worn out by time, were replaced by new ones from the same unfailing source. The gown and the white cravat are still seen occasionally in some of our pulpits, the only badges of office that still remain; and these, too, are passing away, and, so far as relates to the country clergy, will soon be numbered among the things that were.

Great and memorable changes have been witnessed, during the period we are reviewing, in the architecture and internal arrangements of our houses of worship,\* and in the general style and character of our public services. The old church in Worcester (still standing), built for the venerable Dr. Bancroft, was an unsightly structure of small dimensions, standing in what was then a retired spot, now a busy street; with a high pulpit, and galleries on three sides. The church at Lancaster, till the erection of their spacious and beautiful brick church in 1816,

---

\* Not one of these was erected as "a church," or was so called at the time spoken of. They were universally called "meeting-houses," and most of them were used for secular meetings — lectures and town-meetings — as well as for religious worship.

was without spire or cupola or bell. And so late as 1824, when our brother Lincoln was ordained, both his church and that belonging to the Orthodox society in Fitchburg, were barn-like structures, wholly devoid of beauty, unless it were the " beauty of holiness," of which we trust there was no lack. The church in Sterling was a large and costly structure, with high pulpit and wide galleries; the front gallery being occupied by a large and noble band of singers, who performed their part of the service to universal acceptance. Not much unlike it, though a more modern structure and after a better model, was the church in Northborough, till remodelled in 1848, just forty years after its erection; also the church of the West Parish in Marlborough, built about the same time. The church in Shrewsbury, which is still standing, having been raised for the sake of a vestry, and newly arranged, was built, in the style of the middle of the eighteenth century, with tall, pointed spire. The church in Boylston was in a different style, such as prevailed in the latter part of the eighteenth century, with cupola and side-porches for entrance. The churches in Bolton and Princeton differed somewhat from either of the others mentioned, but were without any pretensions to architectural beauty, or adaptation to the comfort either of the speaker or the congregation. But, however varied in form or dimensions, all were furnished with high pulpits, and tall, square boxes, called *pews*, with perpendicular backs and wooden seats, without cushions, furnished with hinges, by which the seats were raised when the congregation rose for prayer, and let down, not without a deafening noise grateful to young ears, when the prayer was ended.

It appears, accordingly, that we had within the limits of the Worcester Association, at its formation forty-seven years ago, specimens of nearly every style of church architecture that has prevailed since the settlement of New England. First, the square, tall building without steeple, cupola, or porch, resembling a large two-story dwelling-house without chimneys, and furnished with a multitude of windows arranged in two tiers. Next, the same, with the addition of a tall, slender steeple and a bell, such as were common in New England one hundred years ago. The next in order, specimens of which may still be seen in remote country towns, was that introduced soon after the close of the Revolutionary War, in which the steeple gave place to the cupola; while porches in front and at each end were added, not certainly for ornament, but much to the convenience and comfort of those who attended public worship. Soon after the commencement of the new century, a greatly improved style of church architecture was introduced, of which there are abundant specimens in Worcester County. In front of the main building is a well-proportioned tower, commonly called the *projection*, surmounted by belfry and cupola; the lower part of which projection forms a convenient hall of entrance, from which flights of steps lead to the gallery, or singers' seats; the space over the hall being formerly used in some instances for holding town-meetings, as was the case of Northborough till the erection of a town-house in 1822. In most places, however, before the erection of town-houses, the body of the church itself was used for this and other secular purposes.*

It may be well to state, for the information of the effeminate generation now on the stage of action, that, at the commencement of the period now under review, furnaces and stoves were wholly unknown in any of our country churches; and that the only means of obtaining or retaining heat, on the part of the worshippers, was the use of foot-stoves, warm clothing, and a brave, manly and womanly spirit, that set at defiance the wintry blasts, and rose superior to all outward hinderances.

The singing in the old meeting-house was performed by a choir of from ten to fifty or more voices, under the direction of a leader furnished with

---

* A still more antique style of church-architecture was introduced at an earlier period of our history, of which a solitary specimen remains; to wit, the church of the First Parish in Hingham, where the bell is suspended in a small cupola, raised from the centre of the roof, the bell-rope coming down in the middle of the broad aisle, by which the minister and the congregation pass to their respective places. The old church in Lynn was built after the same model, and was standing within the last half-century.

a pitch-pipe, or accompanied by one or more musical instruments; the violin and bass-viol, especially the latter, being considered almost indispensable; the flute, the clarionet, and the bassoon finding their way only into some of the more ambitious choirs.

At the commencement of this period, Watts's Hymns were commonly used in our churches. Soon, however, this collection was exchanged for Belknap, or for the New-York Collection, and, in some of our churches, for Dabney's, — all of which afterwards gave place to Greenwood's admirable selection; while the Cheshire Collection, introduced about twenty years since, is the one at present in most general use in the churches connected with the Association.

The *territorial limits* of the Association varied from time to time. At first they embraced, as we have seen, either in whole or in part, nine towns in Worcester County, and one in Middlesex. To these ten were subsequently annexed, in order, Harvard, Fitchburg, Berlin, Grafton, Leicester, Leominster, Southborough, Framingham, Upton, Clinton, and Hudson; making the whole number twenty, represented by the ten original members, and others who have since joined the Association. Several of these latter, however, had but a very brief and slight connection with the body; some of them having met with us only a few times, and never having taken any active part in the affairs of the Association. I have thought it proper, however, to furnish a complete list of their names, with brief notices of each.

One of the leading designs of this and similar Associations from the first has been the intellectual and spiritual culture and growth of its members. For securing this end, various measures have from time to time been adopted, in order to meet the exigencies of the times, and the wants or wishes of individual members. The dissertation, required of the brother at whose house the meeting was held, and which commonly demanded much study and reflection, had special reference to this end; as had also the discussion which followed the dissertation, in which all took part.

Nor do we make light account of the social influence of our meetings. They brought us into intimate relation with one another; gave us opportunities, of which we were glad to avail ourselves, for making the acquaintance of the clerical sisterhood, and the children of the parsonage; and for gathering hints, from what we saw and heard, of which we could avail ourselves in conducting our own domestic affairs. For our meetings were not afternoon or evening calls or fashionable parties, but social religious meetings, commonly lasting a part of two days; the evening being not the least important portion, whether spent in the church or in the parlor. When the number in attendance was too large to allow of all being lodged at the minister's house, as often happened, especially when the members were accompanied by their wives or daughters, the guests were hospitably entertained by members of the parish, who always had a "prophet's chamber" for use on such occasions, and who, in doing a favor, felt that they received as much in return.

Some of the subjects discussed at the private meetings of the Association were theological and critical; but more of them related to matters of practical and professional concern. Occasionally an exposition was given of some obscure or difficult text. Thus an exposition of 1 Cor. xv. 25 — "For he must reign," &c. — was assigned first to one, and then to a second, and then again to a third brother, each of whom shrunk from the task. The fourth assignment was to Dr. Bancroft, who was ready to grapple with any difficulty, and who treated the subject with his accustomed ability.

The subject of one dissertation was, "The Control of Church-members over the Ordinance of the Lord's Supper;" of another, "The Worship attributed in the Scriptures to the Son of God;" "Evangelical Faith;" "The Influences of the Holy Spirit;" "The Duty of a Minister in his Pastoral Visits;" "The Duty of Ministers at the Solemnization of Marriages;" "How are we to understand the precept, 'But I say unto you, that ye resist not evil'?" "Church Discipline;" "The Terms of

Christian Communion;" "The Nature, Design, and Duration of Future Punishment." Such are a few of the subjects treated in dissertations, and discussed, sometimes with marked ability, at the private meetings of the Association.

At a meeting held at Princeton, July 16, 1823, a dissertation was read by brother Clarke on " the Duty of Ministers at the Solemnization of Marriages," the subject assigned him at the previous meeting. After the reading of the dissertation, a committee of three, consisting of Dr. Bancroft and the two Allens, was appointed to report " on the expediency of obtaining or compiling a small book to be given on marriage occasions to young married persons." At the next meeting, the committee reported in favor of adopting Bean's " Advice to Young Married Persons" as a suitable book for the purpose. An edition was struck off for the use of the Association, copies of which may be found on the book-shelves of some who were married by members of the Association thirty or forty years ago. The book was well enough for the price, and it was the best we could find; though far inferior to the one compiled by our brother Livermore, entitled " The Marriage Offering," or " Buds for a Bridal Wreath," by our brother Tilden. The same committee, to which was added Dr. Thayer, were directed to report " on the expediency of adopting a uniform method in admitting persons to our churches." We find no record of any report made by this committee; but we believe that they made a verbal report, to the effect that each minister should be left to take such a course as he thought best.

The subject of admitting persons to church-fellowship by recommendation of other churches, was subsequently, May, 1834, brought before the Association; when it was voted, "That it be recommended to the churches under the pastoral charge of members of the Association, to admit to all the privileges of church-membership, in the several churches, all persons, being members of the church, who shall give satisfactory evidence to the officers of the church, that they are members of some Christian church, in good and regular standing."

Harvard, June 22, 1826, the project of forming a theological library, for the use of the members, was started by brother Blanchard, which was so favorably received, that a committee of three, consisting of Rev. Dr. Bancroft, Dr. Thayer, and the prime mover of the project, Rev. Mr. Blanchard, was appointed to consider the subject, and to report at their next meeting. The committee reported in favor of the measure, which report was accepted by a unanimous vote: and it was agreed, that the assessment for each member for the first year should be ten dollars, and five dollars annually afterwards; that Lancaster should be the place of deposit; and that the minister of the Congregational society in that place, for the time being, should be the librarian.

Agreeably to the provisions of the Constitution, a committee of three, consisting of Drs. Bancroft and Thayer and the writer, was appointed to purchase the books; which accordingly was done, and the library went into immediate operation. A number of costly and valuable works were purchased, and others were presented as gifts; and, for several years, the members availed themselves of the privilege of taking books from the library. It was found, however, after the experience of a few years, that the inconvenience of taking and returning the books was so great, especially to those who lived at a distance from the place of deposit, that the library was of less value to the members than had been fondly hoped; and in July, 1837, a discussion took place, at a meeting of the Association, with regard to the disposition to be made of the library. The subject was, after discussion, indefinitely postponed. Again, however, in August, 1844, the subject was brought before the Association; and a request was made by Rev. Mr. Stebbins, that, if the Association should see fit, some of the books might be transferred to Meadville, for the benefit of the Theological School about to be established in that place, and of which he was to be the first President. The proposition was favorably received; a selection was made; other books were contributed by individual members; and the whole was transmitted to the school in Meadville, then just going into operation. The remnant of the library is still the property of the Association.

The public lecture, or sermon, was delivered in the church; at first in the afternoon, afterwards in the evening; the subject of which had been previously assigned. At first, a subject was given out for the annual course; subsequently, the course was divided into two parts, and a subject assigned for each. This service was specially designed for the use of the congregation; and the subject was chosen with this object in view. I give a list of subjects, taken at random from the records of the Association, which were assigned for the annual or the semi-annual courses: "The Christian Temper;" "Prayer;" "Christian Faith;" "The Design of Religion, Natural and Revealed;" "Early Piety, addressed to the Young;" "Means of Personal Religion;" "Future Retribution;" "Signs of the Times;" "The Dangers and Duties of Unitarians;" "Active Christian Benevolence;" "Peace and Peace Societies;" "The Relative Duties of Ministers and People."

At a subsequent period, the choice of a subject was left with the officiating minister; an arrangement which was found to be most generally satisfactory. At one time, the sermon was followed by the communion service; and some of these occasions were seasons of deep religious interest and high spiritual enjoyment, the memory of which is still fresh and fragrant.

At one time, it was recommended that the brethren, using the liberty claimed by the apostle Paul, — "to lead about a wife, a sister," — should bring with them to the meetings of the Association their wives or daughters; a proposition that was received with much favor, and adopted, we believe, without a dissentient voice, even from the small minority who had failed to comply with the apostolic injunction, that "a bishop should be the husband of one wife." The experiment was satisfactory in the highest degree. The attendance of the brethren from that time was more regular; and the discussions, carried on in the presence of the other sex, and in which they sometimes shared, took a more practical turn, and were marked with a more earnest and fervent spirit. The custom, we are happy to say, has not been wholly discontinued; and we hope that it may be revived and perpetuated, not only as one of the most effective means of keeping up an interest in the meetings of the Association, but for the opportunity it affords for a pleasant, social, and spiritual intercourse between neighboring ministers and ministers' wives and their families.

At one time, a committee, chosen to consider by what means the meetings of the Association might be rendered more attractive, and the means of more extensive usefulness, reported (Nov. 19, 1850) a recommendation, " that there be a social gathering and collation in the different towns at the meetings of the Association, and that the sermon be dispensed with :" but the measure, though regarded with favor by some, was thought by a majority of the brethren to be an unwise experiment; and, accordingly, the proposal was rejected. In justice to those who favored the measure, it should be stated, that it was their object not merely to give new interest and attractiveness to the meetings, but to bring into exercise the social element in connection with religion, and thereby to enlist the favor of the young of both sexes; and, though the sermon should be dispensed with, its place would be supplied by table speeches, as is the custom of our Unitarian brethren in England and Scotland at their anniversary re-unions.

The attention of the Association was called to a consideration of the means of awakening a new interest in our meetings, in a dissertation read at Sterling, November, 1852, by Rev. T. P. Allen, when the following resolution was unanimously adopted : —

" Whereas of late years the Worcester Association has lamentably declined from its former life and vigor, to the great detriment of the interests of true religion among us; therefore *Resolved*, That respect for the labors of our honored predecessors, as well as regard for our own reputation and good, for the progress of Christian truth and the growth of gospel piety among our people, imperatively demand that we bestir ourselves with energy for its resuscitation, and renewed activity and usefulness."

The moderator and scribe were also appointed a committee to make arrangements for a meeting of the Association in January, to consult for its interests. Accordingly, a meeting was held, agreeably to arrangements made for the purpose, Jan. 19, 1853, at the house of Rev. E. E. Hale; ten of the immediate members being present, besides brother Willson, who had just accepted a call to the church in West Roxbury, and brothers Stone, of Bolton, and Livermore, of Clinton, who joined the Association at this time. It was a meeting of more than common interest. Past negligences were candidly acknowledged; and there seemed to be a disposition and determination on the part of all present to do their share in remedying the evil complained of. After an extended and earnest discussion, it was voted, on motion of brother Hale, that "we hold only six meetings each year, and that the time and place of each meeting be specially determined at the preceding meeting." In regard to the character of these meetings, it was maintained that, in these stirring times, we should not be content with coming together for the mere purpose of discussing questions of an abstract and general nature, or of Scripture interpretation, or of pastoral duty; but that we should boldly meet the great questions of the day, those questions which stir up men's minds, and warm their hearts, and enlist their deepest feelings, — questions of present interest and great practical concern, — such as Pauperism; Intemperance; War; Crime, its Prevention and Cure; the Defects in our Systems of Education; our Duty to our Foreign Population; and the Best Means of Supporting Religious Institutions. Thereupon it was voted, that, for our private sessions, each brother be at liberty to choose the subject of his dissertation; and, with regard to the public service, the brother at whose house we meet shall select such topic as in his judgment will be most interesting and useful to his people.

The subject was again called up, June, 1859, when a committee was appointed, consisting of brothers Shippen and Tilden, who in their report at a subsequent meeting, held in Bolton in the following September, "recommended that the individual at whose house the meeting is held, and the brother who is to write the essay for the public, agree on a topic; and that said topic, with the name of the essayist, be published in the notice of the meeting; and that the essay be followed by a conference on the topic discussed; also, that the essayist be confined to half an hour, and the speakers to fifteen minutes each:" which recommendation was adopted with the proviso "that the subject be chosen by the Association."

The experiment was tried, and proved eminently

successful. The subject of the first essay was Slavery. The essay by Rev. Mr. Scandling, of Grafton, was followed by an able and animated discussion on the Duty of Northern Christians growing out of its existence. This was followed by one by Rev. Mr. Forbush, on the Best Means of Promoting the Cause of Temperance.

At a meeting in Worcester, at the house of Rev. Mr. Hale, in May, 1849, the attention of the Association was called by Rev. Mr. Burton, then chaplain of the jail and minister to the poor in Worcester, to the condition of the neglected classes in their respective towns, when the following vote was passed: "*Resolved*, That each gentleman present will devote the next week to visits among the neglected families of his town, and present the results to his people on some ensuing sabbath, and transmit the same to Mr. Burton, for such use as may seem advisable." The result of this measure, so far as it was carried into effect, was the discovery, in most of our towns, of a considerable number of families, principally composed of foreigners, living in the total neglect of public worship, and without Christian nurture and instruction; and, in some instances, increased and successful efforts to raise the fallen, and to save those who were ready to perish. It was at this meeting that the proposal of starting a child's paper was introduced by brother Hale, when it was unanimously voted to bring the subject before the Convention of

Sunday-school Teachers, which was to be held in Northborough the following month. The proposal was favorably received by the Convention, and arrangements were made for starting the paper at once, which resulted in the establishment of "The Sunday-school Gazette," which, under various auspices, has been sustained to the present time.

The education of the young has ever been an object of special interest with this Association. So early as October, 1821, a committee, consisting of Drs. Bancroft and Thayer and the writer, was appointed to prepare a catechism for the use of young children, which was accordingly done; and the first edition of "The Worcester Catechism" was published in the following year (1822), the profits of which were paid into the treasury of the Evangelical Missionary Society.

The profits of several succeeding editions till the year 1830, amounting to fifty dollars, were applied to the purchase of books for the library of the Association. From this date, by a vote of the Association, the profits of this little book were relinquished for the benefit of the compiler.

Before the publication of the Worcester Catechism, several manuals were in use in the different towns represented by the Worcester Association, and in other Liberal churches. Among them was one, bearing the same title, compiled by Dr. Bancroft; another, by Channing and Thatcher; one, by Parker, of Portsmouth; another, by Colman, of Hingham; besides the Geneva Catechisms, in three numbers, an excellent work, republished in Boston, under the auspices of Hon. John G. Palfrey, then minister of the church in Brattle Square. Some of these manuals continued in use for many years, and were found to be valuable aids to the minister in imparting religious instruction to the children of his parish. The Worcester Catechism was followed by other manuals prepared by a member of the Association, and published, if not by their direction, yet by their encouragement and aid.

In September, 1838, at a meeting of the Association at Lancaster, Dr. Thayer communicated a letter from Professor Henry Ware, jun., requesting the views of the Association on the subject of a seminary for the education of pious youth designed for the ministry; which was referred to a committee consisting of Dr. Thayer and the writer, to report at the next meeting. The committee reported in favor of the measure; and a copy of their report was transmitted to Rev. Mr. Ware.

As the subject is one of permanent interest, and one that at the time occupied the earnest and anxious thoughts of many of the friends of Liberal Christianity, both among the clergy and laity, and as the plan proposed met with the warm approval of the members of the Worcester Association, we give the report in full, from a copy which was found among the papers of Rev. H. Ware, jun. The report was written by Dr. Thayer, and is as follows : —

"The committee, to whom was referred the letter of the Rev. Henry Ware, jun., D.D., requesting this Association to co-operate in means for supplying the wants of the Christian community, by increasing the number of ministers of our denomination, respectfully reports : —

"The want of ministers in the class to which we belong has been apparent to us. We are settled in the belief, which has been confirmed by full experiments, that the existing means, including the Theological School at Cambridge, give us no hope of a competent remedy for the evil. We have deeply lamented, and it has exposed us to merited reproach, that there has been in Unitarian Christians a reluctance, next to invincible, to train up, and give them an opportunity to be well qualified for their work, a multitude of young men who would 'contend for the faith which,' we believe, 'was once delivered to the saints.' We duly appreciate the engagedness and zeal of our fellow-Christians of other sects, who, amongst the charities of the age, have assigned to this a prominent place. To us there appear peculiar advantages in the selection of a Christian minister, who shall receive youths into his family, over whom he may exert a direct moral and religious influence. We may hope that he will so far aid in forming their tastes, and in inducing them to a course of serious and religious reflection and inquiry, as that they will give a fair promise of being devoted, faithful, and successful ministers. We presume that we coincide with all the friends of the measure which is contemplated, in the opinion, that the minister who shall superintend this great work shall be a man of experience, have a conciliating mode of imparting knowledge, and one who has attained to eminence in his profession. If a minister of this character can be secured, and the proposed measure shall go into effect, reliance may be placed on the Worcester Association to give it their cordial co-operation. We believe that suitable candidates for the privilege may be found within our limits. We feel also assured, that a sum not less than three hundred dollars annually may be collected in our parishes to advance the proposed object.

"The committee also recommend, that, in reply to the letter of Rev. Dr. Ware, the Secretary forward him a copy of the report.

"NATHANIEL THAYER.
JOSEPH ALLEN.

"A true copy of the original report.
"Attest: P. OSGOOD, *Scribe*."

This letter bears the date of Oct. 20, 1838. The subject had been under consideration for many months. As early as May, 1837, a circular, with the signatures of H. Ware, jun., I. Bangs, and A. B. Muzzey, was sent to the superintendents of the Sunday schools connected with the churches of our faith, asking for distinct answers to the two following questions: —

"1. Are there any, and how many, lads in your school, of talents and disposition suitable for the ministry, who probably might be induced to receive an education in the way we propose?"

"2. Are there any young men among your teachers, or in your parish, who would make zealous and useful ministers, and who might be induced to enter the profession, if sufficient encouragement were offered them?"

To this letter of inquiry, answers were returned from many of our churches, expressing the approval of the plan suggested, and speaking encouragingly and hopefully of its success. One writer knows of eight, another of six, another of three or four, lads of a suitable character; and, in a schedule which lies before me, I find, that, from twenty-four churches therein named, as many as ten or twelve young men are mentioned as suitable candidates for the theological school. Besides the above-named circular, Mr. Ware addressed letters to individual ministers and laymen, in whose judgment he confided, and who had shown an interest in the enterprise. From one of the letters which he received in reply, I venture, without the leave of the writer, to give the following extract. The suggestion that had been made to him by Mr. Ware, to which the extract relates, viz. that the contemplated school should be placed under his care, may possibly have been connected with the subsequent promotion of that gentleman to the presidency of the Theological School soon after instituted at Meadville.

"As for myself," the writer proceeds, "I must say, that I am grateful for the confidence you have manifested in mentioning the undertaking to me. It is not necessary for me to say to one who knows my heart as well as you do, that I am willing to do all I can for that cause. An older, better man, I think, should be employed. I am in no situation to attend to such lads now, and I do not know that I shall be soon, if ever. On one account I should like to do it: I should see the result of my labors. I dare not say no, for it seems too much my Master's work to reject it. I cannot say yes, as I do not see how I can be so situated as to do it now."

The plan of the school was matured by Mr. Ware and his associates and coadjutors; and many looked with confidence and hope to its establishment. But some of our brethren looked upon it with distrust, and some with indifference; and it was finally abandoned, with many regrets on the part of those who had projected it and given it shape. But the discussion which it called forth was not in vain. It directed attention to the wants of the churches and the means of supply; nor can we doubt that it was the means of bringing many young men of promise into the school at Cambridge, nor that it did a good deal to prepare the way for the establishment of the school at Meadville, which has proved so rich a blessing to our churches.

Mr. Ware, whose heart was in the work, proposed the following scheme, which certainly contains many valuable hints and suggestions : —

"In order to an adequate supply of candidates for the ministry, such as shall enable us to discharge our obligations to the importance of our views and the growing wants of the country, it is proposed, that measures be taken to provide for the education of suitable young men, now entering on other pursuits, who would yet prefer the ministry; and also for that of promising boys, whose parents are unable to educate them, but would gladly resign them to this work.

"To this end, the following scheme has been suggested : —

"1. Some competent clergyman should be engaged to superintend an institution for the education of these lads. They should form part of his family, and be at all times under his influence; the object being so to cultivate their tastes, dispositions, and characters, as to form in them a desire and preference of the ministry as their business in life. But they should be left wholly free, and without coercion, to choose or reject it.

"2. In selecting the pupils for such a school, special care should be taken to admit none but those of high promise, both from disposition and from adaptedness of talent, and not at a younger age than ten or twelve years.

"3. They should be educated either with a view to the university, or to a completion of their education elsewhere, as in each case might appear expedient.

"4. The expenses might be defrayed, — 1st, by scholarships provided for the institution; or, 2d, by the friends and parents of the pupils; or, 3d, by the parishes to which they belong; or, 4th, by annual donations and subscriptions.

"5. The number of pupils might be twelve or twenty; and, in order to aid the labors of the superintendent, there might live among them several of the young men above referred to, who should be under his instruction, and, by teaching and other influences, assist his labors with the boys.

"6. The government of such a school might rest with some board or committee, chosen by subscribers, whose office should be to provide the requisite means for supporting it; and, in connection with the superintendent, to form and enforce the rules which would be necessary to its successful operation.

"If a plan like this should be adopted, its practical result would immediately be this: —

"A family, composed of twelve boys of about twelve years of age, and of six young men of about twenty, engaged together in a regular course of moral and religious culture; the young men, while instructed, acting also as instructors of the boys, and essentially co-operating to the great end by their social and moral influence, — such an institution would, in four years, give an addition of six to the number of our preachers; and, in ten years, of eighteen. If the success of it should satisfy, it might be enlarged, or another like it be founded, so as still further to augment the number.

"An estimate has been made by which it appears that the expenses of such a school would probably amount to about two thousand dollars a year. Of this it might be calculated, that one-half would be paid by competent parents and friends, and the religious societies from whose Sunday schools the boys came; while the other half must be provided by the institution itself.

"This project is presented, not as in itself complete, but simply that, by giving the subject a definite shape, the purpose and its feasibility may be more readily seen."

As one of the most effective instruments of early religious culture, the Sunday school has been regarded with favor, and has formed a frequent subject of discussion in the meetings of the Worcester Association. The institution, as is well known, had its origin in Great Britain more than three-fourths of a century since, but did not come into general use in this country till near the end of the first quarter of the present century. It was introduced, not simultaneously, or by the concerted action of our own or of any other denomination of Christians; but at an earlier or later date, as each church or minister deemed it expedient. From time immemorial, it had been the custom in New England for the minister to meet the children of his parish once or twice a year, at the village church, to hear them repeat, *memoriter*, the Westminster Assembly's Catechism, or some other manual, which they were expected to commit to memory at home or at school.

These "catechisings," as they were called, were occasions of much interest to the children, who, on a day appointed, flocked to the village church, where, seated in ranks, on long benches or in pews, they repeated the answers to the questions contained in the manual then in use.

Before the multiplication of rival sects, moreover, a considerable amount of religious instruction was imparted to our children orally, or in the use of manuals, in our district schools. The jealousy of sects rendered this practice obnoxious, and led to the almost total exclusion of religious instruction from our public schools.

In this state of things, the introduction of Sunday schools into our parishes seemed to be called for as a thing of necessity. It was made necessary by the altered state of our ecclesiastical affairs. This necessity was recognized at an early day by most of the ministers of this region; and, before the end of the first quarter of the nineteenth century, a Sunday school had been organized, and was in successful operation in nearly every parish embraced in this Association.

As early as Nov. 21, 1817, a committee, composed of three members of the Association, — Messrs. Osgood, Allen, and Alden, — was appointed to take into consideration, and to report on, the subject of Sunday schools. That committee made their report in the following May, in which, after speaking hopefully and encouragingly of the institution as "an efficient instrument of a Christian education," they recommend "that the ministers of this Association, at the last meeting in each year, be expected to present oral or written reports to this body, communicating such information as they may judge to be expedient respecting the Sunday schools in their parishes, or other modes which they may have adopted for promoting the religious education of the young;" which was accordingly done. Sunday schools formed a frequent subject of discussion at the meetings of the Association for the next six or seven years, till at length, in 1834, measures were taken for forming a Sunday-school Union, composed of the teachers and superintendents (including, of course, the ministers) of the several schools connected with the churches within the bounds of the Worcester Association; the first society of the kind of which we have any knowledge, the parent of all similar associations in our denomination, to which, also, may be traced those Sunday-school conventions which have since become so frequent, and which enjoy so large a share of popular favor.

The subject of forming such an association was introduced Aug. 14, 1834, by a respected brother, recently deceased, who, from his retirement, was indulged the high satisfaction of witnessing the success of the means which he had the wisdom to initiate. Our brother Osgood was chairman of the committee chosen at the above-mentioned date, to consider the expediency of forming a Sunday-school Union. The meeting was held in Sterling; and the subject of the dissertation read by brother Osgood on the occasion was "Sunday schools." After hearing the dissertation, the Association "voted to choose a committee of three to consider," as the record reads, "the expediency of forming a Sunday-school Union within the limits of this Association, and to report at the next meeting. Brothers Osgood, Allen of Northborough, and Thayer, were chosen on this committee." The next meeting was at Fitchburg, Sept. 17, at which meeting "the committee made a report, which was accepted; and a meeting was appointed to be held at Lancaster, on Thursday, Oct. 9, for the purpose of forming a Sunday-school society within the limits of this Association. Brothers Hill, Allen of Northborough, and Lincoln, were chosen a committee to make arrangements for the meeting; and brother Osgood was requested to deliver an address on the occasion."

In giving this brief account of the origin of this society, we have taken the simple record of the scribe of the Worcester Association, who was the first mover in this enterprise, and who gave to it his earnest thoughts and wise counsels. The meeting at Lancaster was an occasion of much interest. A large number of Sunday-school teachers, with their pastors, were present; the discourse of brother Osgood, as well as the other exercises, were appropriate; and all felt that it was good to be there. According to the original plan, the society met but once in the year, usually in May or June, soon after our Sunday schools had been re-organized; having been suspended, as was the case in most of our parishes, during the winter. Afterwards it was thought desirable that a semi-annual meeting should be held in early autumn, at which season it was found that the interest in Sunday schools, both on the part of teachers and of pupils, was apt to flag; and several such meetings were held in successive years with profit, and to the acceptance of all. It was not long, however, before there was a falling-off in the attendance at the semi-annual meetings; and the last attempt of the kind was a failure. It was concluded, therefore, to return to our first plan of having but one meeting in the year, and to make that an object of as much interest and attraction as possible. Such is our present practice; and hitherto our success has been satisfactory and most encouraging.

In the great temperance movement which began to attract general attention about forty years ago, the Worcester Association took an early and active part. Up to this time, it was the custom to provide for our meetings — as, indeed, for all sociable gatherings, as well as for private and domestic use — decanters of wine and strong drinks, of which we were all expected to partake. Indeed, during the first quarter of the present century, the shocking custom prevailed, at least in some parts of New England, of passing round the cup on funeral occasions, just as the band of mourners were preparing to follow the body of their friend to the grave. Alcoholic drinks were partaken of freely by ministers and laymen at ordinations, ecclesiastical councils, and wherever numbers were collected for business or recreation. In consequence of these practices, intemperance had become everywhere alarmingly prevalent; and men and women too, in great numbers, fell victims to the destroyer. At length, thoughtful and patriotic men became alarmed, and were led to inquire if any thing could be done to stay the plague. As early as 1813, the Massachusetts Society for the Suppression of Intemperance was formed, of which Samuel Dexter,

Nathan Dane of Beverly, Chief-Justice Parker, and Dr. John C. Warren, were successively the presiding officers, and which embraced the leading men, ministers and laymen, in Boston and other parts of the Commonwealth, then including the State of Maine. These men were pioneers in the great enterprise; and though groping their way in the dark, and " vaguely floundering about," as one expresses it, " as in a Slough of Despair," they prepared the way for the splendid triumphs of the cause in subsequent times.

At a meeting of the Worcester Association at Northborough, Oct. 18, 1826, a committee, consisting of Dr. Thayer and the writer of these sketches, was appointed to consider and report what measures the members of this Association should individually adopt for the prevention and suppression of intemperance.

April 18, 1827. — " The committee made the following report : —

" *Whereas*, The excessive use of ardent spirits is the prevailing vice of our age and country, — is, in our belief, unfitting many, who would without this be honorable and useful members of society, for their common and religious duties, threatening with ruin their earthly condition, character, and best interests and prospects in this and a future world; believing, also, that it is our duty as Christians and as ministers to do all in our power to restrain and suppress this most alarming vice, and to rid society of the attendant and consequent evils, —

"*Therefore resolved*, That we will, as individuals, be examples of uniform sobriety in the use of ardent spirits; that in our Association they shall not form a part of the usual entertainment; that we will not in our families offer or receive them as an expression of hospitality; that we will continue and increase our exertions, by private and public instructions, counsel, and warnings, to awaken a general alarm at the ruin impending over the community from the sin of intemperance, and to persuade the present generation to be 'temperate in all things.'

"We further recommend to the Association the expediency of appointing a committee to take into consideration the subject of this report, and to prepare such a detail of facts and views relating to the intemperate use of ardent spirits as may be proper and useful, under the sanction of this body, to communicate to our respective congregations."

The report was accepted; and Messrs. Allen of Northborough, Blanchard of Harvard, and Clarke of Princeton, were appointed a committee for the purposes designated.

That committee reported at a following meeting, held at Princeton, June 20 of the same year, which led to an interesting discussion, but to no definite action; the further consideration of the subject being indefinitely postponed. Among the measures recommended in that report, as I well remember, was the instituting of a county savings bank, as an encouragement to young men and others to lay up a portion of their wages, instead of wasting them, as was too commonly the case, in taverns and tippling-houses. The proposal met with favor; the moderator, Dr. Bancroft, promised to talk over the subject with the leading men of Worcester; and the result was the formation of "The Worcester-county Institution of Savings," — the first in the county, and, I believe, in America, — which received an act of incorporation the following winter.*

I think, moreover, that I am not mistaken in ascribing the origin of the semi-annual meetings of Unitarian ministers and laymen, since known as the Autumnal Conventions, to the Worcester Association. The first step seems to have been taken at a meeting of the Association at Worcester, April 15, 1828; at which time, the record says, "Brother Hill, not having prepared a dissertation on the subject proposed, submitted some remarks on the expediency of organizing a Unitarian association in the county of Worcester."

Again, under date of April 18, 1832, we find that

---

* On reading this account at a recent meeting of the Association, some of the older members, who were acquainted with the circumstance, insisted that I should state the fact, that the first suggestion of the measure referred to in the text came from Mrs. Lucy Clark Allen, the daughter of Rev. Dr. Henry Ware, sen., and the wife of the chairman of the committee.

a committee was appointed "to confer with the associations east and west of us upon the subject of an annual meeting of the associations in one body;" and, on the 17th of the following October, the public services in the church (Lancaster) were conducted by the Worcester-county Unitarian Association, — addresses being made by Rev. Mr. Hill, S. M. Burnside, Esq., Lovett Peters, Esq., Dr. Parkman, and Rev. Messrs. Hall and Sullivan.

On the following May, Dr. Bancroft, as one of the Executive Committee of the Worcester-county branch of the American Unitarian Association, made a verbal communication, the purport of which was, that "it was the intention of that Association to hold two semi-annual meetings in different parts of the county, similar to the one held at Lancaster the last year; these meetings to be appointed by the associations of ministers in the east and west parts of the county, and to be conducted by them, provided such arrangement should be agreeable to these associations." With this proposal, the Worcester Association voted its concurrence. Accordingly, on the 17th of the following April, such a meeting was held at Worcester, which took the place of one of the regular meetings of the Association.

Under date of July 11, 1842, the following record was made: "The attention of the Association was called in regard to the desirableness of a meeting of Unitarians in the autumn, for the purpose of awakening mutual sympathy, and considering the wants of the Unitarian body. Whereupon it was voted, that such a meeting be called by the Worcester Association, to meet in Worcester the latter part of September. Messrs. Hill, Allen, and Palfrey, and Joseph G. Kendall and William A. Wheeler, Esqs., were chosen a committee to make arrangements."

At a subsequent meeting (Oct. 25), it was voted, that the thanks of the Association be presented to Rev. Mr. Gannett, for his sermon preached on that occasion at their request; also to Rev. Mr. Peabody, of Portsmouth, for his sermon preached on the same occasion, Oct. 19. This was the first of that series of autumnal conventions which have been held in various places from that time to the present, and which have been attended with so gratifying results.

ACTION OF THE ASSOCIATION RELATING TO THE DIVINITY SCHOOL AT CAMBRIDGE.*

In the summer of the year 1847, the Association took the initiative in some action regarding the Divinity School at Cambridge. In an address to the Alumni of the school, on the 16th of July of

---

* In justice to an esteemed brother, at the time referred to a member of the Association, I feel bound to state, that I am indebted to Rev. E. E. Hale, of Boston, for the succinct account which follows. The documents from which it was compiled are now in my possession.

that year, Dr. Noyes, then, as now, one of its professors, had made an earnest appeal for some enlargement of its force of instruction. The Worcester Association met the next Tuesday, and took this subject into consideration. The plan of action finally determined on in the Association proposed the appointment, in the school, of lecturers not permanently resident there. It was supposed that clergymen could be appointed to such positions without leaving the charge of their parishes. The Association determined to suggest this plan at once, — with the feeling that several such lecturers could be appointed, — and, as a beginning, voted to address the Corporation of the University on the subject, offering to bear the expense of one such lectureship; and suggesting that other similar bodies or societies, interested in theological education, would care for the endowment of others.

A letter containing this proposal was sent to the Corporation the next day. The Association expressed the wish, that, in case their proposal was accepted, Rev. Cazneau Palfrey, who had then recently closed his active connection with their body, might be named as the first lecturer on their endowment. The letter of their committee to the Corporation thus briefly states their plan : —

"The experience of the colleges of Europe, of all the medical schools in our own country, and many of the law and theological schools, leads us to consider favorably the system of instruction by lectures. In a divinity school, where two gentlemen of high talent are retained as resident professors, we conceive that gentlemen who are still engaged in the practical duties of our profession can deliver courses of such lectures, of great value, without abandoning their engagements in their respective parishes. We suppose, that, if the subjects of such courses be properly limited, the ministers of most worth in our denomination may be called in thus, to increase the power of the school; and may furnish instruction and influence of the greatest value to the student.

"If we rightly understand the original plan of the Dexter Lectureship of Biblical Criticism, the method of action which it proposed is that which has thus recommended itself to us.

"We remember also, that the late Dr. Henry Ware, jun., advocated such a system of relieving the professors from some of their onerous duties."

The Corporation declined the proposal at their next meeting. But the letter of President Everett, accompanying this vote, seemed to show that it might be possible to arrange some plan agreeable to that body. When it was laid before the Association, therefore, at a meeting held at Leicester, jointly with the Worcester West Association, the two associations jointly voted to offer to the Corporation an annual contribution of two hundred and fifty dollars towards the purpose proposed, whenever such an enterprise might be undertaken. In reply to this offer, Mr. Everett asked if the Association would not attempt to unite the different societies and associations interested in the object in some plan sufficiently extensive, definite, and permanent, to meet the whole exigency. In compliance with this request, the Association, by a committee appointed for the purpose, invited the various ministerial associations — the Unitarian Association of New York, the American Unitarian Association, and the Society for the Promotion of Theological Education — to send delegates to a meeting in Boston on the 9th of March, 1848, to consider this subject. This meeting was held, and attended by a large number of delegates, who showed great interest in the object sought, and a hearty readiness to co-operate. A committee of the Worcester Association had previously met a committee of the Boston Association and Rev. Dr. Walker, of the Corporation; and, after their conference together, a plan drawn up by Rev. Dr. Lothrop was submitted to the meeting of delegates, and approved by them. The plan contemplated an addition to the endowment of the Hollis Professorship, sufficient to enable the Corporation to fill that professorship at once. It contemplated also the appointment of a "Preacher to the University and Professor of Pulpit Eloquence." To meet the demands necessary for these endowments for ten years, the meeting made arrangements to raise twenty thousand dollars, two thousand dollars annually for ten years. It also proposed to endow two lectureships, one on Early Ecclesiastical History, one on the Pastoral Care. The Boston Association undertook to meet the expense of the first of these; and the other ministerial associations represented at the meeting, to meet the expense of the other.

A committee, consisting of Dr. S. K. Lothrop, Dr. E. B. Hall, and Rev. E. E. Hale, presented these proposals to the Corporation. They had been informally considered in that body, and it was supposed that they were approved there. In the conversation which took place on the subject, it had been supposed that Dr. Peabody, of Portsmouth, would be appointed the "Hollis Professor of Divinity and University Professor of Christian Evidences and Theology;" that Dr. Dewey, of New York, would be "Preacher to the University and Professor of Pulpit Eloquence;" and that Dr. Lamson, of Dedham, and Rev. Calvin Lincoln, of Fitchburg, would be the two lecturers. It was known that the Corporation wished, if possible, to connect these gentlemen with the University.

This plan was submitted to the Corporation of the University on the 25th of March, 1848. But it failed to receive that approval which had been confidently relied upon. When the subject was brought in form before the Corporation, that body determined to give its assent to no plan under which the same officers should render services in the college and in the Divinity School. The committee which reported on the subject said, that the mixed arrangement by which professors in the Divinity School rendered services in the college chapel, and the Hollis Professor rendered service in the school, had always been objectionable on both sides. So unwilling was the Corporation to continue it or to appear to countenance it, that they declined the proposal made by the committee of the Liberal clergy, even after, as had been supposed, it had been arranged in all points in deference to their views. This point may be taken, perhaps, as the period in the history of the University when the Corporation resolved on the policy of separating the Divinity School from it, if possible, and to relieve themselves wholly of its care.

With this refusal on the part of the Corporation, the plan fell wholly through. The system of lectureships, precisely as suggested by the Worcester Association in 1847, was revived ten years after, when Dr. Hedge and Dr. Ellis were appointed, on such foundations, professors of Ecclesiastical History and of Dogmatic Theology. In 1860, Dr. Andrew P. Peabody was appointed Preacher to the University, twelve years after the proposal was declined by the College Corporation.

This Association has not been indifferent to the wants of sister churches within and without their territorial limits; and, either as individuals or in their associate capacity, they have lent their aid to various objects of general philanthropy.

The Worcester-County Bible Society, founded in 1816, derived a large portion of its funds, during the first ten or twelve years of its existence, from the several religious societies connected with the Worcester and the Worcester West Associations; and, during this period, most of the officers of the Bible Society were members of the Worcester Association.

The profits accruing from the sale of several editions of the "Worcester Catechism" were, as we have seen, paid into the treasury of the Evangelical Missionary Society; and annual contributions, for a succession of years, have been made by some of our churches for the same object.

After the formation of the American Unitarian Association, in 1825, most of our contributions for the aid of feeble churches, and for the spread of Liberal Christianity, were made through this channel; and, though our efforts in this direction have been inexcusably feeble, we think, at least, that we have not been more delinquent than our sister churches in other places.

In some instances, we have selected particular churches to be the recipients of our contributions.

At a meeting of the Association at Worcester, October, 1848, the condition of the society at Upton, struggling nobly for existence, was presented by brother Tenney; and, on motion of brother Hill, it was voted, "that Rev. Mr. Tenney be requested to state to the society in Upton, that this Association will raise one hundred dollars for their use."

Through the agency of this Association, in concert with members of the First Congregational Society in Westborough, efforts were made to relieve that society from the pressure of a debt of long standing, in the confident hope, that, by the removal of this incumbrance, the society, which, by great personal sacrifices and praiseworthy exertions, had sustained itself amidst many discouragements, would become a strong and self-sustaining society. For this object, liberal contributions were made by the societies connected with this body; and our appeal made to other churches, without our borders, met with a favorable response.

At length, it was agreed that the several societies connected with the Association should be called upon to raise a sum sufficient to redeem a mortgage held on the church buildings, the mortgage being transferred to the Association; and, in order to make the transaction legal, the Association took measures to become a body corporate, adopting a new Constitution, the main article of which is as follows:—

"Art. 3. Members of this Corporation shall be the ministers of the Second Congregational Parish and of the Church of the Unity of Worcester, of the First Congregational Parish in the town of Grafton, the First Unitarian Society in the town of Upton, the

First Congregational Parish in the town of Westborough, the First Congregational Parish in the town of Northborough, the First Congregational Parish in the town of Bolton, the First Congregational Parish in the town of Harvard, the First Congregational Parish in the town of Lancaster, the First Congregational Parish in the town of Clinton, the First Congregational Parish in the town of Sterling, the First Congregational Parish in the town of Leominster, the First Congregational Parish in the town of Fitchburg, the First Congregational Parish in the town of Lunenburg, in the county of Worcester; and the minister or ministers of the West Parish in the town of Marlborough, in the county of Middlesex, and their successors; also, the ministers of such other parishes in the above-named towns or city, or of such parishes in the towns of Shrewsbury, West Boylston, Boylston, Berlin, and Southborough, in the county of Worcester, which may now exist, or shall hereafter be formed, their successors, as the Corporation shall, from time to time, elect to its body."

On the 20th of April, 1864, this article was amended so as to read as follows: —

"Art. 3. The members of this Association shall consist of the present members, and such other persons as may, from time to time, be duly elected into the Association, by a majority-vote of the members present at any meeting called for the election of members."

At an earlier date, viz. June 25, 1861, it was voted, "That all members of the Old Worcester Association, and all present or future members of this body who shall vacate their parishes within the Association, retain their ministerial relations to it while they remain within its territorial limits."

In April, 1863, by request of the Union Society in Feltonville (now Hudson), that parish was recognized as belonging to the Worcester Association; and their pastor, Rev. Mr. McDaniel, was admitted as a member.

It was at the first meeting of the new organization, April 24, 1861, that Rev. Dr. Hill, by request of the Association, presented the following offer addressed to the Governor of the State: —

"To His Excellency Governor Andrew.

"The subscribers, members of the Worcester Association, heartily sympathizing with their people at this great crisis of the country's peril, hereby cheerfully offer their services to the Government as chaplains, to be attached to such regiments as may be judged advisable; provided, however, that they accept commissions only with the approbation and consent of their several parishes."

But, as some had already offered their services as chaplains, it was thought better to leave each one to consider what his own duty was, and to act accordingly.

Of the members, past and present, of the Worcester Association, who served as chaplains in the army, were the following: Stephen Barker, 14th Reg. Mass. Vol.; George S. Ball, 21st Reg. Mass. Vol.; William G. Scandlin, 15th Reg. Mass. Vol.; E. B. Fairchild; Samuel W. McDaniel, 34th Reg. Mass. Vol.; Gilbert Cummings, 51st Reg. Mass. Vol. While in this service, Rev. Mr. Scandlin was taken prisoner, and was confined in Libby Prison, Richmond, several months.

It will be seen from the above sketches, that this Association has ever kept in view the objects for which it was instituted; viz., the theological and religious culture of its members, and the promotion of Christian knowledge and piety in their respective parishes, and throughout the world. It seems to have been the earnest endeavor of the members to make their meetings, not merely pleasant reunions, or the occasions of drawing closer the bonds of personal friendship, but also the means of intellectual and spiritual life and growth.

The Worcester Association has occupied an honorable rank among similar associations in this Commonwealth, as a living, active, working body. Such, at least, is the reputation it has enjoyed; and, without claiming any thing for the members of which it is at present composed, justice to the absent and the departed demands that it should be said, that that reputation was earned by meritorious services in the cause of truth and freedom and practical religion.

We confess that we are jealous of its honor: and it is our earnest desire, and it shall be our fervent prayer, that its integrity and honor may be maintained and perpetuated; that its activity and usefulness may be greatly increased; that as the fathers are 'not suffered to remain, and the prophets do not live for ever, the sons of the prophets may rise up in their fathers' stead; and that there may be a succession of pastors and teachers imbued with the spirit of "the Master," who shall enter into their labors, and carry forward the work of the Lord with stronger hearts and a truer success.

I feel at liberty to introduce the following extract from a letter I received some months since from a dear friend, a former member of the Worcester Association, written during his residence in Nice, on the shores of the Mediterranean.

"Your discourse [semicentennial] recalls many memories, now over a quarter of a century old: not long, indeed, yet how many, then acting, gone! Never can I forget the pleasant meetings of our Association, when, with our dear wives, we came monthly together for mutual greeting and common counsel. You will remember we assembled on a Tuesday afternoon, quartered among the hospitable families of the parish, and in the evening held our public services, with sermon, followed by an impressive administration of the Lord's Supper. The following morning, about nine o'clock, we all assembled at the house of our brother, who, after an invocation, read a dissertation, at whose close remarks were offered from the juniors to the elders. I well remember *one* of our meetings, at the house of our brother of Lancaster. The subject on which he had prepared himself was the 'plenary inspiration of the Scriptures,' which he discussed with the plenitude of a deep thought, calm conviction, and poetic imagery, characteristic of his rare powers and true spirit. I cannot recall the particular views presented in the discussion which followed; but well do I remember how it brought out the dialectic skill of our brother of Leominster; the calm, lucid sense of our learned brother of Grafton; the earnest, impressive argumentation of those of Worcester and Fitchburg; and the bold, unflinching logic of our brother of Sterling; to say nothing of the large, practised wisdom of the elders and others in our fraternity. I am not aware that I was ever present on a similar occasion more interesting. I well remember it required some skill, when we assembled as usual at our noon repast, to banish all dialectics, and give free vent to the more social entertainment of the festive hour. One thing I can say, that, in a discussion so likely to bring out all eccentricity of opinion, we were never shocked by a bald 'rationalism,' or 'irreverent handling of God's word,' such as have been so often made the flippant reproach of us; but all seemed true, earnest seekers for the sublime truth, which each mind was fain to reach. Ah, how little is understood, even now, the 'liberty of the sons of God,' the toleration of Christian brotherhood, seeking ever 'the truth in love!' I cannot recall, in all my cherished memories of the Worcester Association, a single example of intolerance on the part of the brethren, or one of extreme trespass on their patience. Why cannot *all* Christians be thus trustful, patient, tolerant; leaving with God 'the things of God'? We serve, not rule; not as having 'dominion,' but 'helpers.' Man passes: the truth abides.

"Were it not an intrusion on your better knowledge, I would gladly say more of some named in your discourse, — of Bancroft, *primus omnium*, the Nestor of the Association, whom I knew only in his green old age, but who yet, and to the last, retained the dignified presence, calm wisdom, and genial sympathies, which made his words weighty, and his very presence an inspiration and a benediction. More I knew personally of Dr. Thayer, of Lancaster, from whom I received the 'charge,' at my own ordination, near forty years since. His ample brow, hardly frosted; his commanding yet benignant air; his slow, distinct, impressive enunciation, enforced by the true *ore rotundo* (rarely equalled); his simple, clear, sound reasoning, never wearing by prolixity, always pertinent and persuasive, — all conspired to give him a pre-eminence, which all conceded, all felt.

We shall not soon look upon his like again. One proof of his rare combination of the best qualities of a New-England pastor was, that, while he ever commanded the respect and friendship of men of culture and position, he equally attracted the warm confidence, sympathy, and affection of the humblest of his flock. I ought not to pass by one name, remembered by me with particular respect and affection,— our long-since departed brother, once of Harvard, after of South Natick, where he ended a life of faithful ministerial service, whose promised usefulness and honor had ever the sad drawback of enfeebled health. It was my privilege to see him often and know him well, in his later years, when his suffering was soothed, and his beautiful home was cheered by the yet surviving partner of his struggling life, who recalls to us always a name honored at Harvard and in the churches. Our dear brother, whose early academic honors and really superior powers seemed to promise a high place of usefulness and distinction, will always live in my memory, associated with the beaming intelligence of his eye, his courteous manners, and his large information in theology and letters. I cannot stay these hasty reminiscences without naming one other,— your namesake, of Bolton— whose sound sense, straightforward truth and frankness, ready, sparkling humor, and genial, social qualities, made his presence ever welcome in the pulpit or among his brethren. You well know his physical infirmity. What in others might have seemed a Levitical disqualification never appeared either to impair his professional dignity, or to abate the cheerfulness of his social character. On one occasion in my family, when some encomium was given on his unflagging spirits and joyous temperament, he remarked one could little know at what cost they were maintained. In the frankness of the moment, he divulged that he scarcely ever passed a night without so severe bodily suffering as to oblige him to rise from his bed, and pace his room, to obtain a temporary relief from almost insupportable pain. Our good 'Father Allen' (an epithet all spontaneously gave him) was always a favorite in my pulpit. His crisp, terse way of expressing a homely yet pregnant thought, with the added charms of his genial humor, and the twinkling of his mirthful eye, accompanying his rapid utterance (hardly impaired by an imperfect command of the labial organs of speech), rarely failed to interest his auditory, especially where his personal probity, truth, and generosity were known. For, after all, the *man* lies behind, and inspires all true power in the pulpit, as in all other important spheres.

In speaking above of Dr. Thayer, I was reminded of one, a layman, connected with him by family ties, — the Hon. C. G. Atherton, of Amherst, N.H., — who, with the long-since departed Colonl W. A. Kent, of Concord, and others, did for Liberal Christianity in that State, what was so ably done by the Storys, Lowells, Whites, Sullivans, (where shall I end?) in Massachusetts. Our lay-helpers in the great work of vindicating and carrying forward a liberal faith merit a high place in the record of New-England church history.

*List of Subjects for Essays and Discussions at its Public Meetings, adopted by the Worcester Association.* 1862.

1. The Nature and Origin of Christian Churches; including the question, whether any plan or form of a church was ever laid down by Christ or his Apostles.

2. Episcopacy, Presbyterianism, Congregationalism, and Independency, as Forms of Church Government.

3. The Organization of our Parishes and Churches: how can it be rendered more efficient?

4. Church Art, and the Value of Emblems in Religion.

5. Hymns and Choirs, with some criticism of the different hymn-books in use in our churches.

6. The Importance of Preaching compared with other parts of Public Worship; with some remarks upon the custom of having two sermons on Sunday; also upon the question whether any thing better than a sermon can be substituted for it in the public service for either half of the day.

7. Clerical Morals and Manners.

8. The Difference between the Ministerial and the Priestly Office: and what foundation or authority has either in the Christian Scriptures or the wants of the Church?

9. The Press, the Lyceum, and the Pulpit.

10. The Duty and Concern of the Country Minister, in schools, lyceums, farmers' clubs, and free town-libraries; or in any other means of promoting, not only general intelligence, but a knowledge of educational, economical, and esthetical principles, and the practical application of them to the increase of general thrift, refinement, and social happiness.

11. Epitaphs and Obituaries, and the Good and Bad there is in Eulogies; with some remarks on funeral customs, modes of burial, laying-out of cemeteries, head-stones, monuments, inscriptions, &c.

12. Right and Expediency.

13. The Doctrine of Reserve in the Communication of Truth, especially of Religious Truth. Should our views of truth ever be accommodated to the ignorance or prejudice of others?

14. The Doctrine of the New Testament and of Christian Morality concerning War and Peace.

15. Atheism, Deism, Rationalism, and Scepticism.

16. What is Religion, and the Difference between Natural Theology and Natural Religion?

17. The Moral Views or Doctrines of the Ancient Hebrews: their excellencies and defects. What did they do to prepare the way for the Christian doctrine, or the reverse?

18. The Peculiar and Essential Principles of the Morality of the Gospel; including the question, whether it is in any sense new or original: and also some comparison of philosophic or systematic morality therewith.

19. Does the first Development of the Religious Sentiment in Man lead to the Notion of Unity, or is Polytheism the earlier Religion of Man? and, if the former, how did the Gentile Monotheism become corrupted while the Judaical remained pure?

20. The Mosaic Cosmogony as compared with other Cosmogonies, and viewed in relation to Modern Science.

21. The Garden of Eden, or the ancient Jewish Theory of Sin. The first Sin and its Consequences. Who was the Tempter? Traditions of the Fall and of the Serpent in Profane History. The belief of the Jews and of other nations in an evil Spirit called the Devil, compared with the description of Satan in the Book of Job.

22. The Unity of the Race.

23. The Jewish Sabbath and the Lord's Day; the origin and authority of each; with the use and abuse of Sunday.

24. An Estimate of the Character of Moses as a Statesman, Legislator, and Moralist.

25. The Morality of Judaism, as illustrated in the Book of Proverbs.

26. The Persian Religion, Fire-worship, Astrology, and the Doctrine of Zoroaster.

27. The Doctrine of a Future State, as it may be collected from the Old Testament, and the opinion of the Jews in the time of our Saviour respecting such a state.

28. Dreams or Visions in general, and more particularly in the Old Testament and the New.

29. The Power of the Body over the Mind, and the Connection of Physical Influences with Religious Feelings.

30. How has Christianity affected the History of Mankind?

31. The Worcester Association: what can we do to elevate its character, and increase its usefulness?

32. Mahometanism: its Theology and Morality compared with that of Christianity, and the relation of the Koran to the Hebrew and Christian literature.

33. The Classical Mythology.

34. Compare the Doctrine of Incarnation, in Christianity and in Buddhism.

35. The Relation of Christianity to Judaism, in the Old Testament and in the New Testament; including quotations from the Old Testament by the writers of the New.

36. The Acts and Letters of the Apostles; or Christianity as preached and as developed immediately after the death of its Founder.

37. The Design of the Gospel of John: its peculiar characteristics and their causes.

38. On the Teachings of Christ, with particular reference to the degree in which he adapted his language to the state of mind of his hearers.

39. The Doctrine of Angels.

40 Conversion and Baptism: what is each, and the change in the significance of both in the case of those born of Christian instead of heathen parents? What was the usual mode of baptism in the time of our Saviour? and is there any mode of baptism, which, more than any other, may be supposed to have the sanction of Jesus, or of the Apostles, or of the primitive

Church? What distinction is there between the baptism and christening or dedication of children? — with some remarks on the significance of, and the choice between, different names given to children in our day.

41. Theology and Christianity: what have they in common, and in what respects do they differ?

42. Paul's Idea of Christ.

43. Paul's Idea of Salvation.

44. Prophets and Prophecies.

45. The Teaching of the Hebrew Prophets concerning Christ.

46. What is to be understood by the Gift of the Holy Spirit?

47. The Nature and Value of the Christian Ordinances of Communion and Baptism.

48. Is there any Absolute Evil?

49. Foundation, Nature, and Development of the Christian Consciousness.

50. What is Spiritism, its reliability and importance, in a religious point of view?

51. The Nature and Value of Swedenborgianism as a Theological System.

52. The Nature and Influence of Divine Inspiration on Man, and Book Revelations.

53. The Characteristics of an Efficient and Useful Christian Ministry.

54. What Connection has Christianity with Religious Systems of Former Times? Is it to destroy them at once, as hostile to the wants of mankind, or is it to accept and improve what is good and true in them?

55. The Foundation of Human Action: is it the desire of happiness, or the attainment of virtue?

56. The Nature and Importance of Ecclesiastical Councils, in the Settlement of Ministers of the Gospel.

57. The Gospel a Power: the philosophy of its influence on the lives and characters of men. Is there any known natural power by which its influence on the souls of men can be explained?

58. Do we. as a Christian Denomination. need to adopt a vesper or liturgical service ? If so, should it be written or unwritten ?

59. The Comparative Importance of Unction and Learning in the Christian Ministry.

## REV. IRA HENRY THOMAS BLANCHARD.

Among our departed brethren, we recall, with feelings of affectionate respect, the memory of Rev. Mr. Blanchard, of Harvard. His connection with the Worcester Association dates from May 20, 1823; and during his ministry in Harvard, till his health failed, he was seldom absent from our meetings.

He was born in Weymouth, Sept. 9, 1797, and was the son of Josiah and Elizabeth Blanchard. He pursued his classical studies at first under the direction of Rev. Thomas Williams, of that place; and subsequently at Derby Academy, Hingham, of which Rev. Daniel Kimball was the Principal. He entered college with the class that graduated in 1817; being a classmate of Bancroft the historian, of Caleb Cushing, Samuel J. May, and others who have risen to distinction. He held a respectable rank as a scholar; and, throughout his college course, sustained an unblemished reputation. Young and inexperienced as he was, he needed the counsels of a judicious friend; and to President Kirkland he felt under ceaseless obligations for many proofs of a truly paternal regard. Being of a feeble constitution, and subject all his life-

J. H. L. Blanchard.

time to attacks of illness, he could not pursue his collegiate studies with that persistent application required for the attainment of the highest honors: but he faithfully used the talents and the strength which were given him; and a highly respectable part was assigned him at the Commencement, when he took his first degree.

On leaving college, he spent one year, as private tutor, in the family of Hon. Robert H. Goldsborough, then a United-States Senator from Maryland, where he received the most gratifying proofs of attachment and respect. In 1818, he returned home; and, having chosen his profession, he entered the Theological Seminary in Andover. Owing to the state of his health, and other causes, he left that institution at the end of the year; soon after which, he received the appointment of tutor in Harvard College, the duties of which office he faithfully discharged, devoting his leisure hours to the study of theology. In 1821, he was licensed by the Boston Association as a candidate for the ministry; and, in September of that year, he went to Eastport, where he supplied the pulpit for six months, and was urged to remain as the pastor of that church. Declining the call on account of his feeble health, he returned in the spring much exhausted.

The following August [1822], he was requested by a friend to supply the pulpit in Harvard for a few Sundays, — not, however, as a candidate: but, having given great satisfaction, he accepted a unanimous invitation from the society to be their minister; and the first day of January, 1823, was fixed for the ordination.

The day was cold and dismal; and, before the services were over, a severe north-east snow-storm set in, which before night made travelling difficult. But, notwithstanding the storm and the cold, the old church was filled; and the sermon by President Kirkland, and the other services, were listened to with much interest and satisfaction.

With the exception of the writer, all the clerical members of the ordaining council have long since ceased from their mortal labors; and "nearly all the friends," writes Mrs. Blanchard, " assembled at my father's house on that day have passed to their home above. I venture," she adds, "to extract a few lines, expressive of his feelings in view of the transaction.

" ' A day ever to be remembered as one of the most interesting of my life for the influence it may have upon my future condition and happiness, for the deeply affecting and impressive services by which it has been signalized, and as commencing a period in which the solemn and weighty responsibilities of the ministerial office are devolved upon me. May God strengthen me for the work to which I am called, give me heavenly wisdom for my guide, inspire me with a spirit of diligence and fidelity, assist me in the discharge of all my private and public duties, render successful my endeavors to build up the Society with which I am connected in the order and faith of the gospel, and make me the happy instrument of converting many to righteousness!'"

Such aspirations are naturally enough awakened in the bosom of an ingenuous young man on entering on the work of the Christian ministry; but, alas! they sometimes pass away as the morning cloud and as the early dew. Judging from his life, it was not so with our friend and brother. His ministry, though brief, was active and useful. He took a deep interest in all measures designed and suited to advance the welfare of the church and of the community with which he was connected. He instituted a Sunday school, formed a parish and a Sunday-school library, gave much time to the selection and care of the books, and was gratified by witnessing the results of his labors.

It may be proper to mention, in this connection, what is more fully stated in the preceding history, the fact that the plan of a library for the use of the Worcester Association originated in Mr. Blanchard, and owed its success very much to his exertions.

But his labors were often interrupted by sickness and debility. Frequently, we are told, after preaching in his peculiarly animated and impressive manner, he was too much exhausted to take requisite nourishment of food or sleep; though he never intermitted public or private claims, when not disabled by some violent malady which confined him to his bed.

At length, in the midst of his eminently useful ministry, he was compelled, by alarming illness, to relinquish all his hopes and plans and labors in his chosen field, and to seek the benefits of a milder climate.

In November, 1828, he sailed for Augusta, Ga., where he remained through the winter; preaching, as his strength would admit, to the small Unitarian society in that city.

His health for a time seemed much improved; and he was encouraged to hope that he should be able to return, and resume the care of his beloved flock, early in the spring. But his hopes proved fallacious. In April, 1829, he was suddenly prostrated by a most painful disease, that baffled the skill of the most eminent physicians, the effects of which lasted through four years of suffering and helplessness.

Believing that there was no longer any reasonable prospect of recovery, he wished to resign his place, the duties of which he was unable to discharge: but so strong was the attachment of his people to their minister, that they refused to accept his resignation; and it was not till the spring of 1831 that his connection with the parish was dissolved. At the ordination of Rev. Washington Gilbert as his successor, in 1831, the following vote was passed by the ordaining council : —

"*Voted*, That the council do sincerely sympathize with Rev. I. H. T. Blanchard, under the afflicting visitation of Heaven. We bear our unqualified testimony to his fidelity as a Christian minister. We cordially recommend him as one who, if his health shall be restored, is peculiarly fitted for the sacred office. We pray that the religion he has preached may be to him a continual source of consolation, and that he may be finally received to its highest rewards.

"NATHANIEL THAYER, *Moderator*."

From 1833 to 1835, a gradual improvement was evident, and he ventured to enter the pulpit; declining, however, all invitations to settle as a parish minister, till he received a call from a small society in South Natick, over which he was installed in April, 1835, and where he remained about five years.

In 1840, after the death of his father, he resigned his office, and removed to Weymouth, to spend the remainder of his days with his widowed mother, to whom he was devotedly attached. From this time, his health gradually declined, though he was still able to preach occasionally; and he supplied the pulpit in East Bridgewater for several months, where he was invited to settle as the stated minister. But, in his view, filial duty was paramount; and no personal sacrifice was too great that might contribute to the happiness of a beloved mother.

After his removal to Weymouth, he lingered through five years of weakness, weariness, and suffering, till at length the powers of nature gave way, and, April 9, 1845, his emancipated spirit was released from the burden of mortality, and death was swallowed up in life.

The account given of his last days, by one whose privilege it was to minister to his wants to the latest hour, is so just a tribute to his memory, and presents so beautiful a picture of Christian faith triumphing over pain and death, that I shall give it in her own words. Speaking of the last few months preceding his death, she writes, —

"His patience under every privation, and in all the various sufferings incident to such a daily decay of body, was perfect. Not an instance can be recalled betraying the slightest irritation or fretful uneasiness: but, on the contrary, a most grateful, placid, calm, resigned frame was manifested throughout his long and trying sickness; while he dwelt with devout gratitude on the distinguished blessings and mercies with which he was encompassed. It seems impossible for any words to express his views and feelings when attempting to speak of the goodness of God to him, and his astonishing compassion in providing a Saviour for mankind, and the manifestation of the love of Christ which pervaded his own soul. 'My mind,' he said, 'is filled with peace, — *such* peace as no language can convey.' Every attempt of the doctor or others to alleviate his agonizing distress drew forth expressions of gratitude. From the irritation on the lungs, it was very difficult and painful to talk; which prevented his seeing friends with whom he would have delighted to converse. It was only at intervals, in the day or night, that he could impart, from the fulness of his heart, something of the comfort enjoyed in sweet communion with his God and Saviour, though scarcely breathed aloud from the fear of expressing too much. He had a great detestation of any thing like display and boasting in religious experience, which led him to avoid speaking of himself, and rather to understate his own feelings: he would say, 'I have said thus and thus for your comfort, and it might seem like boasting, which is ill-becoming. I have no claim to assurance and triumph: all I desire is perfect submission to the will of God; this continued peace and trust, and a humble hope through my blessed Saviour. I wish you to pray,' he added, 'that I may have my reason to the last, and an easy death, if it be the will of God.'

"These remarks were made three weeks before his departure, in the wakeful hours of night, which seemed his most favored season. There was no rapturous excitement: all was calm and self-possessed; and, with his habitual thoughtfulness for others, many directions were given and wishes expressed in regard to certain persons and transactions, which might afford them comfort, and relieve me of care. Memory was not impaired, so that minute circumstances were recalled with exactness.

"A few nights before the last, after intense suffering for breath, towards morning he fell asleep, and, awaking just at the dawn, desired me to open the shutter, that he might behold the blessed light, emblem of the glorious light of God, who had graciously spread abroad over all his works this beautiful type of himself. He then expressed devout gratitude, that the eye was so constructed as to receive pleasure from such wonderful displays of goodness; saying that he hoped soon to be in the more immediate presence of that Being who is light, in whom is no darkness at all.

"But it is not possible to recollect many expressions with exactness. Once he said, with great earnestness, 'Oh, I long to be where I shall comprehend more of the glorious character of God, and understand more of the wonderful plan of redemption by Jesus Christ!' During an interval of quiet, after hours of agony, on the day he left us, he asked me how his pulse was. To my reply, that it was very weak and intermitting, he said, 'I am very weak; but, as the body fails, my faith and hope are strengthened: the same peace prevails. Have no fears for me; my trust is firm. I wish I could say more, but am too weak to talk now.'

"Soon another violent paroxysm came on, — it

was the last terrible conflict with this 'body of death,' — which continued for two hours; and he lay faint and exhausted, almost lifeless, till half-past six, when he was raised up to relieve his cough. With clearness of thought and expression, and with earnestness, he commenced praying in an audible voice, with perfect distinctness, to the amazement of all present, as, from extreme weakness, he had for several days previous only spoken in faint whispers. Soon afterwards, he raised his hands and eyes, saying, with strong emphasis, 'Oh, the anchor of the soul is sure and steadfast! The anchor is *sure!*' and then he commenced speaking to those about him with great appropriateness on the duty of each to prepare for his own departure. 'Remember,' he said, with peculiar earnestness, 'that the spirit of Christ — the spirit of Christ — that is every thing — that is all. If any man have not the spirit of Christ, he is none of his.'

"His address to his aged mother was most touching, full of respectful affection and anxious solicitude, that she might so trust in God, the only unfailing support, as to be comforted and sustained through her solitary pilgrimage. At the close of this affecting expression of his tender sympathy, he raised his feeble hands, and, with a clearness of voice and utterance never exceeded in days of health, began, 'Father of mercies and God of all consolation,' proceeding with entire pertinence to implore blessings on each, that all might enjoy the favor of God, the blessedness of religion, be sustained by a hope of immortality, and received at last, through the mercy of God in Christ, into the heavenly kingdom; especially commending his afflicted mother to *the widow's God*.

"It was a long, fervent, humble, confiding, devout outpouring of the soul to his Father in heaven, full of childlike trust, submission, and hope. The doctor was near; and he inquired, 'How long do you think I shall live?' He replied, 'The pulse is very feeble; but I do not think you are dying, though you seem to be sinking very fast.' — 'The will of God be done: I am willing to go; to resign all; to leave all.' Afterwards he said much to me, and referred to the consoling belief in a *re-union*, &c., and evinced his tender concern, not only for the spiritual, but the temporal welfare of friends, whom he was soon to leave. The last words he uttered were, 'I know in whom I have believed. The mercy of God through Jesus Christ is my only hope, — *my only hope;*' and, in a few moments, he fell asleep, without a struggle or a sigh. His death took place April 9, 1845.

"Of his general character," the writer modestly suggests, "I presume you may be far better qualified to judge than myself. But it may not be impertinent to state, that, from a child, his veracity was never impeached. *Sincerity* was a leading feature through life, with a great abhorrence of hypocrisy and ostentation. His reverence for the Scriptures was very great. His manner of reading was emphatic, showing a quick comprehension of the sense, and a deep feeling of the sentiment, which rendered him an interesting preacher, with no pretensions, however, to eloquence or rhetorical flourishes. Consistent propriety marked his public and private actions. He was serious, simple, and devout in his services, delivering his sermons with that impressive earnestness which secured the attention of his hearers. His natural refinement and delicacy of taste never forsook him amidst all his sickness, nor his love of flowers, which were constantly in his room, and afforded him much pleasure, viewed as tokens of God's love."

I do not feel disposed, nor is there occasion, to add a word to the foregoing deeply interesting account of the last days of our dear brother Blanchard. May his example of fidelity in duty, patience in suffering, and strong religious trust in the darkest hours, stir up our minds, and warm our hearts, and lead us to press on with renewed vigor in the race set before us!

Mr. Blanchard was married, May 30, 1825, to Margaret B., daughter of Eliphalet Pearson, LL.D. (H.C. 1773), formerly Professor of the Oriental Languages and of Elocution in Harvard College, and of Sarah, daughter of Henry Bromfield, Esq., formerly of Boston, subsequently of Harvard, where he spent the remainder of his life, occupying the venerable old mansion built in 1732 by Rev. John Seccomb, the first minister of that town. The house and farm came into the possession of Dr. Pearson, and afterwards of his youngest son, Henry B. Pearson, Esq. The spacious mansion, embosomed in a forest of noble elms, was an imposing object; and its destruction by fire, Aug. 3, 1855, was a public loss, as well as a private calamity.

Mrs. Blanchard still has her residence in Harvard, blessed with a competency, and doing good as she has opportunity.

### REV. SETH ALDEN, MARLBOROUGH.

Among the departed members of the Association, who have labored with us in the work of the ministry, and with whom we have interchanged the offices of Christian sympathy and friendship, we recall with sentiments of affectionate respect the memory of our brother Alden, for nearly fifteen years the worthy minister of the West Parish in Marlborough.

Mr. Alden joined the Association on the very day of its re-organization, — May 18, 1820; and he continued an active and valued member till his connection with the society in Marlborough was dissolved, April, 1835.

Seth Alden was born in Bridgewater, May 21, 1793, and was the son of Joseph and Bethiah

(Carver) Alden. He had four brothers, all older than himself, all of whom, himself included, died within the brief period of five years; viz., between the years 1850 and 1855.

Mr. Alden was a descendant of the fifth generation, in a direct line, of John Alden, one of the little band of Pilgrims who came over in the "Mayflower" in 1620. His father, Captain Joseph Alden, was a son of Captain Seth Alden, whose father, Deacon Joseph Alden, jun., was a grandson of the Hon. John Alden, of the "Mayflower." On his mother's side also, he was a descendant of Governor Carver, of the same Pilgrim band.

Mr. Alden entered Brown University in Providence, R.I., in 1810, and was graduated with the class of 1814. The year following his graduation, he was principal of the academy in Wakefield, N.H.: and in 1816 he entered on a course of theological studies in the Divinity School, Cambridge; after completing which, in 1819, he received a call to settle as minister of the Second Congregational Church and Parish in Marlborough, where he was ordained, Nov. 3 of the same year, as the successor of Rev. Asa Packard, the first minister of that parish. Here he led a quiet, peaceful, useful life for fifteen years; faithfully discharging the duties of a Christian pastor, and sustaining a character without reproach. Being settled for life, as was then the custom, and feeling that he had now a home and the means of supporting a family, he built him a house, a neat and commodious dwelling, planted about it trees for ornament and use, and made it attractive, not only to the indweller, but to the passer-by.* He soon found in the daughter of a neighboring minister, Rev. Mr. Miles, of Grafton, a companion and helpmeet, with whom he enjoyed a large share of domestic felicity during the brief period that the union lasted, and by whom he had one son, John Carver Alden, who is still living, and a daughter, who died in infancy. The marriage of Mr. Alden with Mary Denny Miles took place June 4, 1822; and she died, after a long period of weakness and suffering, July 31, 1825. Her early death was a sore disappointment to her husband, who cherished her memory with fond regard, and who felt that he had sustained an irreparable loss. I do not think that he ever fully recovered from the blow, or that, in the midst of the happy domestic circle by which he was surrounded in after-years, he ever forgot his *first love*, the beautiful and accomplished wife of his youth. At the house of a brother minister, Rev. Isaac Allen, of Bolton, there hung, on the walls of the parlor, the picture of a lovely female, one of the Catholic saints, Santa Rosalie; a painting of very great merit, — by one of the old masters, as is supposed, — which bore a striking resemblance, as he thought, to the features of his departed wife. It

---

* The house is now owned and occupied by Deacon Phelps.

was his practice, whenever he called at the house, to repair at once to the parlor to gaze on this picture, from which he seemed reluctant to part. He had often•expressed a wish to become its possessor; and at length, through the generosity of his friend, he had the satisfaction of removing it to his own home, where it was reckoned among his choice treasures.

After the death of his wife, having disposed of his house, he boarded with a member of his parish, till his second marriage, which took place March 8, 1831. He married Persis, a daughter of the parishioner with whom he boarded, Deacon Benjamin Rice, a graduate of Harvard College of the class of 1796, who had been engaged in mercantile life, but had retired to his native place, and become a respectable farmer and citizen of Marlborough.

Mr. Alden now resumed the duties and responsibilities of the head of a family, and became the father of a large household. By his second wife, he had seven children, two of whom, who bore the honored name of William Bradford, died in infancy: the other five, two sons and three daughters, still survive. Their names are Mary Denny, Benjamin F. Rice, Edward Winslow, Adaline Augusta, and Susan Elizabeth.

After a peaceful ministry of fifteen years, with only such vicissitudes and trials as are common among men, his connection with the parish was by mutual consent dissolved; and he left the place, carrying with him the respect and confidence of his brethren in the ministry, and of the people generally by whom he was best known. The separation took place in April, 1834.

In May, 1835, he was installed as pastor of the First Congregational Church and Society in Brookfield, as successor of Rev. George R. Noyes, D.D., the learned Professor of Hebrew, and other Oriental Languages at Cambridge, where he lived in his own house, and discharged faithfully and acceptably the offices of a Christian pastor for another term of ten years; his labors being occasionally interrupted, as they had been during his ministry at Marlborough, by ill health. In May, 1845, he resigned the pastoral care of the church in Brookfield, leaving behind him many friends, and a name without reproach.

The two following years, he remained without a settlement, supplying vacant pulpits as he was able, and had opportunity; and in May, 1847, he took charge, without the formality of a public installation, of a weak and declining society in Southborough, which he labored, with no very encouraging success, to revive. His connection with this society lasted two years and six months, till October, 1849; and, had he met with the encouragement which we had a right to expect from a society which at that time numbered among its members many families of wealth and influence, instead of its declension and ultimate extinction as a religious society, we might have witnessed its revival, and gradual growth; and it might have been at this time one of the living and prosperous churches of our denomination.

From November, 1849, until his decease, he ministered to the Second Congregational Society in Lincoln, where he passed four quiet, happy, and it is believed useful years, as the successor of Rev. Samuel Ripley, formerly the respected and beloved minister of Waltham, whose sudden death two years before, 1847, while on his way to his father's house in Concord to pass Thanksgiving Day, was the occasion of deep grief to his family and friends.

Of the beautiful close of Mr. Alden's ministry and life, we give an account in the words of his surviving companion: —

"On Saturday, Nov. 12, 1853, Mr. Alden rode to Southborough, called on some of his acquaintances, and passed the night at the house of one of his former parishioners and friends. On Sunday morning, Nov. 13, he rode to Westborough, to fulfil an engagement with Rev. Mr. Gage for an exchange on that day. He appeared quite well after the morning services, and during the intermission. While reading the hymn at the commencement of the afternoon services, he expired. It was that beautiful hymn (156th of the "Cheshire Collection") beginning, —

'Father of spirits! Nature's God!' —

and concluded it with the exception of the last line of the last stanza, with an unfaltering voice. 'Joy' was the word uttered with his last breath."

The last two lines of the hymn are, —

> "And fit us for those realms of joy,
> Where nought impure shall enter in."

His death was instantaneous, as he had ceased to breathe when some of his hearers rushed to the pulpit, the moment that he was seen to fall.

From an obituary notice in the "Christian Examiner" for March, 1854, written by one of his clerical friends and neighbors, to the justice of which, from a long and intimate acquaintance, we bear our willing testimony, we make the following extract: —

"The prominent feature of his character was *fidelity*. No duty ever came in his way, which was not conscientiously, punctually, cheerfully performed; no occasion ever waited for him, or found his talent "laid away in a napkin." In his family, he was gentle, yet firm, not more affectionate than wise. In his parish, he was distinguished by soundness of judgment, integrity of purpose, excellent common sense, and unhesitating fidelity. Laboring with his own hands, like St. Paul, that he might not burden a feeble society, he honored toil by his sunny spirit. Notwithstanding his frequent suffering by disease of the heart, he was uniformly cheerful; the regard of his friends, the love of his family, the reverence of his villagers, crowning his exemplary life with peace. Not only was he looked up to by his neighbors as a sincere Christian, but he was justly a favorite with the rural congregations; his manly figure, his dignified address, his sound common sense, his clear conscience, his thorough honesty, making his modest presence acceptable. His preaching was thoroughly liberal, yet with a Puritan solemnity, appealing to conscience rather than to feeling, to judgment more than imagination.

His funeral was attended, date not known, at the village church in Lincoln, where were gathered a large congregation of sympathizing friends, who thus testified their respect for the memory of a good man and a faithful minister of Jesus Christ. An appropriate discourse was preached on the occasion by his friend and neighbor, since deceased, — Rev. Barzillai Frost, of Concord; from which we take the following extracts: —

"He was eminently simple, plain, and open. Like limpid waters, though deep, you could see to the bottom at a glance. He was of Puritan stock, being a direct descendant of John Alden who came over in the 'Mayflower.' And the sober correctness, the honest sincerity, the stern integrity, and unfeigned faith of his ancestors coursed through the currents of his moral being, as their blood did in his veins. . . . A parishioner of his told me yesterday, that, whilst there was something in the language and tone of his preaching that reminded you of Orthodoxy, yet no one was more thoroughly liberal in his views. I interpret this to mean, that, while the light of the nineteenth century had shined full into his understanding, the faith and piety of the Puritan warmed his heart with their original strength. This led him to choose the ministry, and devote himself to it between thirty and forty years with constancy and fidelity. While the community were changing around him, his interest in his profession knew no change; and, as he went from one parish to another, he carried the interest and fidelity of a first love. . . . In the structure of his mind, the solid and useful predominated, rather than the striking and showy. Judgment predominated over imagination; conscience, over sentimentalism; the practical, over the speculative; an humble filial trust and obedience, over religious fervors. . . . His preaching was reverent, rational, practical, and direct. He spent but little time on theories or dogmas, ancient or modern, either to overthrow or defend them. He had God's truth to explain and recommend, and he 'must needs be about his Father's business.' . . . He was not so absorbed in the world as to forget his profession; nor was he so engaged in study and religious exercises as to forget the great practical duties of life."

### REV. HIRAM WITHINGTON, LEOMINSTER.

A Memoir of Mr. Withington, prepared, at the request of the Worcester Association, by his intimate friend and fellow-student, Rev. J. H. Allen, then minister of the Unitarian Society in Washington, D.C., was published in 1849, the year after his death. From that Memoir, and our own recollections, the following sketch is compiled.

Hiram Withington was born in Dorchester, July 29, 1818.

In the district school, he gained the reputation of being a good scholar, and exhibited many of those estimable traits of character for which he was distinguished in his subsequent life. He was grave, thoughtful, and gentle; and at the same time, when among his friends, overflowing with good-humor and mirthfulness. He was very fond of reading, and he delighted in telling humorous stories and ludicrous incidents, and in repeating poetry, of which he was very fond. He loved solitary walks, and enjoyed with a keen relish the beauties of nature. As a boy, he was very little understood, and found almost no sympathy among his schoolmates.

The remarkable cheerfulness by which he was distinguished at a later period, was almost wholly acquired. When a boy, and even when approaching manhood, he had a tendency to sadness, which was only overcome by hard struggling. It was never, indeed, wholly eradicated; for, while he was habitually cheerful, there were times when he gave way to feelings of despondency.

At the age of fourteen, he left the common school, and entered an academy, where he remained for two years. At the early age of sixteen, he began to teach; first in Hanson, and the following year in one of the grammar schools of his native town. At the age of seventeen, his religious nature seems to have been more fully developed. It was his good fortune, at this time, to enjoy the friendship, and to experience the kind offices, of his minister, Rev. Nathaniel Hall, to whom he ever felt under great obligation.

He now took a warm interest in the Sunday school and in teachers' meetings; "and when, in his turn, he came to give the general lesson to the children of the Sunday school, so attractive," we are told, " was his little sermon, so simple and beautiful, delivered in a tone so impressive and sweet, that they would cluster around him, and hang upon his words, enjoying at once the charm of his stories and the music of his voice."

In the spring of 1839, he became an assistant and pupil of the writer, and an inmate in his family; in which situation he continued somewhat more than two years, pursuing the study of Latin and Greek, preparatory to his entering the Divinity School, Cambridge. While here, his time was divided between teaching and study ; the mornings and evenings being wholly at his own disposal. He was now of manly age ; his mind was mature, his tastes formed, his profession chosen. He was looking forward to the ministry ; and his leading object was to qualify himself for the office of a Christian teacher and pastor. He had no special fondness for classical studies, and was never what would be called *a hard student*. But he had an active and thoughtful mind, was much given to speculation ; and he pursued his investigations after truth with great freedom and boldness, and in the absence of that " fear of man which bringeth a snare." He had a brilliant and poetic imagination, which he sometimes indulged in writing verses, humorous or serious, as the occasion demanded. He was fond of writing ; and his correspondence with his friends was conducted on so large a scale, that I sometimes feared that it would seriously interfere with his studies, as it undoubtedly did. But though I sometimes remonstrated with him on what seemed to me, at the time, a misdirection of his talents, and what might prove a hinderance to his success, I am now convinced that he was taking the most effectual method for disciplining his mind, and laying the foundation of that ease and grace in composition for which he was distinguished, and which made him so excellent a writer, and so acceptable a preacher.

On leaving Northborough, he entered the Divinity School in Cambridge in the autumn of 1841, where he remained three years, graduating with the class of 1844. Not," we are told, " without a most serious sense of the greatness of the work " in which he was to engage, yet with a determination "to be more of a man than a minister," and never to suffer books to stand between him and the living heart of men, he entered upon a theological course in the Divinity School. "His method of study was to keep the mind active, and appropriate the food within reach; to search for the materials of thinking and communication with other minds, yet jealously guarding his own intellectual liberty and that of others; and, when occasion demanded, to gather and combine very rapidly what he required for the work in hand." In adopting this method, he consulted his tastes and inclination; and, though it failed to make him a profound scholar and theologian, it made him an original thinker, and gave a peculiar freshness and attractiveness to his writings. With his active and independent mind, he could not follow in the beaten track, nor adopt opinions and views, however sanctioned by age or general consent, which did not approve themselves to his individual judgment. He claimed the largest liberty, and held himself in readiness to receive whatever new truths might reveal themselves to his mind, from whatever source they might come. "Natural good sense, and simple, unaffected piety, were quite as prominent as any traits of character in all his intercourse with the school;" and it was these that, by their controlling influence, preserved him from all hurtful extremes, and made it safe for him to speculate with the utmost freedom.

With such natural gifts, and such preparations of mental and moral culture, it was easy to foresee that he would not remain long without employment. The dissertation which he read on the day of his graduation, July, 1844, and which was inserted in the "Christian Examiner" for November of that year, was regarded as an indication of his ability as a writer, and a pledge of his success. "As a preacher, he seems to have become at once popular; and to have displayed all those qualities of fancy, tenderness, devotion, and gentle earnestness, which always characterized his public ministrations."

He did not wait long for a settlement. In the autumn of the same year, after a probation of a few weeks, he was invited to take the pastoral charge of the First Parish in Leominster, one of the largest and strongest parishes in Worcester County, — a place made vacant by the resignation of Rev. Rufus P. Stebbins, D.D., who had been chosen President of Meadville College, Penn.

His ordination took place on Christmas day, 1844; on which occasion he welcomed to his new home, and introduced to his newly married wife,[*] his breth-

---

[*] Mr. Withington was married, 19th of November, 1844, to Miss Elizabeth Clapp, of Dorchester.

ren of the Association, and other members of the ordaining council. Seldom has a young minister entered on his work with brighter prospects of usefulness and happiness. About two weeks after his ordination, he thus writes to a friend: " Every thing, thus far, is as fair as possible. Nobody ever began under fairer auspices. Everybody is friendly; everybody is pleased. I invited people to come and see me New Year's Eve. About two hundred came, from far and near, — young and old. . . . Just so at the ladies' sewing meeting here on Thursday. There were sixty-eight or seventy ladies present, — the largest meeting ever known. Then, on Sundays, they have come out like "doves to their windows," and filled my great church almost as full as at my ordination. Now, don't be frightened, good brother mine, at all this chuckling. I know, just as well as you do, how much it is all worth, and how little to be depended on. . . . I know them a great deal better than they know me. I cannot rely on present popularity, *and I do not*. It is a fair field of labor, and a wide, — hopeful and pressing. For myself, I am singularly free from exciting feelings, either of expectation or anxiety. I mean to *work*, — I trust, to work successfully. Beyond this, I have hardly any feeling about it."

He soon found his strength inadequate to the demands made upon him by his preparations for the pulpit and the care of the parish. " I have too much to do," he writes, March 2, 1845, "and yet don't do half as much as I might. . . . Don't imagine I am slumping yet. I wrote two sermons yesterday, besides making five calls, some two miles distant, and have got some stuff left, though I have preached at home ever since my settlement, except a day and a half of love-labors. But I know that my spontaneous thought is not just the thing for my people."

We introduce another extract from his correspondence, of the date of March 31, to show the extent of the field, and the amount of his labors: "I have made two hundred and fifty calls, and have a hundred families yet to call on. I am delegate to a temperance convention, but can't go. Have ladies' meeting Wednesday, P.M., and teachers' meeting in the evening. Thursday, Fast, and a wedding; and two sermons to write for next Sunday. Have a bronchitis these three weeks, which is awful; but otherwise in good health and spirits."

It is perfectly evident, that for one never robust, and now suffering from incipient disease, he undertook more than his strength would warrant, and that he must break down under the weight of incessant toil and anxiety. Besides the cares of his parish, he had to bear the burden of domestic trials, some of which were peculiarly severe. An invalid sister was taken sick while on a visit at his house; and in less than a year from the date of his ordination, Dec. 3, his beloved wife, after giving birth to a son, suddenly departed, leaving him to mourn her irreparable loss. Three days after this melancholy event, he writes to a friend : " The Providence that made me a father, has left me a bereaved and desolate husband. My white dove has flown upward ; yet still she cometh again, at times, to bring an answer to my prayers, and minister strength to my fainting heart. . . . How I shall bear it I do not know, — I hope with Christian serenity and cheerfulness. I trust to live so high and pure, that she shall be to me an ever-living presence. . . . I have no right to complain ; all reasons to be thankful. Had I loved her less, I could not bear it so well. But these years of our union have blessed me with more and fuller happiness than often comes in a long life. Blessed be their memory and hers, in ministering sweet influences and sanctifying hopes ; and may God help me to show, in my own example, the serenity of faith that I have preached to others as the Christian's duty and privilege ! "

We will not deny ourselves the pleasure of giving an extract from another letter, written a few days later, Dec. 17 : " True I have stood face to face with stern realities, and the angel of discipline is bruising from my heart the black blood of selfishness ; but the blessed angel of my love stands by me also, to pour the oil of healing on the smarting wound. You know I have had all possible consolations, — the blessed memories of seven years of happiness, full and perfect enough to make me all my life thankful to God, bring the future what it may; the very tenderness and fulness of sympathy from many a heart; and what is dearest of all, next to my faith in immortality, a constant sense — I was going to say a *consciousness* — of the presence of the departed. It is not sight nor sound nor touch, and yet there are times when I see and hear and feel her presence; and now I *know* that I believe what I was not quite sure before could bear such a test."

Two weeks later, he writes: " My health is not very good. Living the last month in a state of extreme nervous excitement, and compelled to do a good deal of mental labor, I have got worn down. I hardly expect to stay here another year. My throat is troublesome again, though I use it as much as I want to. It would be hard to go away, yet you will not wonder that all other trials seem light to me now; and though life still looks cheerful and happy to me, and the world is as far from being a 'vale of tears' as ever, yet you can understand how every thing but duty should seem almost indifferent to me, — every thing but duty and death. Sternly beautiful stands the former to me, and I feel consecrated anew in the baptism of sorrow; but, oh, how welcome at any moment were the latter, how great a privilege, if tonight I could lie down in my last sleep, to wake in the light of her smile, and the morning of her eternal blessedness!"

It is evident, from these extracts, that the discipline of sorrow had not been lost upon him; that it gave him spiritual insight, and brought him into a nearer communion with the Source of all good influence. It will be seen, too, what was apparent at the time to all who knew him, and what his friends lamented as a fatal mistake, that he habitually overworked himself, and neglected to observe the laws of health. Indeed, he acknowledged as much himself. "Both mentally and physically," he writes, "I am suffering the results of high-pressure work." His friends were more ready to excuse him than he was to excuse himself. They knew that it was a self-sacrificing, martyr spirit that urged him on, — the same spirit that led the apostle to say, "But none of these things move me, neither count I my life dear unto myself, so that I might finish my course with joy;" essentially the same spirit that makes martyrs and confessors and Christian heroes. Though his ministry was short, and though his labors were often interrupted by physical weakness and disease, it could not be regarded as a failure. On the contrary, judging from the strong hold that he gained on the affections of a large and united people, and the estimation in which he was held by his brethren in the ministry, and by the public generally wherever he was known, it was an uncommonly fortunate one. He was a man to be loved. His very looks inspired confidence, and won esteem. His connection with the Worcester Association is remembered with peculiar interest. His presence at our meetings was most welcome; for he was always wide awake, and his conversation was replete with wit and wisdom.

But we must hasten to the closing scenes of his ministry and his life.

Feb. 21, 1848, he was united in marriage with Miss Phila A. Field, of Northfield, Mass. His health continued to fail; and he was convinced, at length, that he must retire from the field which he had no longer strength to cultivate in a manner satisfactory to himself. His request for a dismission was reluctantly granted, July 31; and it was "voted unanimously to continue his salary to him till the first day of November next." On Friday, the 15th of September, he removed with his wife and child to Dorchester, and, on the following Sunday, preached at Taunton, the last time that he entered the pulpit. After a severe exposure on his way home, he was taken seriously ill, and soon became alarmingly sick. On being told, some time after, that he was thought not likely to live, he looked up with a smile, and said, "I am ready."

"On the morning of his decease, he was observed to be sinking rapidly, and his wife was called in from her sick-room, where she had been confined for several weeks by a fever. He smiled upon her, and reached out his hand, but was unable to speak."

He died on the 30th of October; and, after func-ral services in Rev. Mr. Hall's church in Dorchester, his remains were conveyed to Leominster, where, on Friday, Nov. 3, his friend and neighbor, Rev. Calvin Lincoln, of Fitchburg, preached an appropriate discourse in the presence of a great and sympathizing congregation. The Worcester Association of Ministers were present on the occasion, and looked once more upon the countenance of their beloved brother, and followed in the melancholy procession that accompanied the remains to their last resting-place.

"There he sleeps beneath the virgin soil; while the spring-flower above him, in its early decay, shall image to the heart his brief life; and the pine-trees, that wave over him in their perennial verdure, shall be the emblems of the influence which he has left behind."

Mr. Withington had, by his first wife, one child, a son, who still lives, I believe, in Dorchester.

A sermon on "Immortality," addressed to children, and the article in the "Christian Examiner," on "Mysticism," already mentioned, were all of Mr. Withington's writings published during his life. The extracts from his sermons and his epistolary correspondence, given in the Memoir above quoted, show that he was an original thinker, as well as an accomplished writer.

### REV. RUFUS A. JOHNSON, GRAFTON.

A division of the old Congregational society in Grafton, in consequence of the dismission of their pastor, Rev. Mr. Searle, took place, Dec. 3, 1831. The church in a body, with a large minority of the parish, withdrew, thereby relinquishing their rights as members of the First Congregational Society, forming a new parish, and erecting for their use a new and handsome church on the west side of the Common. In consequence of this withdrawal of all the members of the church, a new church, consisting at first of nineteen members, was organized Aug. 5, 1832, in connection with the old society, under the auspices of Rev. E. B. Hall, who, after leaving Northampton, supplied the pulpit of the First Parish for several months, previous to his settlement in Providence.

At length, Oct. 16, 1833, Rev. Rufus A. Johnson, a graduate of the Cambridge Divinity School, was installed as minister, where he continued to labor till his dismission, March 12, 1838, — five years and five months. During most of this period, — viz., from April, 1834, till his dismission, — he was an acting and efficient member of the Worcester Association; taking an interest in the meetings of that body, and doing his part to render those meetings attractive and useful.

As I had no acquaintance with him till his settlement in Grafton, I give an account of his early life and character chiefly in the words of another, an associate in his theological studies, and an intimate friend, — Rev. Dr. Lathrop, of Boston : —

"His family was very respectable in character, poor in worldly goods, and with some hereditary tendency to insanity. He learned, or partly learned, a shoemaker's trade; but, being quite ambitious, he qualified himself to keep school, and was employed — not, I think, until he had taught one or two previous winters — in Brighton.

"While there, Rev. Daniel Austin, then a minister in Brighton, became interested in him, and urged him to enter the Divinity School at Cambridge.

"While in the school, he was generally regarded as a young man of high Christian aim, superior ability, and great professional promise; to which last, however, there were the drawbacks of a certain bluntness and impetuosity in his social intercourse, which might fail to conciliate those whom his preaching might edify. During a considerable part of the time that he was at Divinity Hall, he was a dyspeptic; and this disease sometimes made him quite melancholy, though without ever impairing his reason. But, for the most part, he was happy, fond of society, deeply interested in the work of the school, and industrious, though spasmodically rather than continuously.

"On leaving the school, he was ordained as an evangelist in Dr. Channing's church in Boston, with Pittsburgh, Penn., as his destination. I think that he stayed but six months at Pittsburgh; certainly less than a year. While there, he was brought to death's door by a malignant fever, and was delirious for many days. Either while there or on his return, by some casualty, I forget what, he lost his entire stock of sermons and manuscripts, which gave him much uneasiness and trouble. I am inclined to think, that the illness, the casualty, or both, helped to develop the hereditary tendency to insanity. Certain it is, that, after his return from Pittsburgh, he never seemed to me the same man that he was before; and his success fell at the highest very far short of his promise; while there were, both in his speech and writing, for many years distinct outflashings of the man that I remembered. I did not confess to myself that he was insane for several years; but I distinctly remember his appearing very strangely at the time of his marriage: and, after his wife's death, he made me a visit, in which he said and did so many odd things, that it needed all my friendship for him to bear with him; and the family in which I boarded thought him insane. My sincere conviction is, that, so far as he was an accountable being, he was a true-hearted, Christian man; and that the cloud that rests, as I know, over his whole ministry, is a cloud stretched over it by a mysterious Providence, and not by his own folly or sin."

Mr. Johnson was married to Miss Annah Hill, a daughter of the late Aaron Hill, Esq., of Cambridge, in March, 1834; and, in the following July, her sudden death gave him a shock from which he never fully recovered. He continued, however, to hold his place till March, 1838, when, by mutual consent, he took a dismission from his pastoral charge. Some time in the following autumn or winter, he became editor of the "Christian Register," the duties of which office he fulfilled to general acceptance for more than a year. It was during this period, as I learn from the same friend with whom he was in daily communication, that he began to show marks of insanity. "I was observant," he writes, " of its first beginnings and progress, till it broke him down completely. It became so bad in April, 1840, that I conferred with P. upon the subject, who came up to Boston for the purpose; and, at our suggestion, Johnson, as soon as the weather became pleasant enough in May, started on a horseback journey for five or six weeks, I agreeing to take charge of the 'Register' during his absence. The journey did him no good; his letters to me, written almost daily, showing that his delusion was increasing instead of diminishing: and, on his return, he was clearly inadequate to the duties of editor, and I took permanent charge of the 'Register' with brother B.; and Mr. Johnson passed the summer with his friends, and a part of the next winter, I think, at Charleston, S.C., where he had a relative. Subsequently, he boarded in Boston, doing nothing but walking the streets, and writing insane letters to me. In the spring of 1844 or 1845, I forget which, he applied to me, having passed the winter with his friends, to get him back to edit the 'Register.' I made agreement with him, that if, for four weeks, he would write for me as editor, and I liked his articles, and thought that they showed that his mind was not impaired; and if, during all these weeks, he would not speak or write *one* word on the subject he was deluded about,— I would then tell Mr. Reed that I thought he was competent to take charge of the 'Register' again. He assented to the agreement, and kept it. For weeks he was daily in my study; furnished a large amount of original matter for the 'Register,' portions of which I published under the editorial head, others as communications; and, during the whole four weeks, never alluded in any way to the forbidden subject, or to his delusion: but, the very morning that the four weeks expired, I had a letter from him, beginning, —

"'The person who for four weeks can keep absolute silence upon a subject on which his friends think him insane, proves, by that very silence, that the insanity exists only in the imagination of his friends.' He then went on for ten or twelve pages in the wildest and most absurd declarations," &c.

Accordingly, he was at once sent to the hospital

at Worcester, and continued there till about two or three years since, 1857 or 1858, when he was taken out by his friends, with whom he lived till his death. He died in Upton, Sept. 27, 1860, at the age of fifty-one.

"I think," says the friend to whom I am indebted for the interesting account here given of his insanity, "he was a man of strong mind, a sound thinker, and a writer of ability and power." — "He was a man," writes Dr. Hill, of Worcester, "of strong passions and propensities, and of a good deal of mental vigor. Had he been favored, he might have been distinguished."

After these testimonials and statements, coming from gentlemen of the highest respectability, who had ample opportunities to know intimately the subject of this memoir, I hardly deem it necessary to add my own impressions respecting one with whom my acquaintance was but slight. I will say, however, that these testimonials are confirmed by what I remember of our unfortunate brother, whom I occasionally met on our exchanges, and often at the meetings of our Association, which he usually attended. I visited him once while he was an inmate of the hospital, when he conversed freely on common topics, without betraying any symptoms of insanity. He was a man of robust frame, above the medium size, and of a remarkably healthy countenance. He had a strong, manly voice, and delivered his well-written sermons with much force, and with so much labor as in midwinter to cause drops of perspiration to stand on his ample forehead.

## REV. PETER OSGOOD, STERLING.

In the list of deceased members of the Worcester Association we are at length called to place the name of our beloved brother, Peter Osgood, for twenty years the faithful and devoted pastor of the church in Sterling. Mr. Osgood had first joined the Lancaster Association in 1819, and, on the following year, became a member of the Worcester Association, when the two associations were united, and became one body.

Peter Osgood was born in Andover, Mass., Feb. 4, 1793, and was the son of Peter and Hannah (Porter) Osgood. He entered Harvard College in 1810, at the age of seventeen, graduating with the class of 1814; having, for his classmates, Prescott the historian, President James Walker, Rev. Dr. Lamson, and other men of distinction. His college life was irreproachable; and he held a respectable rank among his classmates.

Immediately after graduation, he commenced a course of theological studies at Cambridge, and was a member of the first class that graduated from the Divinity School. He soon received a call from the town of Sterling to be their minister, and was ordained as the immediate successor of Rev. Lemuel Capen, June 30, 1819. His field of labor was large, including the whole town; and his parochial duties were arduous and exhausting. But he gave himself wholly to the work of the ministry, being instant in season and out of season: visiting the sick, comforting the afflicted; caring for all, however humble their condition; seeking earnestly the highest good of all who came under his influence. By virtue of his office, the minister of those days was the superintendent of the public schools; and, in this department of labor, Mr. Osgood was a wise counsellor, and an enlightened and efficient friend. He also took an early and distinguished part in the religious education of the young; interesting himself in the Sunday school, which, under his ministry, became one of the largest and best-conducted Sunday schools in the county. We have given him credit, in a former part of this history, for being the originator of the plan of Sunday-school teachers' conventions, — an honor that is justly his due; for while others assisted in maturing the plan, and in carrying it into successful execution, to him belongs the honor of taking the first step.

He was not a distinguished scholar or a learned theologian; but he had a cultivated mind, and his pulpit services were acceptable to all classes, both at home and in the neighboring churches where he was known. There was in his looks and tone and whole demeanor in the pulpit, and in all places and at all times, a gravity, an earnestness, an air of sanctity, that, without being repulsive, produced the conviction that he was a true man, — one to be trusted, one in whom dwelt in large measure the spirit of the Master, "simplicity and godly sincerity." He loved his profession; he loved his people; and, as he had no family of his own, they were to him as wife and children, and sisters and brothers.

But, though he remained through life unmarried, he did not live a solitary life. It was his great good fortune — a privilege which he highly valued — to be the inmate, during the whole period of his ministry, of excellent, well-ordered, happy homes, where he received the kindest attentions, being treated as a son or a brother. Here he lived in elegant simplicity, free from domestic cares, with sufficient if not ample means, surrounded by kind and sympathizing friends, and with not one, it is believed, who wished him ill. Thus he lived a score of happy years, feeding his flock like a shepherd, leading them into green pastures and beside the still waters, watching lest any should stray from the fold, or seeking to call the wanderers back. A more peaceful, honorable, useful ministry we have seldom had the privilege to witness. His name is held in grateful esteem and lasting affection by many to whom he ministered, who still regard him as their spiritual father, to whom they are indebted for the beginning of a new and higher life.

Mr. Osgood was, in person, below the medium size, and slightly built. He had marked features, rendered more conspicuous by a narrow, thin face, indicative of feeble health. His whole appearance, indeed, gave one the impression that he was constitutionally and incurably fragile; and he had not been long in the ministry before he gave unmistakable marks of decay and the approach of mortal disease. But so strong was his hold on the affections of his people, that they would not consent to his dismission, so long as any hope of his recovery remained.

In a communication to the writer, he speaks of his ministry in the following modest terms: "My ministry in Sterling was a happy one. Though my labors were frequently interrupted by ill health, I lived in harmony with my people at all times, and can call to mind at this time no incident of particular interest which is worthy of notice, so even was the tenor of my way. In the spring of 1839, I sent in my resignation of my pastoral office to the parish. The parish, by vote, requested me to withdraw my resignation for a year, and to give the time to the restoration of my health, they supplying the pulpit. I complied with their request; but at the end of the year, my health not being restored, I withdrew my relation as pastor with the church."

In 1860, in a letter to the same, he thus describes his situation: "Since that time," — that is, the time of his dismission, — "I have resided at North Andover, on the farm where I was born, and have employed myself in agricultural pursuits. I preached occasionally till five years ago, when I had a slight paralytic shock, since which time I have not spoken in public. A year ago last December, I had the misfortune to fall on the ice and to injure my hip-joint. Since that time, I have not been able to walk, except with the help of a crutch and chair. . . . I can read and hear reading, so that I have still many blessings with my privations. . . . My health through the winter (1859–60) was very comfortable; and I was able to attend public worship the first sabbath in May. Since then, I have not been so well, — have suffered from indigestion, and have been confined to the house."

From this time, his health gradually declined. Disease impaired his mental powers, so that, for the last few years, he became insensible to all about him, even to the presence of his friends. From this state of utter helplessness and insensibility he was delivered when his spirit took its flight, and entered into the rest that remaineth for the people of God. He died Aug. 27, 1865, in the seventy-fourth year of his age.

Mr. Osgood, though never a zealot or a partisan in the bad sense of those terms, was not an unconcerned spectator of the course of events that led to the fratricidal war through which this nation has just passed. In January, 1861, he thus writes:

"I take a deep interest in our political history, and feel a strong assurance that all events will be overruled by Providence for the overthrow of slavery, and the establishment of liberty throughout all our country. It may be," he adds, "at the price of much blood; but better sacrifice life than principle."

That price was paid; that sacrifice — oh, how costly! — was made, and our country was saved: but our brother "died without the sight." We will not doubt, however, that he sees it now, and shares in our joyful thanksgivings at the return of peace.

We subjoin the following just tribute to the memory of our brother Osgood, contained in a letter to the writer from a former member of his parish: —

"I have thought it strange," she writes, "that so little notice was taken of Mr. Osgood's decease; for it seemed to me, that, in the work of his ministry, he was in some respects remarkable. To *singleness of purpose* may be attributed the efficiency of his labors. Directness, simplicity, and earnestness characterized all his utterances. A minister's presence and influence was never more a fact. His fitness for the pastoral office commanded the respect and admiration of his people. Although naturally grave and reserved, no one welcomed a lively, genial turn more heartily. By some he was thought cold and austere; but, if he so seemed, it was owing, I think, to his strict conscientiousness, which led him to guard against any appearance of evil. He turned the eye of rebuke upon offenders, and was anxious to guard the lambs of his flock from those who would corrupt their innocence. The latter part of his ministry was more especially directed to the cause of education; and he had the satisfaction of seeing a decided improvement in the tone of society, as the result of his efforts. The standard of school-teachers, books, lectures, &c., was signally advanced. The Sunday school especially was the great burden of his thoughts; and in this department he was eminently successful. Female education he considered of the first importance. In a private conversation on the subject, he remarked, 'I wish to see young women trained up so as to make *good mothers;* for upon them depend the morals of the community.'

"Thus the good man stood in the hearts of his people, who still hold him in grateful remembrance.

"Very truly yours, E. R. WAITE."

## REV. WILLIAM AUGUSTUS WHITWELL, HARVARD.

My acquaintance with Mr. Whitwell was so slight, as he remained with us for so brief a period, that I shall let others, to whom he was better known, delineate his character in their own words. Until he came to Harvard, in 1857, I knew him only by reputation. While he remained in that place, he met with the Association a few times, and took part in their discussions and doings. If not brilliant or original, his remarks were always wise and pertinent. He seemed to have a well-balanced mind, sound, practical views, and a scholarly, cultivated taste ; and I believe that he was generally esteemed as a good and useful minister, — a workman that needed not to be ashamed.

Mr. Whitwell was born in Boston, Jan. 10, 1804, and was the son of William Whitwell, merchant. His mother's maiden name was Hannah Story, daughter of Rev. Isaac Story, of Marblehead.

In 1824, he took his first degree at Harvard College, being a classmate of Rev. Drs. Burnap and Newell. Having completed his course of professional studies at the Divinity School, Cambridge, he began his ministerial life in Walpole, N.H., where he was ordained in 1830. From that place he removed to Rochester, N.Y., supplying the pulpit of the Unitarian church in that place for some time, when he received a call from the Unitarian society in Hallowell, Me. Thence he removed to Calais, Me., where he was installed in 1832, and where he remained about nine years. During his ministry in this place, his services were very acceptable, and his labors were crowned with encouraging success. A new house of worship was erected, and many were added unto the church. In 1841, he was called to Houlton, Me., and supplied the church in that place nearly two years, and where his services are said to have been highly appreciated. Thence, in 1842, he removed to Wilton, where he remained till 1850. He began to supply the pulpit in Easton the same year, from which place he removed to Harvard, in 1857; and thence, in 1860, to Chestnut Hill, Newton, where he remained till his death, Feb. 10, 1865. He was married, in 1837, to Eliza Galvin, of Portland, Me. He had just entered on his sixty-second year at the time of his death. He left a widow, but no children.

From an obituary notice in the "Christian Inquirer," I am permitted to take the following extracts. The notice was written by his friend and relative, Rev. Edward I. Galvin, of Brookfield.

"From earliest childhood, I have regarded him with filial affection; and to me he has been as a father, a teacher, and friend. It is pleasant to dwell upon that pure and beautiful life, whose outlines were filled with Christian virtues. Though his life was an humble and retired one, yet the world was better for his having lived in it. In every community where he dwelt, his true worth was acknowledged. In Calais, Me., in Wilton, N.H., in Easton and Harvard, Mass., where the years of his ministry were chiefly spent, he left large circles of friends, who have always held him in grateful and endearing remembrance. Shrinking from what is commonly known as popularity, he nevertheless exerted a wide influence by the very goodness of his character, which was none the less potent because he was unconscious of it. By his simplicity and childlike confidence, he won the affections of everybody around him. There was nothing like concealment or suspicion in his nature. It was clear and open as the day; and his disposition was ever genial and sunny. The lines on his face were the traces of the cheery smiles which loved to use it for their play-ground. His heart was so warmed by his beautiful faith in the fatherhood of God and the brotherhood of man, that it ever kept his sympathies tenderly alive. The sorrowing and needy found in him a comforter and friend. His charity was full and never-failing. In the world's estimate, he was poor, possessing only the limited means of 'a country parson.' And yet to me he seemed always rich. His purse, like the widow's cruse, never gave out. Like the fairy's wallet, it always had a dollar in it. He dispensed alms regardless of expense, like the good missionary Eliot. He fed the hungry, clothed the naked, and sent the poor from his door with generous gifts and kindest words. There was not a trace of selfishness or worldliness in his disposition; but, on the contrary, he was open-hearted and open-handed.

"During Mr. Whitwell's ministry of more than thirty-five years, he was always faithful and earnest in his labors. His sermons were characterized by sound thought and fervent piety. His words came from the heart, and went to the heart. Liberally educated, he found constant delight in study and in reading. His library, larger than that of the average of country ministers, was composed of well-chosen volumes. Among them were some rare and valuable works, which scholars and antiquarians might covet. . . . Even till the last days of his life, Mr. Whitwell found pleasure in good books. His mind was fresh and active when his bodily powers were nearly exhausted. Only a month before he died, he was engaged in reading a new translation of Homer; and on his sick-bed he read the last number of the 'Christian Examiner.'

"The closing hours of this good man's life were in perfect harmony with his preceding years. Surrounded by an affectionate and appreciative people, at whose hands he had received every kindness, the last three years of his ministry in Chestnut Hill, Newton, had been peaceably and happily spent. He spoke frequently, and with deepest gratitude, of his little flock. To them he had endeared himself, as well by his friendly intercourse in their own homes, as by his weekly ministrations in their beautiful little chapel. Godliness and contentment were his great gain. Death had no gloom to him, because he regarded it as the passing-on of the spirit to a higher and better life. Happy and resigned, he parted with his wife and friends with the brief and tender farewell, 'Let me go : **good-by.**' His death was like a beautiful translation. The words of Dr. Peabody seem most applicable here: 'There sometimes pass away from us those whose death-chamber seems an Ascension Mount, and we can almost see them go, so sure are we that they go home to God. From them we need no parting words; nay, we sometimes feel glad that no strongly marked closing scene intervened to rival the beautiful testimony of a holy life, and to distract our thoughts from their free range over the successive stages of a heavenly pilgrimage. We prefer witnessing, till the last moment, the same blending of social and religious traits and affections which we have seen in them for months and years.'"

The following beautiful tribute to his memory, by another personal friend, Rev. William P. Tilden, of Boston, I take the liberty to introduce. I wish I could give it in the still more glowing words he used in addressing the Alumni of the Divinity School, Cambridge, Commencement week. In a letter addressed to the writer, he thus speaks of his friend: "I knew him well. He was a good man and true; simple as a child, but strong in faith, hope, and love. It was my privilege to be with him, an hour or so, the day before he died. He received me with a sweet smile; was calm and trustful, leaning in childlike faith upon his Father's arm. I expressed my joy at finding him so peaceful. He turned his great clear eyes upon me, lustrous with resurrection-light, and said, 'Why, of course: where have I been for

the last thirty years?' As if he had said, 'Have I been preaching the fatherly love of God during all these years, and shall I not trust him now in the crisis-hour?' It was a most beautiful exhibition of Christian faith, undoubting and childlike, in the fatherly love of God, most refreshing to witness."

In 1848, Mr. Whitwell published a "New Translation of Paul's Epistle to the Romans," which bears marks of diligent study, scholarship, and good judgment. He was also one of the compilers of the "Cheshire Collection of Hymns for Public Worship."

### REV. JARED MANN HEARD, CLINTON AND FITCHBURG.

None can easily forget the shock we received on hearing of the sudden death of our brother Heard, the talented, accomplished, and much-beloved minister of Fitchburg. My acquaintance with him began while he was in Clinton; and, from the first, I was led to form a very favorable opinion of him as a man and a Christian minister. He won esteem at once by his gentle manners, his conversational talent, and his public services. I was attracted, too, by his fine intellectual countenance, beaming, not only intelligence, but benignity, and witnessed with deep interest his growth from year to year in knowledge, wisdom, and Christian manliness. He joined our Association soon after his settlement in Clinton, and at once took a high stand among the brethren, as a skilful writer and a graceful and eloquent speaker. I was not surprised to learn, after a few years, that his services were called for in a larger field; and, while we sympathized with his little flock in Clinton in their disappointment and loss, we rejoiced that he was not removed out of our circle, and that we might still hope to be enriched by his wisdom and gladdened by his presence at the meetings of the Association; while we congratulated our friends in Fitchburg on their good fortune in securing the services of so good a minister. We were not disappointed. He proved to be all, and more than, we had hoped. During his very brief ministry in Fitchburg, he gained a place in the affections of his people, and in the respect and confidence of the whole community, that is seldom secured by years of faithful labor in the pastoral office; and his early death, so sudden, so unlooked for, was felt as a public calamity.

But I shall leave it for others to delineate his character, and to pronounce his eulogy. From the discourse preached at his funeral by Rev. Mr. Sears, of Wayland, who knew him well, and to whom he was a very dear friend, I make the following extracts: —

" Our brother had just completed his thirty-fourth year. This short life was begun at Wayland, on the 16th of March, 1830. There his childhood opened;

there he became familiarized with the fields and streams, and drank the spirit of the hills. . . . There, where he imbibed health and strength of mind and muscle, he had an open eye for all the processes of nature. He loved books, and was one of the best scholars in the school. I think he loved the open book of Nature somewhat more. As his mind unfolded, he studied the habits of insects, watched them in their transformations; studied the habits and diseases of plants, would discourse of them by the half-hour; entered enthusiastically upon comparative anatomy, and preserved skeletons to explain it. Had he devoted himself to these pursuits, he would have been such a disciple as Agassiz would have delighted in. . . .

"At the age of nineteen, he entered Brown University, passed honorably through its course of studies, and graduated in 1853. In that year, and only a day or two previous to his Commencement, an event took place which shaped his whole future course, and exerted a plastic influence over all his spiritual life. You, that never had it, can never know that priceless treasure of a household, an only sister or an only daughter. Such our brother had, — a sister a little younger than himself; who, in beauty, affection, and sweetness of spirit, was all that could draw forth a brother's devotion and love. But the angels beckoned her, and she went away. On the day that she was to start for Providence, to strew flowers upon her brother's opening path, she closed her eyes upon this world for ever, and the flowers were strewn upon her grave. The brother's heart was well-nigh breaking, for his affections were exceedingly strong; and for a long time he could see nothing but that blank spot in the household, and that one grave in the old churchyard. For days and weeks, the charm of life and the charm of nature were completely broken; for all her sights and sounds had been associated with a voice now hushed for ever; and he could only answer to them, in the words of bereavement, —

> 'The wild bee with his buglet fine,
> The blackbird singing free,
> Break both thy mother's heart and mine:
> They speak to us of thee.'

He went to Susan's grave, and knelt upon it, and prayed for light and peace. The light and peace came at length, and ripened into high resolves, lofty aims, and holy vows. . . . Our brother's attention was now turned with great earnestness to the themes of immortality, the mystery of death, and the meaning of life. . . . A self-consecration to the work of life more entire than ever before, and a religious earnestness and zeal which never ceased to burn, came to him from this great sorrow of his father's house. These ripened into resolves so distinct and clear, that they became a voice within him that called him to the ministry of Christ. 'I hear it,' he would say, — 'I hear it urging me on; and I dare not disobey it.'

"'I visited the spot,' he writes, 'where she lies, the morning that I left home. The rising sun had bathed the whole firmament in a flood of liquid gold; and that holy quiet which rests down upon every thing in the country between the hours of day-dawn and sunrise threw its peculiar charm over my spirit, and I felt happy. I could not refrain from exclamations of thanksgiving and praise. My soul instinctively bowed in adoration to the God of the morning, to the God of the resurrection, of whose morning the gilded sky was such a perfect symbol. I kneeled at the head of Susan's grave, and offered an earnest prayer for wisdom to teach me, strength to assist me, as I was again to start from the quiet haven of home upon the boisterous and deceitful ocean of the world. Into that short half-hour were crowded pleasures unspeakable, whose elevating influence even now hangs around my pathway.'

"Such was the spot where he took his consecrating vows. How nobly he kept them!

"Before entering upon his chosen work, he went to Providence as a teacher of one of the public schools. But a new trial awaited him, — one of the hardest trials to a mind ardent and active like his. A partial failure of health compelled him to quit his school, and give over his plans. But friends who prized his worth, and saw the power that was in him, and the good he could do, always crossed his path. A sea-captain generously offered him a passage to the East Indies; and he sought the restoratives of a sea-voyage. On his return, he entered the Theological School at Cambridge; but, before completing the three years' course, was compelled to leave his studies, and return to Wayland. His mind chafed under these restraints and disappointments, and preyed upon itself. . . .

"But the hour at length came, and he rose out of this depression into the clear spiritual activity for which he was longing. An invitation came to him from the society at Clinton to supply their pulpit. He went joyfully, and breathed all his enthusiasm into his work. The body, touched and magnetized by an indomitable will, refused no longer to work in harmony with the spirit within.

"He preached at Clinton with great acceptance, where he was ordained Aug. 25, 1858. His active ministry there of five years was remarkably successful. His parish honored and loved him. His voice, I believe, was gladly heard, not only in his own pulpit, but in the whole circuit of his exchanges. The town appreciated his talents and worth, and selected him as its representative in the Legislature during the session of 1862. . . .

"It was a severe trial to part with his people, with whom his relations had been so kind and harmonious; but he felt that he must do it. He went there with no preparatory experience; and he saw that the exhaustive draughts upon the mind and brain could not be borne much longer. Doubtless he decided wisely; and he came among you resolved to use the results of his five years' labor, and began his ministry anew. With how much self-devotion and ability, in the pulpit, in the parish, in the Sunday school; and how these promised to your society a new era of increase and prosperity, — you know yourselves: and you manifested to him your appreciation of his worth by tokens of kindness and generosity, which he felt deeply and gratefully. One short year of his ministry had revealed him to you, and endeared him to your hearts."

We here leave the funeral discourse, and quote from an obituary notice in the "Christian Register" of April 2, 1864, the following truthful portrait of our lamented brother, drawn by the same hand: —

"Few preachers, in one short year, ever impressed themselves more deeply upon the minds and hearts of an intelligent community. With a voice of great depth, compass, and power, which could sweep the largest congregations with the utmost ease; with a countenance 'whose look drew audience;' in the large brow and dark eye, which answered to the kindlings of thought or affection; logical powers strong by nature, and drilled under the peculiar training of Dr. Wayland; rare extemporaneous gifts, by which he would pour his rapid thoughts into a discourse, and make it more impressive than his written words; an enthusiasm that breathed itself into every good cause, and inspired it; love of children, that touched every sabbath school he entered, and woke it into life; sympathies exceedingly warm and tender; kindness to the poor, whom he sought out with open hand; above all, a conscientious devotion to his profession, to which he had consecrated himself by early vows, — by gifts like these, in one year he won the hearts of his people and of the whole town, as few have ever done. At the burial service, the church where he had ministered was crowded, not only by his own people, but by those of his former charges; and friends from the other societies, who honored and loved him as a brother, and old men and little children, wept together."

The account of his last days and dying hours is peculiarly touching and impressive: —

"He died at the age of thirty-four years. The disease, diphtheria, made rapid progress; but, up to the Sunday evening before his death, his friends were not greatly alarmed. At midnight, the watchers came down with the intelligence that he could not be roused. The physicians were called, and the family gathered around his bed. At length they succeeded, for a moment, in calling him back to consciousness. He seemed to know that the grasp of death was upon him; and, as if feeling a conquering power over it, he raised himself, leaned his elbow upon his pillow, and, turning his clear, dark eye upon the friends around him, spake in the full, deep tones of his voice: 'Immortality! How they perplex and mystify!' And, pressing his hand to his breast, — 'Here is the proof; here is demonstration.' Then he added, 'I am; *therefore God is:*' and turning to his wife with a smile, that seemed to beam a farewell and a conscious triumph of faith, he sank into the embrace of death. The smile seemed to linger on the countenance when the spirit had gone, and gave it the appearance of peaceful slumber."

Another writer, over the initials of "G. A. T.," in the same number of the "Register," thus speaks of this talented and excellent young minister:—

"As a preacher, his talents were of the highest order; and, had his life been spared, he would have stood among the first in the denomination of which he was a member. Possessed of a clear and vigorous mind, of great intellectual activity, of an easy flow of language, and a striking and forcible style of delivery, he attracted many around his pulpit who had seldom been accustomed to attend church; and, while there, held them in fixed attention, by preaching the great truths of religion with eloquence and power, and with a simplicity and clearness adapted to the taste of the most cultivated and the understanding of all. His people flourished under his ministry, and he had the satisfaction of seeing his labors crowned with success. . . .

"Deeply imbued with Christian principles, he was not satisfied with preaching them from the pulpit, but endeavored to show them in his daily walk and conversation. Of strong religious views, he was practical and earnest, without a particle of hypocrisy; zealous in the faith, he was yet without bigotry, but embraced the whole brotherhood of man in the bonds of Christian fellowship. Ever ready to yield to the wishes, and to listen to the advice, of others, as far as was compatible with right, he sternly refused to be tempted from the path of duty by the calls of expediency or ease. In the closing hours of his life, as throughout his whole existence, he was cheered by the hopes of immortality. With his expiring breath, he expressed his earnest conviction that those hopes were not in vain; while his last words signified that his faith grew stronger and brighter as it approached a glad fruition."

Mr. Heard was born in Wayland, March 16, 1830. He married in Providence, R.I., Oct. 19, 1858, Ellen Balch, daughter of Joseph Balch, Esq., of that city, who survived her husband but about eighteen months. Mrs. Heard died in Sandwich, N.H., Oct. 6, 1865, aged thirty-five years, leaving one orphan child.

"Beloved by all, and doing good to all; exerting a strong power over youthful and often mature minds, partly by her quick perceptions, and still more by her sympathetic nature, — she proved, beyond the ordinary measure, an efficient co-worker in a ministry whose arduousness few understand, whose honor and usefulness a true woman may largely promote. At the very height of happy opportunity and diligent well-doing, she was bereft of the right hand of her power by the painful illness and death of her husband, leading to a total change of relations and prospects. Returning to her early home, and passing another year in scenes of former activity and usefulness, which she could not at once resume, she was just gathering up her strength to the renewal of services, so highly prized by us, in the Sunday school, and other walks of duty, when she was arrested by the messenger whom she well knew, and whom she was willing to follow. Expressing, in her first sickness, the belief that her work was finished, and committing her only child to a sister's care, she tranquilly departed." (Dr. Hall's Funeral Sermon, in the "Christian Register" for Nov. 25, 1865.)

FITCHBURG, Jan. 11, 1867.

DEAR SIR, — In reply to your letter of a recent date, requesting me to state my impression of the character of the late Rev. Jared M. Heard, derived from an intimate personal acquaintance during the last year of his life, I send the following hasty sketch.

The remarkable success which Mr. Heard achieved during his ministry among us was due to no single quality of mind or heart, but rather to the perfection of his character, and the various range of his ability. It is not alone to be attributed to his influence as a preacher, to his untiring zeal in every good work, to his watchful care for his people's welfare, nor to the excellence of his life and conversation. He won the hearts of all who knew him, because, in every duty of life, he faithfully employed the talents with which he was so liberally endowed. Not satisfied to atone for an opportunity neglected to-day by an excess of zeal to-morrow, he earnestly endeavored to do all things well.

He had already taken a high rank as a writer, and, had his life been spared, would have become one of the most prominent preachers in the denomination. His sermons were marked by clearness of thought and force of expression. He thoroughly mastered his subject, and illustrated it by a style forcible rather than elegant, but vivid and pure, adapted alike to the taste of the critical and the comprehension of the unlearned. In interpreting the Scriptures, he was peculiarly efficient; applying to the study and exposition of the sacred text the sagacity and practical wisdom which pervaded all his actions. His delivery was earnest and effective. Every sentence conveyed an idea; there was nothing superfluous, nothing added solely for ornament; every word composed a part of the edifice of thought, without which the structure would have been imperfect.

No preacher, not even the most acceptable writers and speakers in the denomination, hold the attention of an audience more closely than he did. Though he seldom exchanged, there was no one to whom the people more gladly listened. His familiar face was anxiously looked for; and, when he was present, the attendance upon the afternoon service, the practical test of a preacher's popularity, bore witness to the high estimation in which he was held. As an extemporaneous speaker, he was fluent and persuasive. He spoke with the clearness and force with which he wrote.

But his success as a pastor was owing, in a great measure, to his personal character. Of great decision and firmness; with a perseverance which overcame every obstacle; a mind ever anxious in its search after truth, and courage to proclaim it when found, — during his short ministry, he performed the work of years. Having unbounded charity for others' failings, he seemed to have none for his own, and never considered his duty done as long as any thing remained to be accomplished. His mind was constantly in a state of restless activity, which far outran his bodily strength. He was ever learning, ever studying God and his works.

An enthusiastic lover of nature, he passed much time out of doors. The trees and flowers, with their ever-changing beauty, spoke to him of the goodness of God; and the wonderful structure and various motions of the minutest insect shadowed forth the glory of its Creator. The very sunlight was a source of pleasure to him. I have often seen him, exhausted by excessive toil, cast himself down in the full glare of the midday sun, and seem to derive renewed life and strength from his gladsome rays. So ardent a lover of nature, he abhorred every thing unnatural or assumed in behavior and conversation. He despised affectation. Unassuming himself, shining forth his character in its true light, he expected the same in others. He did nothing for effect, nothing to be seen of men. Hence he inspired a confidence that was never weakened, and a trust which he never betrayed.

Nor did he study God only in his inanimate creation, but also in the nature of man. Few understood human nature better. Few could be less easily deceived by outside professions, or more readily looked beneath them, and searched the heart.

Thus acquiring knowledge from every source, he was an exceedingly agreeable companion. His conversation was original and striking, humorous or grave, as occasion required; always entertaining and instructive, and always sincere.

His Christian charities were unfailing. Almost an invalid, his own sufferings never detained him from the bedside of the sick, where he ministered alike to the weary body and the troubled soul. He soon won the warmest regard of his people, and held it without interruption to the last. Nor was the circle of his friends confined to the society to whom he ministered. As a citizen, as a friend of the needy and erring, as a leader in every good work, he was always active. Though he lived with us but a single year, he had gained the affection and esteem of all who knew him; and it can be safely said, that, at the time of his decease, there was no one in this vicinity whose loss would have been more deeply or widely felt. As the tidings of his sudden death rapidly spread throughout the town, hardly a tongue repeated them without a tremor, or a listener heard them without a tear.

To the stranger, this brief sketch may seem rather a panegyric than a portraiture; but, to those who knew and loved him, it will appear but an imperfect likeness of him they held so dear.

Very respectfully yours,

GEO. A. TORREY.

Rev. Dr. JOSEPH ALLEN.

## WARREN BURTON.

Mr. Burton became a member of the Worcester Association May 16, 1849, while a minister at large in Worcester, and was connected with it till his removal to Salem in the following year.

He was born in Wilton, N.H., Nov. 23, 1800, and was the son of Jonathan and Persis (Warren) Burton.

At the age of seventeen, he entered Harvard College, taking his first degree in 1821; being a classmate of Ralph Waldo Emerson, Ex-Governor Kent, Josiah Quincy, and others more or less distinguished.

Having pursued a course of theological studies, he entered the ministry, and was ordained over the Unitarian society in East Cambridge, March, 1826. After leaving that place, he had, for limited periods, the charge of several religious societies, positively declining the fixedness implied by the ceremony of installation. Among the number may be mentioned that in South Hingham, where he remained two years; and that in Waltham, where he was greatly esteemed as an earnest and devoted minister, and where he sustained an irreparable loss, in the death of a beloved wife, — a blow which, for the time, quite unmanned him, and from which, it is believed, he never fully recovered. She had been his cherished companion and friend from their earliest days, his schoolmate, and first love; and her early death, Oct. 11, 1836, almost broke his heart. Sarah Flint (for that was her maiden name) was married to Mr. Burton Sept. 18, 1828, and had therefore lived with her husband a little more than eight years. Their only daughter, Sarah Warren, a most estimable young lady, died in Cambridge, Aug. 17, 1858, at the age of twenty-three. They had also one son, Arthur William, who died in Wilton, March 26, 1831, just one year old to a day.

Mr. Burton was married to his second wife, Mary Meritt, of Salem, Sept. 18, 1845, who, in the long years of weakness and weariness he was called to pass through, was permitted to watch by his side and minister to his wants. He died June 6, 1866.

"His disease, supposed to be cancer," writes Rev. Mr. Willson, of Salem, "left his mind clear and active. His whole soul was kindled with religious fervor. He became, in the latest years of his life, a most earnest student and apostle of the 'New Church' doctrines, which, however, he held in no narrow spirit; for he found them kindred with much of the best thought and deepest faith of other churches. It was good to see and hear him. Though prostrate upon his bed, and with little change of position, he welcomed the entrance of any visitor willing to converse with him of the things of the spirit and of his true life. His cordial hand and voice and speaking eye all said, '*Glad to see you;*' and immediately he plunged into rapid question and talk, his face glowing, his manner eager, as if afraid the minutes of the interview would have flown before he could say what his soul was burning to utter.

"I used to see him as often as I could consistently with other engagements, — once in two or three weeks, perhaps, — and always found it difficult to come away, and always good to have been there. He stirred me by his zeal. Agreeing or disagreeing with him in his peculiar views, there was only benefit and help from coming in contact with a spirit so enthusiastic in its faith, and so thoroughly alive to the reality of spiritual things. I was absent when he died, and had not seen him for two weeks before; but I understand that he continued in the same frame to the end. He was buried in Wilton, N.H., where a marble stone marks the place of his rest."

To these remarks of Mr. Willson, I may add, from my own personal acquaintance with the subject of this notice, that, with feeble health and very limited means, he devoted himself with singleness of aim to the cause of popular education, especially to domestic education or home culture, which he justly regarded as of paramount importance as the foundation of the future character. His views on this subject, as illustrated and enforced in lectures and addresses delivered in many places, a summary of which is contained in the volume he published with the title, "Helps to Education," are exceedingly valuable, and must approve themselves to the judgment of all considerate persons. In many of our churches and public halls, he has spoken on his favorite theme with that true eloquence, which, while it convinces the understanding, goes directly to the heart. On one occasion, he gave a course of three lectures in Northborough, in the Town Hall. The hall was completely filled on each successive evening; and then he was invited to deliver a fourth in the church, which also attracted a large and delighted audience. He seemed to care very little for pecuniary compensation; asking only for the means and opportunities of usefulness in the field he had chosen, and for which he was so admirably fitted. He literally " went about doing good ; " and it would be difficult to estimate the amount of substantial, permanent good which he wrought by his wise and well-directed labors in this cause.

In a letter written in 1860, he writes: " I have lived without a permanent parish settlement for many years, because I preferred this independent mode of life. I entered on 'the Ministry at Large,' as it were led by Providence. In this department of labor, and in behalf of 'home education,' I feel, that, for ten years, I have been under providential guidance. In this I am continuing." And so he labored on with unabated zeal, till strength failed, and he was compelled to retire from the field, and to rest from his labors.

"And I heard a voice from heaven saying unto me, Blessed are the dead who die in the Lord; for they rest from their labors, and their works do follow them."

Besides the volume mentioned above, — " Helps to Education," — Mr. Burton published, many years since, a charming little volume, full of wit and wisdom, entitled " The District School as It Was," which was followed by another with the somewhat enigmatical title of " The Scenery Show-er," containing valuable lessons for the young, leading them to observe the beautiful and wonderful objects which nature presents to the view. He was also the author of a work entitled, "Cheering Views of Man and Providence." Boston: 1832. 12mo.

# APPENDIX.

# APPENDIX.

The names of the present active members of the Association are printed in italics. Names of deceased members (of whom biographical sketches will be found in the preceding pages) are marked thus, †.

|  | Admitted. |
|---|---|
| †Ira Henry Thos. Blanchard, Harvard, H.C. 1817 | May 21, 1823. |
| Calvin Lincoln, Fitchburg; H.C. 1820 | July 20, 1824. |
| *Alonzo Hill, D.D.*, Worcester; H.C. 1822 | April 18, 1827. |
| Robert Folger Walcutt, Berlin; H.C. 1817 | April 21, 1830. |
| Washington Gilbert, Harvard; W.C. 1826 | April 17, 1833. |
| †Rufus A. Johnson, Grafton; Div. Sch. Cam. 1832 | April 17, 1834. |
| Samuel May, Leicester; H.C. 1829 | Aug. 14, 1834. |
| David Lamson, Berlin; not a graduate | May 20, 1835. |
| Rufus P. Stebbins, Leominster; Amherst Col. 1834 | Oct. 25, 1837. |
| Cazneau Palfrey, Grafton; H.C. 1826 | June 20, 1838. |
| William H. Lord, Southborough; D.C. | Nov. 20, 1838. |
| William Morse, Marlborough; not a graduate | Nov. 20, 1839. |
| David Fosdick, Sterling; Amherst College, 1831 | April 20, 1841. |
| Edmund H. Sears, Lancaster; Union Col. 1834 | May 19, 1841. |
| William Barry, Framingham; B.U. 1822 | Aug. 30, 1842. |
| *Richard Sullivan Edes*, Bolton; B.U. 1830 | 1843. |
| Edmund Burke Willson, Grafton; a student of Yale College, but not a graduate | April 18, 1844. |
| Horatio Alger, Marlborough; H.C. 1825 | April 23, 1845. |
| †Hiram Withington, Leominster; Cam. D.S. 1843 | Sept. 16, 1845. |
| Edward Everett Hale, Worcester; H.C. 1839 | May 20, 1846. |
| Thomas Prentiss Allen, Sterling; H.C. 1842 | Dec. 16, 1846. |
| William G. Babcock, Lunenburg; H.C. 1841 | June 15, 1847. |
| *George M. Bartol*, Lancaster; B.U. 1842 | Nov. 17, 1847. |
| William C. Tenney, Upton; H.C. 1838 | April 18, 1848. |

                                                                Admitted.
Amos Smith, Leominster; H.C. 1821 . . . . . . .   May  16, 1849.
John J. Putnam, Bolton; not a graduate . . . . .   Sept. 19, 1849.
George S. Ball, Upton; Meadville, 1847 . . . . .   Aug. 21, 1850.
Horatio Stebbins, Fitchburg; H.C. 1848 . . . . .   Nov. 19, 1851.
Thomas T. Stone, Bolton; B.C. 1820 . . . . . . .   Jan. 19, 1853.
Leonard J. Livermore, Clinton; H.C. 1842 . . . .   Jan. 19, 1853.
Thomas W. Brown, Grafton; Cam. D.S. 1852 . . .   April 17, 1855.
William P. Tilden, Fitchburg; not a graduate . . .   Sept. 26, 1855.
James Thurston, Lunenburg; H.C. 1829 . . . . .   May  5, 1856.
Trowbridge B. Forbush, Northborough; Meadville, 1856   Feb. 11, 1857.
William Henry Knapp, Sterling; not a graduate . .   May  5, 1857.
†William Cushing, Clinton; H.C. 1832 . . . . . .   Nov. 5, 1857.
†William Augustus Whitwell, Harvard; H.C. 1824 .   Aug. 12, 1857.
George G. Withington, Lancaster; Meadville, 1854 .   April 21, 1858.
Stephen Barker, Leominster; Cam. D.C. 1856 . . .   April 21, 1858.
William G. Scandlin, Grafton; Meadville, 1854 . .   Aug. 17, 1858.
Farrington McIntire, Grafton; H.C. 1843 . . . .   Aug. 17, 1858.
Rush R. Shippen, Worcester; Meadville, 1849 . . .   Jan. 19, 1859.
Jared M. Heard, Clinton; B.U. 1853 . . . . . . .   April 20, 1859.
E. B. Fairchild, Meadville, 1859 . . . . . . . . . .   1860.
C. B. Josselyn, Meadville, 1858 . . . . . . . . .   1860.
Eli Fay, Leominster . . . . . . . . . . . . . . .   1860.
Gilbert Cummings, Meadville, 1859 . . . . . . .   1860.
Nathaniel O. Chaffee, Bolton . . . . . . . . . .   1861.
Henry H. Barber, Harvard . . . . . . . . . . . .   1862.
Edwin L. Brown, Bolton . . . . . . . . . . . . .   1863.
J. H. Allen, Northborough . . . . . . . . . . . .   1863.
S. W. McDaniel, Hudson . . . . . . . . . . . . .   1862.
A. S. Nickerson, Sterling . . . . . . . . . . . .   1864.
John B. Green, Leominster . . . . . . . . . . .   1864.
James Salloway, Clinton . . . . . . . . . . . . .   1865.
Rushton D. Burr, Uxbridge . . . . . . . . . . . .   1866.
H. C. Dugan, Hudson . . . . . . . . . . . . . .   1865.
Eugene DeNormandie, Marlborough . . . . . . .   1866.
George N. Richardson, Westborough . . . . . . .   1865.
Henry L. Myrick, Northborough . . . . . . . . .   1866.
Jefferson M. Fox, Harvard . . . . . . . . . . . .   1867.
Henry F. Jencks, Fitchburg . . . . . . . . . . .   1867.

# BIOGRAPHICAL NOTICES

OF

## THE LIVING MEMBERS OF THE WORCESTER ASSOCIATION.

### I.

Joseph Allen, D.D., the only one surviving of the original members of the Worcester Association formed in 1820, is a native of Medfield, born Aug. 15, 1790, son of Deacon Phineas and Ruth (Smith) Allen. Having commenced the study of Latin at the district school of his native town, he continued his preparatory studies for one year with Rev. Dr. Prentiss, the worthy minister of Medfield, and entered Harvard College in 1807, graduating with the class of 1811.

After leaving college, he remained in Cambridge as a student in theology (under the direction of Rev. Dr. Ware, Hollis Professor of Divinity), in company with several classmates, and others who were preparing for the ministry. Having received approbation from the Boston Association in the autumn of 1814, he preached his first sermon for Rev. John White, of West Dedham, in October of that year.

In consequence of protracted illness, he was prevented from fulfilling an engagement to supply the pulpit at Weston, made vacant by the death of Rev. Dr. Kendall. In the spring of 1815, his health being partially restored, he preached several Sundays for his friend, Rev. John E. Abbot, in the New North Church, Salem, before his ordination, and subsequently, for a few Sundays each, for the Third Congregational Church in Dorchester, the Second Church in Boston, Dr. Bancroft's church in Worcester, the First Congregational Church in Sherborn, the First Congregational Church in Lexington; spending the most of the winter of 1815–16 in West Boylston. After fulfilling an engagement to preach in Topsfield eight weeks in May and June, he came to Northborough the 1st of July, which from that time has been his home. He preached his first sermon there July 7, and was ordained as *minister of the town*, Oct. 30, 1816. After a ministry of forty years, at his request the First Parish settled a colleague, Rev. T. B. Forbush, Jan. 1, 1857; the senior pastor having relinquished the care of the pulpit, and the responsibilities as well as the emoluments of the office. Mr. Forbush having resigned his office July, 1863, a second colleague, Rev. Henry L. Myrick, was installed as junior pastor in June, 1866.

Mr. Allen was married, Feb. 3, 1818, to Lucy Clarke Ware, eldest daughter of Rev. Professor Ware, D.D., of Cambridge, and of Mary (Clarke) Ware, daughter of Rev. Jonas Clarke, of Lexington.

Their children are,—

1. Mary Ware; married Dr. J. J. Johnson.
2. Joseph Henry; H.C. 1840.
3. Thomas Prentiss; H.C. 1842.
4. Elizabeth Waterhouse.
5. Lucy Clarke; married Albert E. Powers, of Lansingburg, N.Y.
6. Edward Augustus Holyoke.
7. William Francis, H.C. 1851.

During most of the time since his graduation in 1811,

he has had the charge of pupils, some of whom he fitted for college, and a few for the ministry, in whole or in part. Seven months in 1813 he passed in the family of the elder Theodore Lyman, Esq., of Waltham, as teacher of his younger children. While his sons were fitting for college, and while students at Cambridge, to meet his increasing expenses, he kept a home school for boys, employing an assistant. At other times, he had charge, for limited periods, of young men from college, who were received into his family, and whose studies he conducted. Several theological students, and several members of the medical profession, pursued a course of classical studies under his tuition.

Mr. Allen received from his Alma Mater, in 1848, the honorary degree of D.D.; and, in the following year, he went as a delegate to the Peace Congress in Paris, availing himself of the opportunity to visit places of interest in England and on the Continent. On his return, he gave, by invitation, an account of the reception of the delegates in Paris, and of the deliberations of the Congress, both at home and in several other towns in Worcester county.

Since retiring from the active duties of the ministry, he has found pleasant employment in his study, his garden, and his orchard, in superintending the schools, and in visiting his people and friends. He trusts it has not been an abuse of his leisure, that he has spent many happy hours in preparing for the press these sketches and memoirs of the living and the departed.

*Publications.*

1. A Funeral Discourse on the Death of Winslow Brigham, jun., December, 1818.
2. A New Year's Sermon, delivered in Shrewsbury, at a Meeting of the Worcester Association, 1822.

3. An Historical Discourse, delivered on Thanksgiving Day, 1825; which, by request of his parishioners, was enlarged, and published in the "Worcester Magazine," and in pamphlet form, under the title of "An Historical Account of Northborough," July, 1826.
4. A Fast Sermon, "Sources of Public Prosperity," 1829.
5. A Sermon on Family Religion, in "Liberal Preacher," 1831.
6. In 1832, he compiled the first volume of the "Christian Monitor," containing his Sermon before the Society for Promoting Knowledge, Piety, and Charity; and Remarks on the Lord's Supper.
7. An Address to the Parish at the Ordination of Rev. Robert F. Walcott, Berlin, 1830.
8. A Minister's Account of his Stewardship: a Sermon on completing the Twenty-fifth Year of his Ministry, 1841.
9. An Address at the Ordination of Rev. H. Withington, Leominster, 1844.
10. A Centennial Discourse on Completing a Century from the Organization of the Church, 1846.
11. A New Year's Sermon, in "Monthly Religious Magazine," 1855.
12. An Address before the Worcester Sunday-school Society, Lancaster, 1854.
13. A Catechism, prepared at the Request of the Worcester Association, 1822.
14. Easy Lessons in Geography and History, for Schools, of which several editions were published, the first in 1825.
15. A Memoir of Rev. Dr. Lathrop, of Springfield, 1823.
16. Questions on the Gospels, in Two Parts, and Questions on the Acts, prepared in the leisure hours of three successive winters; of which many editions have been called for, the first being published in 1829.
17. Part I. of a Series of Questions on the Old Testament was published in 1837, under the title of "Questions on the Pentateuch;" but, as the work was not called for, he abandoned the project.

18. An Address at the Centennial Celebration of the Incorporation of Northborough, Aug. 22, 1866, and a Half-century Sermon on the Fiftieth Anniversary of his Settlement in Northborough, Oct. 30, 1866, were also printed.

In the early days of the "Christian Disciple" (now "Christian Examiner") and the "Christian Register," he was a frequent contributor to those periodicals.

## II.

I should like to speak as freely and as *eulogistically* of our brother LINCOLN, as I have felt at liberty, or rather have been constrained, to do of some of our departed brethren. But propriety forbids. He is still with us; still in active service, in the midst of useful labors, occupying an important post, — where we hope he may be permitted to remain yet many years, ere any one is called to pronounce his eulogy.

CALVIN LINCOLN, son of Calvin and Linda (Loring) Lincoln, was born in Hingham, Oct. 27, 1799. From ten to sixteen, he studied under the care of Rev. Daniel Kimball, then the Preceptor of the Derby Academy, Hingham, who afterwards removed to Needham, where he recently died at an advanced age, respected and honored. He maintained a highly respectable rank, and an unsullied character, during his college life at Cambridge; graduating with the class of 1820, of which Drs. Gannett, Hall, Furness, and Young were members. After leaving college, he entered at once the Divinity School, then just organized under the care of the elder Dr. Henry Ware and Andrews Norton. In the summer of 1823, he was licensed to preach by the Boston Association of Ministers; and, June 30, 1824, he was ordained pastor of the First Congregational Society in Fitchburg, Mass. He was married, Oct. 10, 1826, to Elizabeth Andrews, daughter of Thomas and Catherine Andrews, of Hingham. Mrs. Lincoln was "a faithful wife, a devoted mother, and a good woman." Their children were Calvin Lincoln, jun., a merchant doing business in Boston, but living with his father on the old homestead; and Elizabeth, married to Henry Harding, Esq., of Hingham. Mrs. Harding died October, 1864, while on a visit to her friends in St. Louis, Mo., deeply lamented by a large circle of friends.

"After a ministry of more than twenty years," he writes, "my health, which had never been firm, very sensibly declined; and in June, 1850, having been chosen Secretary of the American Unitarian Association, with the consent of my people I left Fitchburg, removed my family to Hingham, to the house in which my father and I were born, and commenced my labors as Secretary of the American Unitarian Association. This office I resigned at the meeting in May, 1853. The same spring, I was invited to take charge of the Bulfinch-street Society, Boston, for one year, during the absence of its pastor, Rev. Frederic T. Gray, at San Francisco. Before the close of my labors in Boston, I was invited to preach to the First Parish in Hingham; and in May, 1854, I left Boston for this place, and, the following spring, was installed associate pastor (with Rev. Joseph Richardson) of the above-named parish. My ecclesiastical relation to the society at Fitchburg was not dissolved until the time of my installation at Hingham."

I would add to the above account which our brother gives of himself, that his ministry at Fitchburg was a very successful one; that he was highly esteemed and loved by his parishioners, and held in honor by his fellow-citizens of all parties and sects; and, further, that the

THE NEW YORK
PUBLIC LIBRARY

ASTOR, LENOX AND
TILDEN FOUNDATIONS

Worcester Association, with which he was connected, highly appreciated his services, and regarded him with peculiar affection. *Sero in cœlum redeat!*

### III.

Next in order of time who joined the Worcester Association was Rev. Dr. HILL, the colleague and successor of Rev. Dr. Bancroft, of the Second Congregational Church in Worcester. His connection with the Association has, moreover, lasted longer, with a single exception, than that of any other member; having extended from April 18, 1827, to the present time. And it is but simple justice to say, that to no one is the Association more indebted for the respectable position it occupies than to him.

Alonzo Hill, son of Oliver and Mary (Goldsmith) Hill, was born in Harvard, June 20, 1800. He was, for a time, a student at Groton Academy, now Lawrence Academy, where he pursued his studies preparatory to his entering Harvard College. He graduated with the class of 1822, and at once was appointed Assistant Preceptor of Leicester Academy, in which office he remained two years. In 1824, he entered the Divinity School, Cambridge, where he remained two years, having entered a year in advance, graduating with the class of 1826. Having been licensed to preach, he was soon invited to become the associate pastor with the venerable and excellent Dr. Bancroft, and was ordained March 28, 1827. He was married, Dec. 29, 1830, to Frances Mary Clarke, daughter of Hugh Hamilton Clarke, Esq., of Boston. Their children are — Hamilton Alonzo Hill, Esq., H.C. 1853, who lives in Boston; and Frances Ann, living with her parents.

From 1851 to 1854, Dr. Hill was one of the Overseers of Harvard College, which honored him with the degree of D.D., conferred in 1851. On account of his health, he spent the winter of 1837–8 in Cuba, W. I.; and, with the consent of his people, he made the tour of Europe, in company with his wife and daughter, being absent eight months, in 1856.

The following is a list of Dr. Hill's publications: —

1. A Sermon at the Ordination of Rev. Josiah Moore, Athol, Dec. 8, 1830.
2. Sermon in the " Liberal Preacher," August, 1836.
3. Sermon at the Interment of Rev. Dr. Bancroft, Aug. 22, 1839.
4. Sermon at the Interment of Rev. Dr. Thayer, June 28, 1840.
5. A Review of Edes's and Sears's Sermons on the Death of Rev. Isaac Allen, in " Christian Examiner," September, 1844.
6. Article on the Life and Works of Rev. Jonathan Farr, in " Christian Examiner," November, 1845.
7. Sermon preached in Boston, May 27, 1847, published in " Sermons on Christian Communion."
8. Sermon in " Monthly Miscellany " for October, 1848.
9. Article on the Life and Character of Rev. Hiram Withington, in " Christian Examiner," January, 1849.
10. Sermon on the Death of General Taylor, July 31, 1850.
11. Sermon preached in the Ancient Meeting-house in Hingham, Sept. 8, 1850.
12. Sermon preached at the Dedication of the New Meeting-house in Worcester, March 26, 1851.
13. Sermon preached on the Twenty-fifth Anniversary of his Ordination, March 28, 1852.
14. Discourse on Occasion of the Death of Hon. John W. Lincoln, Oct. 10, 1852.
15. Address before the Worcester New-England Temperance Union, at Sterling, April 13, 1853.
16. Sermon on the Death of Hon. John Davis, April 23, 1854.

17. Address before the Alumni of Leicester Academy, Aug. 7, 1855.
18. Address before the Guardians of the Orphans' Home, Feb. 5, 1857.
19. Discourse commemorative of the Hon. Thomas Kinnicutt, Jan. 31, 1858.
20. Speech before the American Antiquarian Society on Prescott the Historian, Feb. 10, 1859.
21. Commemorative Discourse on Rev. Samuel Clarke, of Uxbridge, Dec. 11, 1859.
22. Sermon delivered Sunday after the Funeral of William Hudson, Aug. 17, 1862.
23. In Memoriam: a Discourse on Lieutenant Thomas J. Spurr, mortally wounded at the battle of Antietam, Oct. 5, 1862.
24. A Speech on the Death of Hon. Edward Everett, before the American Antiquarian Society, Jan. 17, 1865.
25. Before the Same. On the Life and Services of George Livermore, Esq., Oct. 21, 1865.
26. Address at the Funeral of Mrs. Lucy C. Allen, Feb. 14, 1866, in the "Monthly Religious Magazine," for March, 1866.
27. Speech on the Life and Character of Jared Sparks, LL.D.
28. Pastor's Record: Sermon at the Close of Forty Years' Ministry, March 28, 1867.
29. Semi-annual Report of the American Antiquarian Society, April 24, 1867.

Dr. Hill is the oldest ordained clergyman, having the sole care of a parish, within the limits of Worcester County.

The fortieth anniversary of his ordination was observed with appropriate services the 28th of March, 1867; an account of which, with his address, has been printed in a handsome pamphlet of sixty-six pages, containing portraits of himself and also of Rev. Dr. Bancroft.

## IV.

Robert Folger Wallcot was a member of the Worcester Association from April 21, 1830, till the 1st of January, 1834, when, at his request, he was dismissed from his parochial charge. He was born in Nantucket, March 16, 1797, and graduated at Harvard College, 1817. Having pursued his theological studies at Cambridge, he was settled at Berlin, as successor of Rev. Reuben Puffer, D.D., Feb. 10, 1830. A portion of the society had seceded, and formed a new church and parish, before his ordination; but the number left was sufficient to form a respectable society; and, during the first two years of Mr. Wallcot's ministry, his labors among, and in behalf of, his people, were crowned with encouraging success. After the secession, the number of communicants was very small; but by the blessing of God on his preaching, and his labors out of the pulpit, a goodly number of men and women, from among the leading members of the parish, connected themselves with the church by a public profession; and, for a time, every thing looked prosperous and encouraging. It seemed to be a revival of pure religion; and we were encouraged to hope, that a ministry so auspiciously begun would last for many years, and be fruitful in spiritual good. But as too often happens, sometimes without any apparent cause, by what seems to be a law of the human mind, the religious interest that had been awakened, gradually and insensibly declined, on the part, as is likely, both of the minister and the people; and, after a ministry of less than four years, his connection with the church in Berlin was, by mutual consent, dissolved. He left behind him those who regarded him with affectionate respect, as a wise counsellor and a faithful and devoted pastor, to whom they felt that they were under lasting obligations.

Mr. Wallcot was married in Boston, Sept. 25, 1832, to his second cousin, Mary Ann Powers. Their children are Mary R. and Annie E. Wallcot.

After his dismission, he was appointed general agent of the American Antislavery Society. His residence is in Boston.

## V.

WASHINGTON GILBERT was born in Atkinson, N.H., March 18, 1800, and graduated at Williams College, Mass., in 1826. His theological studies were pursued at Cambridge. After completing the prescribed course, he preached for a year and a half in Meadville, Penn. And, after a term of probation, he received a call, and was ordained as pastor of the First Congregational Church in Harvard, as successor of the lamented Blanchard, April 13, 1831. His connection with the society in Harvard ceased on the 13th of April, 1855, after a ministry of twenty-four years. Soon afterwards, he removed to West Newton; and on the 7th of October, 1853, took charge of the Unitarian society in West Newton, which he held for two years.

Mr. Gilbert was admitted a member of the Worcester Association, April 17, 1833, and faithfully discharged his duties as such; gaining the respect and esteem of his brethren, who were always sure of finding, at his pleasant home, a hospitable reception.

He was married, May 23, 1833, to Achsah, eldest daughter of Hon. Stephen P. and Achsah Gardner, of Bolton. Their children were — Augusta Gardner, born Dec. 9, 1834, married to Samuel Lane Wheeler, merchant in Boston; and Frances Allina, who died in infancy. Augusta was a young lady of great purity and loveliness of disposition and character; and there were many out of the family circle who sympathized with her bereaved husband and parents, on her early and lamented death, which took place Dec. 3, 1855, at the age of twenty-one.

Mr. Gilbert published, at the request of his parishioners, in 1831, a sermon on the "Connection of Religion with Morality," and, in 1834, a sermon on the "Law of Liberty." His present residence is Longwood, Mass.

## VI.

Samuel May, son of Deacon Samuel and Mary (Goddard) May, of Boston, was born April 11, 1810.

Having fitted for college, partly with Deacon Samuel Greele, and afterwards at the Boston Latin School, he entered Harvard College, where he graduated in 1829.

Having gone through a course of theological studies, he was ordained minister of the small Unitarian society in Leicester, Aug. 13, 1831. The society was harmonious and compact, and numbered among its members several persons of wealth and cultivation; and Mr. May entered on his ministry hopefully, and with favorable auspices. He had the confidence and love of his parishioners, and the respect of all who knew him; and we anticipated for him a long and peaceful and prosperous ministry. With his labors among his people, he united a strong interest in the philanthropic movements of the times, particularly that for the abolition of slavery. Some of his parishioners did not sympathize with their minister in these matters, and signed off, seriously weakening the society, which was never strong. Other leading members died, or removed to other towns; so that, before the close of his ministry, the society was much reduced in numbers and strength. His health, too, failed; and, in 1843, he was induced to make the tour of Europe, for health and pleasure. After a ministry of fifteen years, his connection with the society was dissolved in July, 1846; and he removed to Boston with his family, retaining his pleasant and hospitable home in Leicester for a summer residence. He soon became general agent of the Massachusetts Antislavery Society, in whose service he labored for many years.

Mr. May was married Nov. 11, 1835, to Sarah, third daughter of Nathaniel P. Russell, of Boston. Their children are Adeline, Edward, Joseph Russell, and Elizabeth Goddard.

## VII.

DAVID LAMSON was born in Charlton, Mass., June 6, 1806; obtained his education in the common schools of his native town, with one term in an academy. He subsequently was employed in a cotton factory in West Boylston, where he met with an injury, which caused the loss of a limb, and where he was married to Mary S. Moore, daughter of Dr. John Smith, of that village. He was settled in Berlin in 1834. For a few years after his settlement, his ministry was prospered, his society increased in numbers, and he seemed to be firmly established in the affections of his people. About this time, he became interested in the movement which resulted in the establishment of the Hopedale Community, and labored to awaken an interest among his people in the peculiar views entertained by the leaders of that movement. It formed the subject of his preaching, and became so prominent as to cause a good deal of complaint and disaffection, which led him to ask for a dismission. This was granted; and the dismission took place in 1840. After leaving Berlin, he became connected with the Hopedale Community in Milford, Mass., of which he was one of the original members; and he was a contributor to the "Practical Christian," a periodical published under the auspices of the community. Having become dissatisfied with the management of that institution, he, with his wife and two little children, joined the Shaker establishment in Hancock, near Pittsfield, Mass., where they remained two years, when he left, and returned to West Boylston, where he has since resided with his family. In 1848, he published a small duodecimo volume, with the title, "Two Years' Experience among the Shakers;" from which it appears that he failed here, also, to find that "little heaven below," for which he longed, and for which he had sacrificed so much.

## VIII.

Rufus P. Stebbins, son of Luther and Lucina Stebbins, was born in Wilbraham, Hampden County, Mass., March 3, 1810. He worked with his father and older brother upon the little homestead, till the death of his father, when he was fifteen years of age. His opportunities for education were such as were enjoyed forty or fifty years ago by children in the remote districts of a country town, — a few weeks of schooling, both summer and winter, till ten years of age, and then a few weeks in the winter only, till fifteen or sixteen. A few years after his father's death, having failed of success in his endeavors to learn a trade, he gratified his thirst for knowledge, by obtaining the consent of his mother to prepare himself for college, which he did at the Wesleyan Academy in his native town; keeping school in the winter, and working the month of July to pay for his board and tuition. He entered Amherst College, August, 1830, in the twenty-first year of his age, in the class of which the late Professors Adams and Gray, and Henry Ward Beecher, were members. On the day of his graduation, he left Amherst for Cambridge, and entered the Divinity School, August, 1834. Of his classmates in the school. only Dr. Bellows, of New York, and Rev. E. H. Sears, of Wayland, are now in the ministry. After supplying the pulpit in Leominster four Sundays, he was invited to settle as pastor, by a "yea and nay" vote of 165 yeas, 0 nays; and was ordained Sept. 20, 1837. — Dr. Henry Ware, jun., preaching the sermon on the occasion.

Mr. Stebbins is of robust constitution, ardent temperament, and an unwearied worker. He took most decided ground on the subject of temperance, of peace, and of anti-slavery; and, as might be expected, he soon found strong and active opponents in his parish. But he maintained his ground; and had the satisfaction to see most of those who had felt cold or hostile, returning to friendship after a few years.

In the summer of 1844, he was appointed President of the Theological School to be established in Meadville, Penn., by the American Unitarian Association, which was to pay him five hundred dollars a year for five years; and the Unitarian society in that place also called him to be their pastor for the same time, with the same sum for a salary. He accepted the appointment; and left Leominster Sept. 20, 1844, after a successful ministry of seven years, to the regret of his parish, and of his associates among the neighboring ministers. During his ministry, the Sunday school connected with his society averaged from three hundred and fifty to four hundred members, including teachers and pupils; and the additions to the church were about a hundred and twenty. In this work he was aided not a little by his excellent wife, Eliza Clarke, daughter of Deacon Nathaniel and Elizabeth Livermore, of Cambridge, Mass., to whom he was married Sept. 11, 1837.

The school founded at Meadville was in the interest both of the "Christian" and the Unitarian denominations. It was a very difficult and a very laborious work to succeed in. For five years, Mr. Stebbins, assisted by Professor Huidekoper, gave the whole strength of both his body and mind to the school and the society; preaching every Sunday, and lecturing three or four times a day during the week. At the end of five years, he resigned his pastorship, and Rev. N. S. Folsom was chosen in his place. Another professor was also appointed in the school, Professor Huidekoper having resigned a part of his labors. It had been the purpose of Mr. Stebbins to leave the school at the close of the seventh year; and accordingly, at that time, he handed in his resignation, but was prevailed upon by the friends of the school to withdraw it.

The pressing necessities of the school requiring better accommodations, W. J. Huidekoper, Esq., father of the professor, and a most worthy man, offered the trustees the sum of ten thousand dollars, on condition that they should raise forty thousand dollars more. Mr. Stebbins was appointed agent to raise this large sum. He was absent from his home nine weeks, and during that brief period secured the money. In 1851 he was honored with the degree of D.D. by Harvard College. In 1856 he resigned his situation at Meadville, leaving the school in a prosperous condition, and returned to Cambridge, where he resided a year, when he received a call to settle as pastor of the First Unitarian Society in Woburn, where he remained six years. He has but one child, — a son, Nathaniel Livermore, born Jan. 9, 1847.

Dr. Stebbins wrote much, when in college, for the newspapers of his county (Hampden); and, while at Leominster and Meadville, for the "Register" and the "Inquirer." He has also written several articles for the "Examiner;" and he assisted in editing the "Christian Repository," which was published monthly, for one year, at Meadville.

He has also published three peace addresses: one delivered before the Bowdoin-street Peace Society, Boston, Feb. 7, 1836; one before the Peace Society of Amherst College, July 4, 1838; and one before the American Peace Society, May 28, 1857.

He has published a Centennial Discourse, Leominster, Sept. 24, 1843; Two Sermons on leaving Leominster, Sept. 15, 1844; a Sermon at the Ordination of Frederic W. Newell, Aug. 1, 1847, at Brewster, Mass.; a Sermon on Renovating the old Meeting-house, Leominster, July 22, 1847; Acceptable Worship, Meadville, Sept. 30, 1849; a Discourse at the Dedication of Divinity Hall, Meadville, Oct. 24, 1844; an Address before the Natural History Society, Meadville, Nov. 6, 1855; an Oration on Academic Culture, before the Literary Societies of Alleghany College, Meadville, July 1, 1851; an Address before the Middlesex Agricultural Society, Concord, Mass., Sept. 28, 1859; and a handsome volume, containing an Historical Address, delivered at the Centennial Celebration in Wilbraham in 1863.

He writes, under date of Jan. 18, 1866: "After leaving Meadville, in the summer of 1856, I removed to Cambridge, and, for the sake of rest, declined to preach as a candidate: but I supplied vacant pulpits, and the pulpit in Woburn, for four months. At the expiration of six months, they gave me a call; and I was installed April 30, 1857. I remained in Woburn till November, 1863, when I resigned my pastorship, and removed to Cambridge, where I have since resided, supplying pulpits as opportunity offered, and, during the last year, giving my time, as President of the American Unitarian Association, to the renewal of its life, and raising funds. More than one hundred thousand dollars were raised; and, the Association being in good condition, I resigned the office of President, or, rather, I declined to be a candidate for re-election, and withdrew from the Executive Committee."

Mr. Stebbins at present resides in Cambridge, supplying vacant pulpits as his services are called for, and declining all offers of a settlement.

## IX.

CAZNEAU PALFREY, son of William Palfrey, for many years an officer in the Boston Custom-house, was born in Boston, Aug. 11, 1805. His mother's name was Lydia Cazneau. His parents were parishioners of Rev. Dr. John Elliot, by whom he was baptized in infancy; and, afterwards, of Rev. Francis Parkman, D.D., his successor, under whose ministry Mr. Palfrey was brought up. He received his early education, and was prepared for college, in the public schools of Boston, and entered Harvard College at the age of seventeen, graduating in 1826. During his course of study in the Theological School, he was for one year a tutor in the Latin department in the University. On the 5th of October, 1830, he was ordained pastor of the Unitarian church in Washington, D.C. His ministry in that city terminated in January, 1836. On the 25th of April, 1838, he was installed pastor of the First Congregational Church in Grafton, Mass., where he continued till April 25, 1843, just five years. From April, 1844, to October, 1847, he ministered to the Congregational Church in East Barnstable, Mass.; and on the 19th of April, 1848, was installed pastor of the First Parish in Belfast, Me., which post he still occupies.

Mr. Palfrey was married, May 30, 1838, to Anne Parker, eldest daughter of Rev. Jaazaniah Crosby, D.D., of Charlestown, N.H. Their children are — Hersey Goodwin, born in Grafton, Oct. 9, 1839, graduated at Harvard

College, 1860; Mary Walker, born in Grafton, 27th of December, 1840; Rebecca Salisbury, born in Barnstable, 9th of May, 1844; and Charles Follen, born in Barnstable, July 4, 1846.

His published writings are the following: —

1. On Forming Good Resolutions: a New Year's Sermon, delivered in Washington.

2. Two Sermons, in the "Liberal Preacher:" Ways of Pleasantness, and Influence of the Gospel on the Domestic Relations.

3. Two Tracts of the Unitarian Association; viz., Change of Heart, and Retribution.

4. Four articles in the "Christian Examiner;" viz., on the Life and Character of Rev. Hersey B. Goodwin, of Concord, Mass.; on Retribution; a Review of Peabody's Sermons of Consolation; and a Review of Wayland's University Discourses.

Mr. Palfrey was the first editor (1839) of the "Monthly Miscellany of Religion and Letters," of which the present "Monthly Religious Magazine," now so ably conducted by Rev. Messrs. Ellis and Sears, is the successor. He has also been a frequent contributor to the last-named periodical, since it passed out of his hands; and has published several funeral and other occasional discourses in the Belfast papers.

## X.

WILLIAM H. LORD. — After the death of Rev. Jeroboam Parker, of Southborough, a new society was formed, by a respectable minority of the legal voters of the old parish, assuming the title of the Evangelical Congregational Church in Southborough; leaving the old meeting-house, and the church property, in the hands of the majority that remained. The old society, though thus diminished in numbers, weakened in its resources, and held together by rather loose bonds, resolved to support public worship, and settle a minister. Accordingly, they invited to settle among them Mr. John Davis Sweet, a graduate of Bowdoin College of the year 1829, and of the class of 1832 in the Divinity School, Cambridge. Accordingly, he was ordained as minister of the First Congregational Parish in Southborough where he continued for a time, gaining a strong hold on the affections of his people. His request for a dismission was the occasion of much surprise and regret; and the society never fully recovered from the wound inflicted upon it by the withdrawal of their beloved pastor.

They were not, however, wholly discouraged; and, in 1838, they were united again in giving a call to Mr. William H. Lord, a graduate of Dartmouth College; who, having pursued a course of theological studies at Andover, was licensed to preach, by an association of Orthodox ministers, under whose auspices he offered himself as a candidate for settlement. Sometime after this, his theological creed having undergone a radical change, his license was withdrawn. After spending six months at Cambridge, he was again licensed to preach by another association, when he began to preach in Unitarian pulpits. After a probation of a few weeks, he was invited by the First Parish in Southborough to become their minister; and in September, 1838, he was ordained. He held that office for four years, and asked a dismission, which was granted in September, 1842. After preaching in various pulpits for three years without a settlement, he was invited, in the spring of 1845, to take charge of the Unitarian church in Milwaukee, Wis., as the successor of Rev. William Cushing, now of Clinton, Mass., who had been compelled by ill health to relinquish that office, after a brief but pleasant and successful ministry. Mr. Lord was a popular preacher, and was received at Milwaukee with a hearty welcome. The society in that place had just built a neat and commodious house of worship, which was filled by a very respectable congregation; and, at the commencement of Mr. Lord's ministry, all appearances indicated health and prosperity. But appearances proved fallacious. Mr. Lord's ministry was brief: for reasons unknown to us, he soon (in 1847) asked a dismission, abandoned the ministry, engaged in other occupations, and is at present, I believe, connected with some publishing firm or newspaper establishment in New York or Philadelphia. He was married, Jan. 1, 1840, to Persis, daughter of the venerable Dr. Kendall, of Plymouth, Mass. Of their five children, all sons, three — Francis, Ernest, and William — died in infancy; the other two — Arthur and Eliot — live with their mother in Plymouth.

## XI.

WILLIAM MORSE was born in Pomfret, Conn., May 7, 1798. He began his ministry in connection with the denomination of Universalists, and was ordained over a Universalist society in Philadelphia, June 18, 1824, where he officiated two years. In the same connection, he preached in Nantucket five years; and, subsequently, two and a half years in Milton and Quincy. After the resignation of Rev. Mr. Alden, the Second Congregational Church and Society in Marlborough invited Mr. Morse to be their minister; and he was installed there, June 25, 1834. He closed his labors in Marlborough, July 14, 1844, after a faithful and peaceful ministry of ten years. Sept. 24, 1845, he was again installed over the Unitarian society in Tyngsborough, where he remained nine years. From

25

Jan. 1, 1854, he supplied the pulpit in Chelmsford for several years, and now resides in Franklin, N.H.

Mr. Morse was married while in Philadelphia, Dec. 24, 1824, to Sophronia Kneeland, daughter of Abner Kneeland. Their only child was married to Daniel Barnard, Esq., a lawyer in Franklin, N.H.

Mr. Morse received an honorary degree of A.M. in August, 1852, from Harvard College.

## XII.

DAVID FOSDICK, jun., son of David and Joann (Skilton) Fosdick, was born in Charlestown, Mass., Nov. 9, 1813, and graduated at Amherst College in 1831, at the early age of eighteen. Having pursued a course of theological studies at Andover, he entered the ministry, and was ordained over the First Congregational Church and Society in Sterling, March 3, 1841, as the immediate successor of Rev. P. Osgood. Here he remained about five years. Shortly after his dismission,—viz., March 4, 1846,—he was installed as pastor of the Hollis-street Church, Boston, as the successor of Rev. John Pierpont, where he remained till September, 1847; after which, he suppl, the pulpit in other places, till April 16, 1854, when a became the minister of a Union society formed at Gro; Junction, where he continued to preach till July 1, 186(

He married, March 10, 1841, Sarah Lawrence Wo bury, a niece of Amos and Abbott Lawrence, wh widowed sister, the mother of Mrs. Fosdick, lived Groton. She had been the wife of Rev. Samuel Wo bury, Orthodox minister of North Yarmouth, Me., married Mary Lawrence, of Groton. Mrs. Fosdick ( Nov. 25, 1860, three weeks after the birth of their ni. child. Their children are, Samuel Woodbury, Mary,

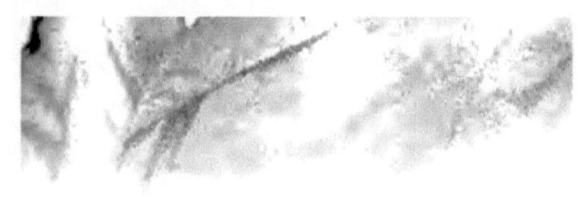

Yours sincerely
EHLear

George, Charles, Frederic, David, Rose, Lucy, Sarah Woodbury. George and David have deceased. Mr. Fosdick, with his motherless children, now lives in Groton.

## XIII.

EDMUND HAMILTON SEARS, son of Joseph and Lucy (Smith) Sears, was born in Sandisfield, Berkshire County, Mass., April 6, 1810; being in direct descent from Richard Sears, one of John Robinson's congregation, who landed at Plymouth in 1630. Having graduated at Union College, Schenectady, N.Y., in 1834, he entered the Divinity School at Cambridge, in the class of 1837,— the same class with Rev. Drs. Bellows and Stebbins. Feb. 20, 1839, he was ordained over the First Congregational Church and Society in Wayland, as successor of Rev. John Wight, where he remained till October, 1840. Dec. 23 of the same year, he was installed as successor of Rev. Dr. Thayer, over the First Congregational Society in Lancaster. After a happy ministry of seven years, he was compelled, by the state of his health, to ask a dismission, which was reluctantly granted; and his connection with his people was dissolved in March, 1847.

He now went back to his old friends in Wayland; who received with gladness the pastor from whom they had been separated for a season, and who was re-installed over them in 1848. In May, 1867, he was installed as colleague pastor with Rev. Dr. Field, of the First Congregational Society in Weston.

Mr. Sears was married, Nov. 7, 1839, to Ellen Bacon, daughter of Hon. Ebenezer Bacon, of Barnstable. Their children are three sons; viz., Francis Bacon, Edmund Hamilton, and Horace Scudder. Their only daughter, Katy, a promising child of ten years, died in 1853. Most of Mr. Sears's publications are well known, as he is one of our most popular writers. The following list comprises all of those which are published under his name, or which are known to be his: —

1. A Treatise on Regeneration, in 1853.
2. Pictures of the Olden Time, as shown in the Fortunes of a Family of the Pilgrims, 1857.
3. Athanasia, or Foregleams of Immortality, 1858.

*Discourses and Addresses.*

1. Address at Lancaster, before the Washington Total Abstinence Society, 1841.
2. Good Works: a Sermon, 1843.
3. Voices of the Past, Lancaster, the last sabbath of the year, 1845.
4. A Discourse on the Death of Rev. Isaac Allen, of Bolton, 1844.
5. Discourse at the Funeral of Deacon Samuel F. White, of Lancaster, 1843.
6. Worship: a Tract of the American Unitarian Association, 1850.
7. Revolution or Reform, preached soon after the assault on Hon. Charles Sumner, 1856.
8. Hindrances to a Successful Ministry, preached at the Ordination of Mr. J. M. Heard, at Clinton, Mass., 1858.
9. A Discourse delivered in Fitchburg at the Funeral of Rev. J. M. Heard.

Mr. Sears has rendered an acceptable service to the public, by his speeches and written addresses at conventions and conferences, and especially by his contributions to the "Monthly Religious Magazine," of which he has been co-editor, with Rev. Rufus Ellis, since January, 1859.

From a late communication from Mr. Sears, I quote the

*with kind memories*
Wm. Barry.

following: "I prepared for college, in part, at Westfield Academy, then in charge of Emerson Davis; was educated under old Calvinism, though never converted to it; entered Union College in 1831; graduated in 1834, under Dr. Nott; entered my name in the law-office of Thomas Twining, Esq., of Sandisfield, with whom I studied law about nine months, especially Blackstone, and books on the laws of evidence. I owe much to these law studies. Entered the Cambridge Theological School late in 1834; graduated in 1837, under the Wares, senior and junior, and Dr. Palfrey,— most invaluable teachers; ordained at Wayland, Feb. 20, 1838. My two years' ministry at Wayland, something less than seven years at Lancaster, at Wayland again sixteen years, at Weston nearly three years,— all stored with most delightful memories, though I broke down at Lancaster with exhausting labor.

"The partial failure of voice led me more to the use of the pen. Hence my three books, — two of them published by the American Unitarian Association, — which have passed through, I believe, six or seven editions. The 'Pictures' passed through two editions. The books," he adds, "were not written with any idea of profit; though, very unexpectedly and providentially, they became profitable, and enabled me to preach in a small parish, with small salary, to which I was compelled by failure of voice."

## XIV.

WILLIAM BARRY was born Jan. 10, 1805, in the north part of Boston, and was the son of William Barry, Esq., and of Esther (Stetson) Barry, youngest sister of Major Amasa Stetson, of Dorchester. Having studied in Woburn under the direction of Rev. Thomas Waterman, and in Hingham under the charge of Rev. Joseph Richardson, he entered Brown University in the class of 1822, with Hon. Isaac Davis and Judge Kinnicut of Worcester, Professor Caswell, and others who have been distinguished. After graduation, he studied law with Judge Shaw, of Boston, for about a year and a half; but, the state of his health not allowing him to continue his studies, he left Boston, and visited New Orleans, and other parts of the Southern States. Thus he passed two years, without being able to resume his studies. Entering the Divinity School at Cambridge, he continued there till July, 1828, when he sailed for Europe, with the Rev. James C. Richmond as a companion. They together entered the University of Göttingen, having been favored with letters to Blumenbach and Heeren, the well-known veterans of that institution, whose lectures, with those of Ewald the Hebraist, Lücke, &c., they attended. The following year, Mr. Barry proceeded to Paris, passing some months in attendance on the lectures of the Sorbonne, and in historical researches in the Royal Library; and, in the summer, travelled, in company with a young English physician, in Switzerland and Holland, and subsequently in England, pursuing historical researches in the British Museum in London. Thence he proceeded to Copenhagen with the same design, returning to America from Elsineur in the autumn of 1829. In June, 1830, he was licensed to preach by the Boston Association; and after supplying, for a few weeks each, the pulpits of the First Church in Roxbury, and that of Medfield and Philadelphia, in May of that year he commenced his labors with a new society formed in Lowell (the South Congregational Society), consisting, at first, of about twenty-five families, over which he was ordained as pastor, Nov. 17, 1830, — Rev. Dr. Lowell, of Boston, preaching the sermon of ordination. Here he continued till July, 1835, when a renewed failure of health compelled him to suspend his labors; and he resigned his ministry. The society at that time numbered over two hundred and fifty families, involving arduous and exhausting labors, quite beyond his strength. In the mean time, a substantial church edifice had been erected; and a parish association, of an efficient character, had been organized, to provide, with the aid of a library, for an effective administration of the Sunday school, for charities to the poor, for the diffusion of religious knowledge, &c. The church, at the same time, numbered nearly a hundred and fifty communicants.

After some months' retirement, Mr. Barry resumed preaching, and Dec. 16, 1835, was installed pastor of the First Parish in Framingham. Here he continued for a term of ten years, in the faithful discharge of his duties as a pastor, gaining the esteem and love of his parishioners, and enjoying the friendship of the venerated Dr. Kellogg, his predecessor, till his death, and also of Rev. Charles Train, the esteemed minister of the Baptist church in that town, who, for some time, was an attendant on his ministry. The society in Framingham, after the secession of the Orthodox members, who formed a new society after the resignation of Dr. Kellogg, was never large; but it retained much of the traditionary spirit of the ancient New-England churches, and embraced many substantial and worthy men.

Mr. Barry interested himself in the public schools of the town, as also in its history, on which he prepared an extended and elaborate work, in a handsome octavo volume of four hundred and fifty pages, published in 1847.

In June, 1844, failing health obliged him again to seek relief; and, in company with his wife and other friends, he visited Europe, passing some months in Nismes, in the south of France, whence he returned, but partially benefited, in December.

The following year, he declined an invitation to take the charge of a new society and church in Lowell; and, in December, he resigned his ministry in Framingham, not preaching at all for two years.

In October, 1847, at the renewed invitation of his friends in Lowell, he commenced a ministry, without installation, at that place, where he continued until May, 1853; during which period the new society erected a substantial church edifice (the Lee-street Church), provided for an active ministration to the poor of the city, and to the neglected children of a large and destitute neighborhood.

Continued feebleness of health required a recess from active labor, and, in 1851, he once more crossed the ocean; at this time visiting Asia, travelling in Syria, and returning through Italy and France. Successive attacks of illness resulted in his final retirement from the ministry; and, in obedience to his medical advisers, he removed to the West, taking up his residence in Chicago, which has since been his home.

Upon the organization, in 1856, of the Chicago Historical Society, Mr. Barry was invited to take charge of its operations, as its secretary; a position for which his early acquisitions and historical tastes had well prepared him. Here he found pleasant employment; passing five or six hours a day in his office, in arranging the books and pamphlets received from the friends of the institution, in waiting upon visitors, and in carrying on a large correspondence with similar institutions in various parts of the world. The society, through the centre of its operations in Chicago, contemplates the broader field of historical research for the State of Illinois and the entire North-west. Mr. Barry has been associated, as a member, with the American Antiquarian Society, with the Massachusetts, New-England, Vermont, and Iowa Historical Societies, with the Essex Institute, and with the Chicago Academy of Science. He has also been a trustee of the Ministry at Large, and of the Charitable Eye and Ear Infirmary at Chicago. He was formerly President of the Lowell Missionary Association, and a trustee of the academies at Derry, N.H., and at Framingham.

Mr. Barry was married, Nov. 11, 1835, to Elizabeth C. Willard, daughter of Cephas Willard, Esq., and Clarissa Willard, of Petersham, Mass., who was niece of Rev. Dr. Willard, of Deerfield, and grandniece of President Willard of Harvard College.

Their children are two daughters. Elizabeth married Lawrence Proudfoot, Esq., counsellor-at-law; and Julia Dalton married Belden F. Colver, Esq., a merchant, both living in Chicago. Their only son, a beautiful boy, died in Lowell, at the age of five years.

At the invitation of the Regent of the Mount-Vernon Ladies' Association, Mrs. Barry took charge of the collections for that association, as vice-regent for the State of Illinois.

*Publications.*

1. Farewell Sermon at Lowell, 1835.
2. Two Discourses on the Rights and Duties of Neighboring Churches, Framingham, 1844.
3. Thoughts on Christian Doctrine: Tract of American Unitarian Association, 1844.
4. The History of Framingham, 1847.
5. The Twenty-fifth Report of the Schools of Lowell, 1852.
6. The Antiquities of Wisconsin, in Transactions of the State Historical Society of Wisconsin, Madison, 1857.

Mr. Barry also published, in the "Christian Register" for 1845, Letters on the Religious Condition of France; also, in the "Lowell Journal" of 1851, Letters from the East; and has been a contributor to the journals of Chicago, on historical, agricultural, and sanitary subjects, &c.

## XV.

Richard S. Edes, son of Rev. Dr. Henry and Catherine (May) Edes, was born in Providence, R.I., April 24, 1810. He was fitted for Harvard College, to which he was admitted in 1826; but, on the accession of Dr. Wayland as President of Brown University, he removed his connections from Harvard to Brown, graduating in 1830; and from the Divinity School, Cambridge, in 1834. Dec. 1, 1836, he was ordained over the Unitarian society in Eastfort, Me., where he remained till Sept. 6, 1842, when, in consequence of impaired health, he sent in his resignation, which was reluctantly granted; the society "bearing their testimony to the conscientious and constant efforts which we have witnessed in you, to fulfil, to the utmost, the duties given you in charge, and to make your labors here promotive of our highest good." May 24, 1843, he was installed over the First Congregational Society in Bolton, as colleague of the Rev. Isaac Allen, whose health had now begun to fail, and who lived less than a year after the installation of Mr. Edes. After Mr. Allen's death, March 18, 1844, Mr. Edes continued the minister of Bolton for the term of about five years and a half, when, to the great regret of his many friends, he felt constrained, in consequence of difficulties in his parish, to ask a dismission. His connection with the parish, as its minister, was dissolved Dec. 25, 1848. When it was known that he contemplated this step, his brethren of the Worcester Association, with whom he had been pleasantly associated, anxious to retain him among them, sent to the parish a pastoral letter, signed by all the members present, proffering their mediation. The letter was favorably received; and the parish, soon after, addressed a letter to Mr. Edes, requesting him to withdraw the notice he had given, and expressing the belief that "the difficulties were of such a nature, that they might be buried to rise no more, and that the harmony of feeling which constitutes the beauty and usefulness of the connection between a pastor and his people might be restored." This letter was signed by sixty-one voters, while thirty-four declined signing it. The difficulties continuing, however, the connection terminated, as stated above, on Christmas Day, 1848.

Mr. Edes still lives in Bolton, on the snug little farm owned by his predecessor, Mr. Allen, and occupied by him till his death. It was purchased by Dr. Robert Thaxter, of Dorchester, who, at his death, bequeathed it to Mrs. Edes, his niece.

Mr. Edes was married April 19, 1837, to Mary Cushing, daughter of Jerome and Mary (Thaxter) Cushing, of Hingham.

Their children are — Robert Thaxter, born Sept. 23, 1838, H.C. 1858, a student in medicine; Richard Henry, born Aug. 3, 1840, died Dec. 29, 1854; Abbie May, born July 10, 1842, died July 19, 1842; Elizabeth Cushing, born Sept. 21, 1843; Edward Louis, born Nov. 19, 1845; Sophia Augusta May, born Feb. 2, 1848; Mary Cushing, born Sept. 6, 1850; Francis Cracoft, born Aug. 25, 1853; William Cushing, born Jan. 14, 1856; John May, born Feb. 27, 1859.

### *Publications.*

1. A Sermon at the Funeral of Rev. Isaac Allen, March 21, 1844.
2. A Discourse at the Dedication of the Church, Dec. 26, 1844.

Also, School Reports and communications to the papers.

## XVI.

EDMUND B. WILLSON, son of Rev. Luther and Sally (Bigelow) Willson, was born in Petersham, Aug. 15, 1820. He entered Yale College, but, on account of ill health, did not graduate with his class. He studied divinity in Cambridge with the class of 1843, and received, the honorary degree of A.M. from Harvard College in 1853. He was ordained, Jan. 3, 1844, as minister of the First Congregational Society in Grafton, succeeding the Rev. Mr. Palfrey in that office; and after a useful ministry of more than eight years, in which he had endeared himself to his people, and made himself favorably known in the neighboring churches, he was dismissed, at his own request, July 1, 1852; and in the same month, July 18, was installed over the Second Church in Roxbury (West Roxbury). From this charge he was dismissed, at his request, May, 1859; and, on the 5th of the following June, was installed over the New North Church in Salem, left vacant by the resignation of Rev. Charles Lowe; which office he still holds. He was married to Martha Ann Buttrick, daughter of Stephen and Patty (Wheeler) Buttrick. Their children are — Sophia Edgell, born March 1, 1845; Martha Buttrick, born Nov. 3, 1845, died Feb. 8, 1853; Lucy Burr, born Nov. 13, 1849; Alice Brooks, born Aug. 5, 1851; Robert Wheeler, born July 20, 1853; Edmund Russell, born April 21, 1856.

Mr. Willson has published two valuable historical discourses, — one entitled the " Church Record," preached in Grafton, Dec. 27, 1846; the other, " An Address delivered in Petersham, July 4, 1854, in Commemoration of the One Hundredth Anniversary of the Incorporation of that Town." Also a sermon, preached in the North Church, Salem, March 4, 1860, entitled " The Memory of Christ."

## XVII.

HORATIO ALGER, son of James and Hannah (Bassett) Alger, was born in Bridgewater, Nov. 6, 1806.* He graduated at Harvard College in 1825, and at the Divinity School in 1829, with the class of which Hersey B. Goodwin and Cazneau Palfrey were members. He was ordained in Chelsea, Sept. 2, 1829, as the successor of Rev. Dr. Tuckerman, of blessed memory, and retained that office nearly fifteen years. His connection with that society was dissolved April 4, 1844; and in the following year, Jan. 22, 1845, he was installed over the Second Congregational Society in Marlborough, as successor of Rev. William Morse, retaining his connection with it till July 18, 1859. His engagement with the society in South Natick commenced on the third Sunday in June, 1860.

Mr. Alger was married March 31, 1831, to Olive Augusta Fenno, daughter of Deacon John and Olive (Pratt) Fenno, of Boston, deacon of the New North Church (Dr. Parkman's). They were the first couple married in East Boston. Their children are — Horatio, born Jan. 13, 1832, H.C. 1852, D.S. 1860; Olive Augusta, born Nov. 19, 1833; James, born March 11, 1836, lives in California; Anna M. C., born Oct. 24, 1850; Francis, born Aug. 21, 1852.

Mr. Alger has contributed several articles to the "Unitarian Advocate," and to the "Monthly Religious Magazine;" and in 1850 printed a small pamphlet, entitled "The Church Record," being a concise "Sketch of the Origin and History of the West Church in Marlborough," &c.

Mr. Alger is at present pastor of the Unitarian Congregational Church in South Natick.

---

* Mr. Alger's father was a deacon of Rev. Dr. Sanger's church, and his mother a descendant of the Cushman family, her mother being Phebe Cushman.

## XVIII.

EDWARD EVERETT HALE, son of Hon. Nathan Hale, for many years the editor and proprietor of the "Boston Daily Advertiser," was born in Boston, April 3, 1822. His mother was Sarah Preston (Everett) Hale, daughter of Rev. Oliver and Lucy (Hill) Everett, of Dorchester, and sister of Hon. Edward Everett, for whom he was named. His father, Nathan Hale, was the son of Rev. Enoch and Octavia (Throop) Hale. He was fitted for college at the Boston Latin School, and graduated at Cambridge in 1839. He studied for the ministry with Rev. Dr. Lathrop, of Boston; and after supplying the pulpit of the Unitarian church in Washington, D.C., during the winter of 1844–5, was ordained at Worcester over the Church of the Unity, April 28, 1846. He relinquished the charge of that church the last Sunday of July, 1856, and was installed as the third minister of the South Congregational Society in Boston, as the successor of the Rev. Dr. Huntington, Oct. 1, 1856.

Oct. 13, 1852, he was married to Emily Baldwin Perkins, daughter of Thomas Clapp and Mary Foote Perkins, of Hartford, Conn., a daughter of Rev. Lyman Beecher, D.D. Their children are Ellen Day, Arthur, Charles, Edward Everett, Philip Lesley, and Herbert; the eldest born in 1855, the youngest in 1866.

*Publications.*

1. The Rosary, Boston, 1848.
2. Margaret Percival in America, in conjunction with his sister, Lucretia P. Hale, 1850.
3. Sketches of Christian History, 1850.
4. Kansas and Nebraska, 1855.
5. A Prize Essay, "Juvenile Delinquency," Philadelphia, 1855.
6. Life and Letters of Sir Ralph Lane, Arch. Americana, vol. iv., 1860.

7. Ninety Days' Worth of Europe, 1860.
8. Elements of Christian Doctrine and its Development, in Five Sermons.
9. Sermon at the Ordination of Charles B. Ferry, in Peterborough, N.H.
10. The Christian Ministry in Large Cities.
11. Thirty Years of Boston, 1861.
12. The Future Civilization of the South, 1862.
13. The Desert and the Promised Land, 1863.
14. The Man without a Country, 1864.
15. A Sermon before the Western Conference, 1865.
16. Edward Everett: "The Ministry of Reconciliation," 1865.
17. The Public Duty of a Private Citizen, 1865.

Mr. Hale was the editor of the Boston edition of Lingard's "History of England," and for four years joint-editor with Rev. Dr. Hedge of the " Christian Examiner;" and it would not be easy to reckon up all the occasions in which he has been called to take a prominent part, — *ad omnia semper paratus.*

## XIX.

JOHN J. PUTNAM was born in Chesterfield, N.H., May 21, 1823; prepared for college at Kimball Union Academy, Meriden, N.H., but did not enter college. He studied divinity under private instruction, and was ordained over a society in Lebanon, N.H., June 7, 1843, and resigned that office September, 1845. His second settlement was in Bolton, where he was installed Sept. 26, 1849; and he joined the Worcester Association the same month. He resigned his place in Bolton, June 6, 1852, and was reinstalled over the First Congregational Society in Petersham, July 11, 1852. That connection was dissolved Oct. 7, 1855; and his fourth settlement was in Bridgewater, where he was installed Jan. 16, 1856, and where he remained till June, 1864.

He was married, May 9, 1860, to Isabella, daughter of Dr. William Parkhurst, of Petersham. They have two children, — Charles Converse and John Parkhurst.

He is at present general agent of the New-England Mutual Life Insurance Company of Boston, and lives in Worcester.

## XX.

Amos Smith was born in Boston, Nov. 29, 1816, and was the son of Amos and Catherine (Langdon) Smith, daughter of Timothy Langdon (H.C. 1765). He attended the Latin School, Boston, from 1829 to 1834, when he entered Harvard College, and graduated in 1838. He was a private tutor at the South one year, after which he entered the Divinity School, graduating with the class of 1842. He was ordained as colleague pastor with Rev. Francis Parkman, D.D., over the New North Church, Dec. 7, 1842. That connection was dissolved June 7, 1848; and he was installed in Leominster, as successor of Rev. H. Withington, Nov. 26 of the same year. His pastorate in Leominster ended Sept. 2, 1856; and he is at present pastor of a new church in Belmont.

He was married in Boston, Oct. 25, 1845, to Mary E. Williams, daughter of Thomas Williams, Esq., of Chelsea, and of Eliza (Avery) Williams, daughter of John Avery, Esq., formerly Secretary of the Commonwealth.

## XXI.

William C. Tenney, son of William and Phebe (Wheeler) Tenney, was born in Newmarket, N.H., July 26, 1817. He graduated at Harvard College in 1838; studied in the Divinity School, Cambridge, two years; was ordained over the Unitarian Society in Kennebunk,

THE NEW YORK
PUBLIC LIBRARY

ASTOR LENOX AND
TILDEN FOUNDATIONS

Yours truly
George M. Bartol

Oct. 7, 1845, where he remained till March, 1848. Having supplied the pulpit in Upton fourteen months, he received a call from the First Congregational Society in Northfield, where he was installed Sept. 9, 1849, where he continued nine years. He was re-installed over the Lee-street Church, Lowell. Oct. 26, 1859; and in October, 1861, took charge of the Unitarian society in West Marlborough; resigned the charge July 1, 1864; and assumed the charge of the Unitarian church in Lawrence, Kansas, Oct. 27, 1865.

His first marriage was with Catherine P. Clarke, of Auburn, N.H., who died in Northfield, July 8, 1850, leaving one child, — Isabella Caroline, born Jan. 6, 1845.

He was again married, June 15, 1852, to Elizabeth E. Bruce, of Grafton, whose children, besides one who died in infancy, are — William Edward, born Jan. 7, 1859; and Elizabeth Bruce, born March 22, 1861. Two other children, by his first wife, died in infancy. His daughter Isabella is an accomplished and successful teacher.

## XXII.

GEORGE M. BARTOL, son of George and Anna (Given) Bartol was born in Freeport, Me. Having graduated at Brown University, in 1842, he entered the Divinity School, Cambridge, and graduated with the class of 1845. He was ordained at Lancaster, as the immediate successor of Rev. Edmund H. Sears, Aug. 4, 1847, where he still remains, the respected minister of the old parish church. He was married, June, 1856, to Elizabeth Kimball Washburn, daughter of John M. and Harriet (Kimball) Washburn, of Lancaster, and grand-daughter of Rev. Daniel Kimball, formerly Preceptor of Derby Academy at Hingham, who died at an advanced age in Needham, a few years since.

Their children are George, Anna, Elizabeth W., John M. W., Mary W.

Mr. Bartol preached a discourse occasioned by the death of Mrs. Sarah Thayer, widow of Rev. Dr. Thayer, in 1857; which was printed.

## XXIII.

THOMAS PRENTISS ALLEN, second son of Joseph and Lucy C. Allen, was born in Northborough, July 7, 1822, and graduated at Harvard College in 1842. After leaving college, he took charge of the Northfield Academy, Franklin County, for one year; and then entered the Divinity School, Cambridge, graduating with the class of 1846. He was ordained Nov. 18, 1846, over the First Congregational Society in Sterling, and was admitted to the Worcester Association, Dec. 16 of the same year. His connection with the society in Sterling continued till the year 1852; after which, he devoted himself to the charge of a large family school for boys in that place until July, 1855, when he was invited, in conjunction with his brother, Edward A. H. Allen, to take charge of the Friends' Academy in New Bedford. In 1864, he removed to West Newton, where he now resides, as Associate Principal, with his cousins Nathaniel T. and James T. Allen, of the English and Classical School at West Newton. He was married, Nov. 17, 1846, to Sarah A. Lord, of Northfield, Mass. Their children are — Gertrude, born in Sterling, Aug. 31, 1847; Otis Everett, born June 17, 1850; Annie Ware, born June 14, 1852, died March 17, 1854; Caroline Putnam, born March 18, 1855, died Aug. 19, 1855; Helen Ware, born at New Bedford, April 16, 1858. Gertrude, the oldest child of Rev. T. P. Allen, accompanied her uncle, William F. Allen, to Charleston,

S.C., in the spring of 1865, as a teacher of a school for colored children, where, after a period of about three months, she was seized with a typhoid fever, and, after a week's sickness, died June 10, 1865, in the eighteenth year of her age.

## XXIV.

WILLIAM G. BABCOCK, son of Samuel H. and Eliza Babcock, was born in Milton, June 1, 1820. He graduated at Harvard College in 1841, and at the Divinity School, Cambridge, 1844; was ordained at Providence, R.I., as an evangelist, April 8, 1846. After preaching as minister at large in that city more than two years, from August, 1844, he was dismissed from that charge March, 1847; and in May, 1849, he was installed over the First Congregational Society in Lunenburg, where he continued a little more than six years. In September, 1855, he left Lunenburg, and was installed at Harvard, Nov. 18, 1855, where he remained one year, and then became minister of the First Parish in South Natick, where he remained till the spring of 1860. His next removal was to Scituate, where he was installed Sept. 16, 1860. He was married, May 27, 1847, to Clarissa Louisa, daughter of Joshua B. and Clarissa Clapp. Their children are Clara Maria, Mary Elizabeth, and Lucy Frances, living. They have buried two, — Harriet Louisa and Charlotte Augusta.

Mr. Babcock has published several sermons and miscellaneous articles in the periodicals. He is at present employed as a minister at large in Boston.

## XXV.

GEORGE S. BALL, son of Micah and Rachel (Lincoln) Ball, was born in Leominster, May 22, 1823, being a descendant of one of the first settlers of Northborough.

He was educated in our common schools, and is a graduate of the Meadville Theological School, of the class of 1847. He was ordained as minister of the Unitarian society in Ware, Oct. 13 of the same year, where he remained till the close of the year 1849. In January, 1850, he was installed over the Unitarian society in Upton, and resigned the office November, 1854. After a few months' service in the employment of the American Unitarian Association, he supplied the pulpit of the First Parish in Plymouth, as associate pastor with Rev. Dr. Kendall, for one year; commencing his labors there April 1, 1855. In April, 1856, he was welcomed back to his former charge in Upton, where he still remains.

He represented Upton and Northbridge in the House of Representatives, to which office he was chosen in 1861; resigning his place to serve in the army as chaplain of the Twenty-first Regiment, a regiment from Worcester County, under Colonel Morse, which fought their first battle with Burnside at Roanoke Island, under Colonel Maggi, in which Mr. Ball rendered important service in the care of the wounded, of which honorable mention is made by Colonel Maggi, in his report to Governor Andrew. His services in other battles are also acknowledged in the reports of other officers. After his return, he was re-elected to the Legislature for the years 1863 and 1864, in the former of which he was chaplain of the House; and, in 1865, he was chosen as a member of the Senate, which office he has held for two consecutive terms. He was also a member of the Convention for revising the Constitution in 1852.

Mr. Ball was married, June 18, 1848, to H. B. Nourse, daughter of Caleb and Orissa (Holman) Nourse, of Bolton. Their children are six. — Clinton D., Susan A., Lydia M., George W., Elizabeth F., and Walter Seaver.

## XXVI.

Horatio Stebbins, son of Calvin and Amelia (Adams) Stebbins, was born in South Wilbraham, Aug. 8, 1821. He was fitted for college at Exeter Academy, and graduated at Harvard College in 1848, and at the Divinity School in 1851. Nov. 5 of the same year, he was ordained at Fitchburg, and was dismissed, at his request, Jan. 1, 1855; being called to take charge of the First Congregational Society in Portland, as the successor of Rev. Dr. Nichols, over which he was installed Jan. 29, 1855.

In 1864, he accepted an invitation to take charge of the Unitarian society in San Francisco, as successor of the lamented Starr King; which important post he still occupies.

He was married in Northborough, June 3, 1851, to Mary Ann, daughter of Samuel and Mary (Bowman) Fisher, of that place. Their children are Mary Louisa, Annie, and Roderick. Annie is not living.

## XXVII.

Thomas T. Stone, son of Solomon and Hepzibah (Treadwell) Stone, was born in Waterford, Me., Feb. 9, 1801. He graduated at Bowdoin College in 1820, and was ordained in Andover, Me., Sept. 8, 1824, at the early age of twenty-three. He was installed at East Machias in 1833, and became the minister of the First Church in Salem, July 12, 1846; which office he filled till Feb. 22, 1852. He commenced his labors as minister of the First Congregational Church and Society in Bolton, in November, 1852, and took leave of that parish in the autumn of 1860. In 1830 and 1831, he was Principal of Bridgeton Academy, Cumberland County, Me., at the same time preaching in the Academy Hall. He became a member of the Worcester Association, Jan. 19, 1853; and, during the time of his connection with it, was an active and efficient member. He is at present supplying the pulpit of the Unitarian society, Brookline, Conn. Jan. 13, 1825, he was married to Laura, daughter of Silvanus and Mary (Merrill) Poor, of Andover, Me.

Their children are — Thomas Treadwell, a farmer in Danvers; Henry, a graduate of the Cambridge Divinity School of 1860; Lincoln Ripley, a physician in Salem, Mass.; Alfred, an architect, Providence, R.I.; Hepzibah, George Herbert, William, Martha Elizabeth. Four other children died in infancy.

*Publications.*

1. A Volume of Sermons on War, 1829.
2. Sketches of Oxford County, Me., 1830.
3. Volume of Sermons, 1854.
4. The Rod and the Staff, 1856.

*Discourses and Addresses.*

1. Address on Temperance, 1829.
2. Lecture on History, 1831.
3. Sermon at the Ordination of Rev. Eber Child, Calais, 1835.
4. Sermon before the Maine Missionary Society, North Yarmouth, 1837.
5. Sermon on Justification, 1847.
6. Sermon to the Senior Class, Divinity School, Cambridge, 1856.
7. Address before the Female Antislavery Society, Salem, 1852.
8. Sermon on the Murder of Lovejoy at Alton, Ill., 1838.

Besides the above, Mr. Stone has furnished many articles for the periodicals of the day; as the "Quarterly Review," "Biblical Repository," "Literary and Theological Review," "The Dial," "The Monthly Religious Magazine," besides two articles for the "Liberty Bell."

## XXVIII.

Leonard Jarvis Livermore, son of Solomon K. Livermore, Esq. (H.C. 1802), and Abigail Adkins (Jarvis) Livermore, was born in Milford, N.H., Dec. 8, 1822. He is grandson of Rev. Jonathan Livermore (H.C. 1760), the first minister of Wilton, N.H., and great-grandson of Deacon Jonathan Livermore, one of the first settlers of Northborough, whose life extended over one complete century, having been born Aug. 16, 1700, and having lived till April 31, 1801. He is a graduate of Harvard, of the class of 1842, and of the Cambridge Divinity School of 1846. He was ordained over a church in East Boston, March 24, 1847. In April, 1851, he removed to Clinton, where he continued to officiate as pastor of the Unitarian church till May 1, 1857; and, on the 1st of the following October, he became minister of the old Congregational church in Lexington, where he remained till 1866, when, at his request, the connection was dissolved. He has recently accepted an invitation to fill the vacancy in the Board of Directors of the American Unitarian Society, caused by the death of John A. Andrew; also to take charge of the Unitarian society in Danvers for one year. His present residence is Cambridge.

He was married, March 18, 1847, to Mary Ann C. Perkins, of Groton, daughter of Aaron and Mary (Gilbert) Perkins. Their children are Allina Mary, Clara Perkins, Joseph Perkins, Henry Jarvis.

Mr. Livermore has contributed articles for the periodicals, but has, I believe, published nothing under his own name.

## XXIX.

THOMAS W. BROWN was born in Portsmouth, N.H., Aug. 15, 1829, and graduated at the Divinity School, Cambridge, in 1852. He received ordination at Portsmouth, Dec. 24, 1852, as minister of the Unitarian church in Trenton, N.Y., and remained in that connection one year; and Feb. 2, 1854, was installed as pastor of the First Parish in Grafton, where he remained two years; and, shortly after his dismission, he became minister of the Congregational society in Brewster, on Cape Cod. Since 1854, he has been the minister of the Unitarian society in Sandwich.

He was married, Jan. 5, 1853, to Annie M., daughter of John H. Bartlett, of Portsmouth.

## XXX.

WILLIAM P. TILDEN, son of Luther and Philena (Brooks) Tilden, was born in Scituate, May 9, 1811. He "graduated" at the district school, in his native town, at about the age of seventeen; then served an apprenticeship at ship-building, and worked at the business till about the age of twenty-five. By the advice of Rev. Samuel J. May, now of Syracuse, N.Y., and under his direction, he prepared himself for the ministry, keeping school during the winter months; and at length, at the mature age of thirty, received from the Old Colony Association license to preach. He was ordained at Newton Corner, April 21, 1841; and, in the summer of 1844, went, in poor health, to take charge of the Unitarian church in Concord, N.H., where he remained about three years. He then supplied, for one year, the pulpit of Rev. John Parkman, of Dover, N.H., who was then travelling in Europe; and, in the autumn of 1848, he went to Walpole, N.H., and remained minister of the Congregational society in that place nearly seven years. At length, June 3, 1855, he was installed over the First Parish in Fitchburg, and afterwards became the minister of the church on Church Green, in Boston, as successor to the late Rev. Alexander Young, D.D. He is at present minister of a Free Church in the south part of Boston.

He was married in Scituate, in 1834, to Mary J. Foster, daughter of Timothy and Hannah (Clapp) Foster. Their children are Laura, Joseph, William Phillips, and George Thomas.

### *Publications.*

1. Sermon on the Evangelical Alliance, 1846.
2. A Discourse on the Death of Lieutenant Edward Eastman of the United-States Army, who died at Camargo, 1846.
3. A New Year's Discourse for 1847.

During his ministry in Fitchburg, he published a small volume entitled "The Bridal Wreath;" also a sermon on temperance.

Besides the above, he published a sermon in the "Religious Magazine," and one in the "Keene Sentinel," and has made many valuable communications to our periodicals.

### XXXI.

JAMES THURSTON was born in Newmarket, N.H., Dec. 11, 1806; fitted for college at Phillips Academy, Exeter, under Dr. Abbott; graduated at Harvard College in 1829; was employed as a teacher in the English High School, Boston, three years; graduated at the Divinity School, Cambridge, 1835. After leaving the school, he was sent as a missionary to the West for one year; and was ordained over the Unitarian society in Windsor, Vt., in 1838. After leaving that post, he preached in several places, and at length, in 1844, took charge of the First Congregational Society in Billerica, where he continued till 1850. He then supplied the pulpit in South Natick two years, when, in 1853, he was installed as pastor of the Allen-street Church, in Cambridge. He resigned that charge the following year, on account of severe illness; and, in 1855, entered on an engagement to supply the pulpit of the First Congregational Church in Lunenburg, where he remained till 1857.

Mr. Thurston was married in Charlestown, Mass., Sept. 11, 1844, to Elizabeth, daughter of William Austin, Esq. Their children are James Peabody, William Austin, Elizabeth Peabody, Charles Abbott, and Charlotte Williams.

## XXXII.

Trowbridge B. Forbush, son of Lowell and Elizabeth (Stone) Forbush, was born in Westborough, Jan. 15, 1832. He pursued a course of classical studies, partly under the direction of Rev. Nathaniel Gage, preparatory to his entering the Theological School at Meadville, Penn., where he graduated with the class of 1856. He was ordained, Jan. 1, 1857, associate pastor of the First Congregational Society of Northborough, with Rev. Dr. Allen. Having resigned the pastorate, July 1, 1863, he at once took charge of the Unitarian society in West Roxbury, which office he still retains. He is at present Secretary of the New-England Emigrant-aid Company.

He was married to Rachel L. Byard, of Meadville, June 29, 1856. Their children are Harry Robinson and William Perry.

## XXXIII.

WILLIAM HENRY KNAPP, son of Abiathar and Nancy Knapp, was born in Norton, Mass., Sept. 19, 1811. He obtained his education by himself, and in our common schools; was ordained Sept. 28, 1833; and settled in Danvers, April, 1835, where he remained two years. He then preached two years in Chelsea, at Winnisimmet Village. He began to preach at Nantucket, May, 1844, where he remained six years, till 1850. He then preached two years for the Unitarian society in West Newton; and Feb. 14, 1856, was installed as minister of the First Congregational Society in Sterling. His connection with that society terminated May, 1858. He now (1867) resides at Cambridgeport.

Mr. Knapp was married, Sept. 28, 1833, to Emily Thompson, daughter of Timothy and Sarah Thompson, of Charlestown, Mass. Their children are — Emma T., married to George A. Stephenson, of West Newton; Henry C.; Marianne, married William A. P. Willard, of Sterling; Arthur M.; Timothy T.; Abby H.; and Eugene R. Arthur M. Knapp has just accepted a call to take charge of the church in Providence, lately under the care of Rev. E. B. Hall, D.D.

Mr. Knapp has published sermons and essays in various reviews and magazines.

## XXXIV.

GEORGE GARDNER WITHINGTON, son of George R. M. Withington, Esq., and Laurinda, daughter of General Gardner, of Bolton, was born in Lancaster, Mass., and is a graduate of the University of Vermont, of the class of 1825. He graduated at the Meadville Theological School in 1854, and was ordained at Hillsborough, Ill., October, 1855, where he remained as pastor of the First Congregational Society till July, 1857. He was admitted to the Worcester Association in 1858, while residing with his parents in Lancaster. June 19, 1858, he became pastor of the First Congregational Society in Easton, where he still resides, and where he was married, Jan. 22, 1860, to Ellen J., daughter of Hon. Elijah Howard, of Easton.

## XXXV.

Stephen Barker, son of Henry and Lois Barker, was born in Andover, Mass., January, 1829; graduated from the Divinity School, Cambridge, in 1856; and was ordained as minister of the First Congregational Society in Leominster, Sept. 2, 1857. He resigned his office June 1, 1860. He was married, Sept. 14, 1858, to Louisa Jane, daughter of William and Hannah Whiting, of Concord, Mass. Mr. Barker served as chaplain of the Fourteenth Regiment of Massachusetts Volunteers in the late rebellion. He has, I believe, left the profession, and is at present engaged in business in the State of Vermont.

## XXXVI.

William G. Scandlin was born in Portsmouth, England, Feb. 16, 1828. He left home at the early age of seven years and a half; previous to which time he had attended a primary school in that place. "The balance of my education," he writes, "I obtained from eleven years' experience on the ocean, where I came in contact with the customs of the different nations of the world; and, in the language of the Psalmist, became familiar with the works and wonders of the Lord on the deep." Before he came of age, he landed on our shores, made a voyage to the West Indies, and, on his return to Boston, found a temporary home for himself, and as many of his comrades as he could persuade to join him, in the Sailors' Home. He had, by this time, become deeply interested in religion; and he now formed the purpose to devote himself to the Christian ministry. He entered the Meadville School in 1850, and graduated in 1854. In November of the same year, he commenced the Hanover-street Mission, under the auspices of the Boston Fraternity of Churches; and was ordained as a minister at large at the Hollis-street Church, Jan. 14, 1855, Dr. Gannett preaching the sermon on the occasion. In this service he continued till the end of May, 1858. The duties of this office proving too arduous for his health, and having received an invitation to settle over the First Congregational Church in Grafton, he removed to that place, where he was installed June 23, 1858, and where he still remains.

At the beginning of the late war, he offered his services to Governor Andrew, and was appointed chaplain of the Fifteenth Regiment of Massachusetts Volunteers; at the same time resigning his charge of the society in Grafton. His resignation was not accepted; but his people gave him leave of absence for twelve months, thinking, as we all did, that twelve months would suffice for the overthrow of the rebellion. At the expiration of his leave of absence, he returned to his parish; soon after which, his church was destroyed by fire.

After making arrangements for erecting a new building, at the solicitation of the American Unitarian Association, he obtained another leave of absence for three months, to go on a missionary expedition to the army; and, to facilitate his movements, he became a member of the United-States Sanitary Commission. In this service, while engaged in conveying food and comforts to the sick and wounded at Gettysburg, he was taken prisoner by Stewart's cavalry, and, with many others, conveyed to Richmond, and confined nearly three months in Libby Prison, and subsequently in Castle Thunder. "I look upon the opportunities," he writes, "opened to me during my imprisonment, as the richest of my experience."

The following testimonial is from Dr. McDonald, one of his fellow-prisoners, published in the "Sanitary Commission Bulletin:" — "Mr. Scandlin proved to be all, and more than all, he professed. Constantly engaged in some good work, cheerful under the most adverse circumstances, ever ready to render aid and comfort to all in distress, he has become endeared, not only to the agent of the Commission, with whom he has been so long associated, but to most of the officers and men whom chance and the fortunes of war have placed in his path. He sought out the sick and inquiring, gave them freely, cheerfully, temporal and spiritual comfort, at all times and in all seasons. He has proved himself to be an honest, faithful worker, and a TRUE man, — 'the noblest work of God.'"

Mr. Scandlin was married, Dec. 13, 1853, to C. S. Adrain, who lived only till the following April. On the 24th of April, 1855, he married Mrs. Eliza M. Sprague at Eastport, Me. Their children are Willie Ira, Elizabeth Frances, Fanny Maria, and John Winthrop. His second wife had, by her former husband, one son, — Horace Bacon Sprague.

## XXXVII.

FARRINGTON McINTIRE became a member of the Worcester Association, Aug. 17, 1858, while living on his farm in Grafton, at the head of a family school. He was born in Fitchburg, June 29, 1819, and graduated at Harvard

College in 1843, and at the Divinity School in 1846. In June, 1847, he was ordained over the Unitarian society in Brattleborough, Vt., where he remained one year. July 1, 1849, he sailed from New York for California, where, more fortunate than many adventurers, he recovered his health, and accumulated a handsome property. Returning after a residence of a year and a half, he was married, on the 23d of April, 1851, to Caroline C. Frost, of Kennebunk, Me., with whom he lived a little less than three years.

On the 9th of February, 1857, he was married to his second wife, Caroline Fisher, daughter of Jacob and Orricy (Hills) Fisher, of Lancaster, Mass.

## XXXVIII.

Rush R. Shippen, son of Henry Shippen, was born at Meadville, Penn., Jan. 18, 1828. He is of English descent, of a family Episcopal and Quaker, long resident in Pennsylvania. His mother was Elizabeth W. Evans, of Welsh and English descent. Mr. Shippen entered as student of Alleghany College (Methodist), Meadville, where he remained till the middle of his senior year (1843), when the college suspended operations for a year. He then taught a district school for nine months, after which he entered the Meadville Theological School, then just going into operation under President Stebbins and Professor Huidekoper. He was at this time only sixteen years old; but it was thought to be the best school to which he could have access. Having remained in the school three years, he spent one year in Nashville, Tenn., as a teacher, and then re-entered the Meadville School, where he graduated in 1849. After three or four months spent in New England in itinerant preaching, he accepted an invitation to take charge of the First Unitarian Church in Chicago, Ill.; and, on his way, was ordained as an evangelist at Meadville. — President Stebbins preaching the sermon, and Professors Folsom and Huidekoper assisting.

At the expiration of the six months for which he was engaged, he accepted an invitation for permanent settlement, and continued his labors without installation. He resigned his charge July 1, 1857, and, after a four months' vacation, spent a year in Meadville, preaching most of the time. He then returned to New England; and at the invitation of the Church of the Unity, Worcester, was installed their pastor, Dec. 22, 1858, which office he still holds and adorns.

Mr. Shippen was married, Oct. 10, 1855, to Zoviah Rodman, who was born in Egremont, Mass., but who from childhood had resided in New York, near Utica. Their children are Sarah, Henry, Marion (died Oct. 16, 1864), and Eugene.

## XXXIX.

E. B. FAIRCHILD, son of Curtis and Miranda Fairchild, was born in Sunderland, Sept. 17, 1835. He graduated at Meadville Theological School in 1859, and was ordained as minister of the First Parish in Sterling, Jan. 19, 1860.

He was married in Meadville, December, 1859, to Maria H. Smith, of that place. He left Sterling near the beginning of the great Rebellion, and served for a time as chaplain in the army, and in other capacities. He is now pastor of a church gathered mostly under his own ministrations, in Webster, Mass.

## XL.

Caleb B. Josselyn, son of David and Mary Josselyn, was born in Pembroke, March 4, 1831. At the age of eleven, he joined the Episcopal Church (St. Andrew's), of Hanover. "My change to Liberal sentiments," he writes, "was gradual, and probably the work of natural development." He pursued a select course of study at Brown University, R.I., in 1853; thence went to Meadville Theological School, where he graduated in 1858. He preached six months at Austinburg, Ohio, and was settled in Lunenburg, October, 1859. On account of failure of his health, he soon took a dismission, and engaged in other pursuits, occasionally supplying vacant pulpits. At present he lives in Malden.

## XLI.

Eli Fay was born in Fenner, Madison County, N.Y., Nov. 8, 1822, and was ordained as a minister of the Christian denomination in Lyndonville, Orleans County, N.Y., Oct. 23, 1844. His installation over the First Congregational Society in Leominster took place Jan. 1, 1861. He is at present the minister of the Unitarian church in Woburn.

## XLII.

Gilbert Cummings, son of Gilbert and Margaret Jane Cummings, was born in Boston, Sept. 15, 1825. When nearly thirty years of age, he relinquished the business in which he was engaged, entered the Theological School in Meadville, where he graduated in 1859. He was ordained as minister of the Unitarian society in Austinburg, Ohio, Oct. 20 of that year, and was installed over the Unitarian church in Westborough, Jan. 3, 1860. Here he remained till the breaking-out of the rebellion, when he received an appointment as chaplain of a regiment. Having served in this capacity for some time, he returned, and engaged in other business. He afterwards removed to Grafton, having been appointed as teller in the Grafton Bank, where he still remains.

## XLIII.

NATHANIEL OTIS CHAFFEE, son of Nathaniel and Tabitha Chaffee, was born in South Wilbraham, Jan. 28, 1812. He received his theological education at Meadville, and was ordained at Montague, Jan. 10, 1849. He was married, July 1, 1841, in Sutton, to Martha P. McKnight. He lives at present in West Bridgewater. He became a member of the Worcester Association while supplying the pulpit in Bolton.

## XLIV.

HENRY H. BARBER, son of Deacon Hervey and Hannah Barber, was born in Warwick, Dec. 30, 1835. He received his theological education at Meadville, where he graduated in 1861; and, Oct. 24 of the same year, he was ordained over the First Parish in Harvard. In 1867, he was installed pastor of the Unitarian church in Somerville. He was married in Deerfield, June 30, 1857, to Eliza H. Pratt, of that place.

## XLV.

EDWIN C. L. BROWNE, son of Erastus and Anna Browne, was born at East Cambridge, April 22, 1833. He is a graduate of Meadville, of the class of 1861, and was ordained over the First Congregational Church in

Bolton, April 22, 1863. He was married, Jan. 1, 1862, to Elizabeth Lincoln, daughter of David P. and Susan L. Rowe, of Hingham.

## XLVI.

JOSEPH HENRY ALLEN, eldest son of Joseph and Lucy C. Allen, born in Northborough, Aug. 21, 1820; graduated at Harvard College in 1840, and from the Divinity School, Cambridge, in 1843; was ordained as pastor of the church in Jamaica Plain, Oct. 18, 1843, the venerable John Quincy Adams being one of the ordaining council; became minister of the Unitarian church in Washington, D.C., in October, 1847, and of the Independent Congregational Society in Bangor, Me., October, 1850. His connection with that church was dissolved, May, 1857, since which time he has been associated in the editorial charge of the " Christian Examiner." Besides the charge of the " Christian Examiner," he has supplied vacant pulpits; among others, those at West Newton, from 1858 to 1860, and at Northborough, from 1864 to 1866.

He was married, May 22, 1845, to Anna Minot Weld, of Jamaica Plain, West Roxbury. Their children are Lucy Clarke, Margaret Weld (died Aug. 17, 1861), Mary Ware, Richard Minot, Gardner Weld, and Russell Carpenter. Their present home is in Cambridge.

### Publications.

1. Ten Discourses on Orthodoxy, 1849 (pp. 227).
2. Memoir of Hiram Withington, 1849 (pp. 190).
3. Manual of Devotions for Families and Sunday Schools, 1852 (pp. 163).
4. Hebrew Men and Times, from the Patriarchs to the Messiah, 1861 (pp. 435).

Also, twelve occasional sermons, — including one preached in Washington, on the death of Senator Fairfield, and one on the day following the funeral of John Quincy Adams; two preached in Bangor, December, 1850, published in a pamphlet, entitled "The Great Controversy of States and People;" and one entitled "A Reign of Terror," preached in June, 1856, during the troubles in Kansas: and many articles in the "Christian Examiner," — among them, the following: Comte's Positive Philosophy, March, 1851; Prospects of American Slavery, September, 1854; Comte's Religion of Humanity, July, 1857; Latin Christianity, January, 1862; The Reformation and its Results, March, 1862; Africans in America and their new Guardians, July, 1862; Our War Policy, and how it deals with Slavery, September, 1862; The Peace Policy, How it is Waged and What it Means, January, 1863; The New Homeric Question, May, 1863; Conditions of Belief, July, 1863; A Month of Victory and its Results, September, 1863; Weiss's Life of Theodore Parker, January, 1864; Federalism and its Present Tasks, March, 1864; Doctrine and Theory of Inspiration (read before the Worcester Association), November, 1864; The Eighth of November, January, 1865; The Fourth of March, March, 1865; The Nation's Triumph and its Sacrifice, May, 1865; The New Nation, July, 1865; State Crimes and their Penalty, September, 1865; The President's Reconstruction, November, 1865; More Open Questions, March, 1866; Some Conditions of the Modern Ministry, January, 1867; The Cambridge Divinity School, September, 1867; also, a large proportion of the articles in the "Review of Current Literature" since July, 1857.

## XLVII.

SAMUEL W. McDANIEL, son of Joseph A. and Hannah (Boyer) McDaniel, was born in Philadelphia, Nov. 18, 1833. He was educated in the public schools of Philadelphia, prepared for the ministry under the care of his pastor, Rev. John G. Wilson, Ex-President of the Maryland Literary Institute, and pastor of the First Independent

Christian Church in Philadelphia. Having been licensed as a preacher of the gospel, he was ordained Dec. 1, 1856, and preached in Luzerne County, Penn., where he organized a Liberal church, serving it as pastor till Oct. 15, 1858. He then removed to Lewisburg, Penn., and became pastor of the Christian church in that town, and also of the Unitarian society in Northumberland, founded by the eminent Dr. Joseph Priestley. He assumed the charge of the Union society in Feltonville (now Hudson), June 5, 1862, where he remained two years. In 1864, he took charge of the Unitarian society in Neponset; and, in 1866, was installed pastor of the First Church in Brighton, Mass. He was married, in 1854, to Elizabeth Kesbaugh, of Philadelphia, who died about five months after their marriage. In 1856, he was married again to Anna M. Brunner, of Bucks County, Penn. At the breaking-out of the rebellion, he assisted in forming a company of militia for the protection of the capital, was elected captain, and accompanied it to the seat of war. He was subsequently chosen chaplain of the regiment. His second wife died a few months since.

## XLVIII.

ALPHEUS S. NICKERSON, son of Captain Theophilus and Mary (Sanford) Nickerson, was born in South Dennis, Mass., April 29, 1830. He graduated at Amherst College in 1854, and at Andover Seminary in 1857; was ordained at North Woburn, and afterwards installed over the Unitarian church in Chelsea, where he remained about three years. He was re-installed over the First Congregational Church in Sterling, July 27, 1864.

He was married, in 1858, to Jeannie Humphrey, of Boston, by whom he has three children, — Nellie H., Frank E., and Mary S.

## XLIX.

James Salloway, son of Henry and Elizabeth (Faulkner) Salloway, was born in Queen Anne's County, Md., May 21, 1828. He pursued a course of studies at Oberlin College, and graduated at Antioch College, Ohio. Having completed his theological studies at the Divinity School, Cambridge, he was ordained, Jan. 21, 1863, over the Unitarian church in Billerica, the charge of which he resigned October, 1864; and Nov. 9, of the same year, he was installed over the Unitarian church in Clinton.

He was married, June 22, 1864, to Nellie S., daughter of George Bacon, Esq., of Billerica.

## L.

Rushton Dashwood Burr, son of Samuel S. and Harriet (Bodge) Burr, was born in Haverhill, Feb. 5, 1828. He graduated at the Cambridge Divinity School in 1852; was ordained at Medfield, Jan. 12, 1853; installed in Brookfield, Nov. 9, 1858, and at Uxbridge, Nov. 12, 1862.

## LI.

John Bremner Green, son of James and Susan (Bremner) Green, was born July 18, 1833, in Fochabers, Morayshire, Scotland. He received his theological education at Meadville, Penn.; was ordained at Bernardston, Mass., Feb. 5, 1862; installed at Leominster, Aug. 3, 1864, and at Chelsea, June 19, 1867.

He married, Aug. 5, 1855, Maria Holmes Spalding, of London, Canada West.

## LII.

Hiram C. Dugan, son of John Clark and Lydia (Holmes) Dugan, was born in Franklin, Lycoming County, Penn., Nov. 27, 1830, being the seventh of a family of eleven children. His father, a *pioneer* farmer, built his block-house in the forest, ploughed and sowed and subdued the stubborn soil, was always poor, and died from hard labor at the age of fifty-nine. Of course, he was able to give his children only a scanty common-school education. Mr. Dugan studied for the ministry at Meadville, and graduated in 1856. "I have no other course of study to tell of," he writes, — "I say it in sadness, — but a few weeks now and then in the old school-house, two miles from my father's house, and the long winter evenings by a pitch-knot light and the open fire, after a hard day's work, with wet feet, in the lumbering woods." He was ordained pastor of the Christian church in Lubec, Me., Nov. 1, 1857; Rev. H. F. Edes and Rev. T. D. Howard taking part in the exercises. "The Christians," he writes, "with whom my ministry has been chiefly given, never install or settle their pastors: they *hire* their preachers from year to year. Hence they have a changing ministry, amounting almost to an itineracy, without the system of the Methodists. Five years previous to my coming to Feltonville, I preached in New Hampshire; two years in Andover, where the denomination sustains a feeble school; and three years in Franklin. I have supplied Unitarian pulpits in Calais, Me., Chelmsford and Sandwich, Mass.

"I was always," he adds, "a Unitarian. I was a small boy when my sister told me that 'some folks believed that Jesus Christ was God.' For some time I was transfixed to the spot where I stood with profound astonishment. I could go back now to the old homestead, and point out the spot where I stood when she told me this. I supposed then that but few believed it, — some little sect of fanatics who were not in the full possession of their reason. And even that seemed almost impossible. The doctrine has never appeared more absurd to my mind in my mature judgment, than it did then to my childish instinct. Since that day, it has been impossible that I should become a Trinitarian."

Mr. Dugan, having supplied the pulpit in Feltonville (Hudson) for some time, was installed as pastor of the Lawrence church, Nov. 22, 1865; which office he resigned in 1867.

## LIII.

Eugene De Normandie, son of James and Sarah B. (Yardley) De Normandie, was born in Philadelphia, Jan. 3, 1832. He received his collegiate education at the University of Lewisburg, Penn.; graduated at Meadville in 1855; and was ordained as pastor of the First Congregational Church in Littleton, where he remained eight years. After spending one year in Fitzwilliam, N.H., he was installed over the Second Congregational Society in Marlborough, Oct. 19, 1866.

In 1860, he married Ann F. Nye, of Sandwich. Their children are Abram Emerson, Richard Currier, Eugene Fitzwilliam, and Sarah.

## LIV.

George N. Richardson, son of Erastus and Mary (Johnson) Richardson, was born in Eastport, Me., 27th of November, 1827. He graduated at Bowdoin College in 1847, and was ordained over the First Congregational Church in Westborough, Feb. 28, 1865.

## LV.

HENRY L. MYRICK was born Dec. 5. 1826, in the city of New York, and is a graduate of the Cambridge Divinity School, of the class of 1852. After receiving ordination as pastor of the First Church in Plymouth, he had the charge of the pulpit for a longer or shorter period in Brookline, Conn., Eastport, Me., Marblehead, and other places; and in June, 1866, became associate pastor with Rev. Dr. Allen, of the First Congregational Society in Northborough.

He married Lucy C. Whittemore, of West Cambridge, now Arlington. Their children are Francis Tiffany (died), Frederic Frothingham, Lockwood, Cora, George Herbert, and Horatio Fiske.

## LVI.

JEFFERSON M. FOX, son of John and Cinderilla (Myers) Fox, was born in Pottsville, Penn., Dec. 5, 1831. He was a student in Hobart College, Geneva, N.Y., and is a graduate of Meadville Theological Seminary. He was ordained over the Unitarian church in Trenton, N.Y., Oct. 7, 1862, and installed at Harvard, March 27, 1867. He married, Aug. 31, 1859, Libbie Marvin; and their only child is Lillian A. Fox.

## LVII.

HENRY F. JENCKS, son of John Henry and Mary Rand (Fitch) Jencks, and a grandson of the late venerable William Jencks, D.D., of Boston, was born in Boston, Oct. 17, 1842. He graduated at Harvard College in 1863, and at the Cambridge Divinity School in 1866, and was ordained as pastor of the First Congregational Society in Fitchburg, April 10, 1867.

## LVIII.

WILLIAM S. HEYWOOD, son of John and Betsey E. Heywood, was born in Westminster, Mass., Aug. 23, 1824. He was ordained in May, 1849; and, after keeping school and supplying the pulpit in several places, was installed as pastor of the Lawrence Church, in Hudson, Oct. 11, 1867. He married Abby S., daughter of Rev. Adin Ballou, of Hopedale. Their only child is Lucy Florence, born July 28, 1864.

www.ingramcontent.com/pod-product-compliance
Lightning Source LLC
Chambersburg PA
CBHW032003300426
44117CB00008B/887